책은 일단 샀는데, 언제 다 외우지?

또 귀찮게 깜지 쓰면서 외울 거야?
눈으로만 대충 외울 거야?
그럼 시험기간 안에 절대 못 끝내!

밀당PT 영어 가 외우는 속도를 절반으로
줄여주는 문장 암기 프로그램 을 보내줄게!

짧은 시간 안에 가장 빠르게
내신 문장이 외워지도록
설계된 학습 프로그램 이야.

다음 페이지로 넘겨봐!

잘 왔어! **문장암기 정말 어렵지 않아!**

별도로 시간 쓰고 노력하지 않아도, 우리 프로그램만 따라오면 돼!

본문에 있는 QR을 찍으면 쌤이 말한 암기 프로그램이 뜰 거야

2과 본문 ❶

FROM TRASH TO TREASURE

Every day during lunch, Jamie enjoys a soft drink and has a decision to make: What should he do with the empty can? Many people would answer, "Recycle it!" Obviously, recycling is good for many reasons. We can reduce the amount of trash thrown away, use less energy than we would to make new products, and conserve natural resources by recycling. However, recycling is not a perfect way to manage waste. It still requires large amounts of energy to purify used resources and convert them into new products. So, what about trying to creatively reuse, or "upcycle," them instead? …

김온택

여러 가지 프로그램이 있네요?

순서 맞추기

문장을 순서대로 선택해 내용을 완성해주세요.

문장을 선택하면 여기에 나타나요 👀   7 COMBO 🎳

> Why Do People Learn Foreign Languages?

> Many others learn them for fun.

> Learn a New Language, Find a New World

> How can I improve my Spanish?

⋮

맞아! 프로그램만 순서대로 따라가면 그 지문은 완전 **쉽게 암기** 할 수 있어

앞으로도 이 프로그램만 잘 따라가면 정말 잘 외워질거야

2과 본문 ❷

Through upcycling, a seemingly useless object can be transformed into something completely different that is useful for everyday life. What do you think can be done with old truck tarps, car seat belts, and bicycle inner tubes? …

2과 본문 ❸

Along with small everyday items, much bigger things can also be upcycled — even old buildings that cannot be used for their original purpose anymore. The German government showed us an excellent example of this with a former steel plant that closed in 1985. Rather than destroy the plant's buildings or abandon the entire facility, they decided to give it new meaning as a series of useful public structures. …

+   ☺ #

김온택

게임하듯이 재밌게 하는데 정말 쉽게 암기가 되고 있어요!

2과 본문 ❹

When artists add their own creative touches, things that most people consider junk are reborn as beautiful works of art. The giant pictures made from trash by environmental artist Tom Deininger are one of a kind. Up close, these brightly colored creations look like a mixed-up mess of broken plastic, unwanted toys, and bent wire — all things that cannot be recycled. From farther away, however, they appear to blend together into marvelous landscapes or other paintings. There is also an artist who shows that even disposable cups can be reused as artistic material. For years, Gwyneth Leech has turned used coffee cups into brilliant art exhibits. After a cup is used by someone, she paints a unique design on it and hangs it with many other painted cups in front of a window or pretty background. ...

2과 본문 ❺

As you can see, creative thinking has the power to make many positive changes to the environment. By giving old products more value, we can lessen the amount of waste in a way that is even more eco-friendly than recycling. So what would you say to Jamie now as he decides what to do with his cans? Perhaps he could upcycle them to make lanterns, toys, or sculptures for his friends and family. The options are endless, and all he needs is a little creativity to think of them. In the same way, stop and think before you throw something out. Who knows? ...

전보다 더 빠르게 외울 수 있지?

After You Read

a: Using recycling bins is a great way to save the Earth. Everyone should separate things that can be recycled from their trash and put them in the bins.

b: If we creatively reuse the things thrown away, we can make the Earth greener by reducing trash and saving more energy.

c: Reusing items several times before throwing them away cuts down on the amount of waste we produce. It saves you money, too.

김온택

이젠 진짜 단어만 봐도 쉽게 문장을 만들 수 있을 것 같아요.
시간도 오래 안 걸렸는데 문장이 외워졌어요!

그치? 학생들이 가장 쉽고 빠르게 외울 수 있도록 학습이 설계됐거든!

생각보다 더 쉽지? 앞으로 우리 책 공부하면서,
암기 걱정은 **밀당PT 영어** 로 해결해 봐!

✂ 페이지를 오려서 활용해 봐! :)   ☺ #

능률 PT

집　　　　필　아이헤이트플라잉버그스㈜ 영어콘텐츠본부
편　　　　집　설북
표 지 디 자 인　㈜다츠
내 지 디 자 인　엘림
맥　편　　집　엘림
영　　　　업　한기영, 이경구, 박인규, 정철교, 하진수, 김남준, 이우현
마　케　　팅　박혜선, 남경진, 이지원, 김여진
펴　낸　　이　주민홍
펴　낸　　곳　서울시 마포구 월드컵북로 396(상암동) 누리꿈스퀘어 비즈니스타워 10층
　　　　　　　㈜NE능률 (우편번호 03925)
펴　낸　　날　2023년 4월 14일 초판 제 1쇄
전　　　　화　02-2014-7114
팩　　　　스　02-3142-0357

능률 내신 PERSONAL TEACHING

능률PT

NE능률 고등영어 (김성곤)

Lesson 2.
The Power of Creativity

내신 만점을 위한 성공적인 준비
Personal Teaching for Your Precious Time

능률PT는 고등영어-NE능률(김성곤) 교과서 해당 시험 범위의 중간·기말고사를 대비하는 학생들을 위해 기획된 교재입니다. 본 교재는 실제 전국 내신 기출문제 100세트를 문장 단위로 철저하게 분석하여, 한 단원 기준 평균 300개 이상의 출제 포인트를 정리하였습니다.

실제 기출문제에 자주 등장한 출제 포인트 순서대로 내신 고득점을 위해 꼭 알아야 하는 내용을 먼저 학습할 수 있도록 구성하였고, 핵심 출제 포인트 내용 설명과 내용 이해를 확인할 수 있는 문제를 제시함으로써 필수 학습 내용을 완벽히 익힐 수 있도록 돕습니다. 핵심 포인트를 확실하게 학습할 수 있는 기출 변형 문제를 포함한 충분한 연습 문제를 제공하며, 최중요 출제 포인트를 모두 포함하는 시험 문제 미리보기를 통해 효율적이고 성공적인 내신 준비를 책임집니다.

본 교재로 학습하는 경험을 통해 출제 포인트에 접근하는 인사이트(insight)를 바탕으로 자기 주도적이고 효과적인 내신 대비 감각을 기를 수 있도록 설계되었습니다.

교재의 특징

- **실제 내신 기출문제 100세트 분석**
  해당 범위 내신 기출문제 100세트와 각 단원 내용과 관련된 시험 문제를 분석하여
  데이터화하였습니다.

- **문장 단위(sentence-by-sentence) 분석**
  본문을 문장 단위로 분석하여, 각 문장에서 시험 문제의 출제 포인트가 된 부분을 정리하고,
  각 출제 포인트의 출제 확률을 산출하였습니다.

- **우선순위 순으로 출제 포인트 제시**
  실제 기출문제에 많이 등장한 출제 포인트들에 대해 빈도순으로 학습 자료를 제공하여
  학습의 우선순위를 명확히 제시하였습니다.

- **풍부한 연습 문제 제공**
  기출 변형 문제, 출제 포인트 연습 문제, 시험 문제 미리보기 등 300문항 이상 수록하였습니다.

교재 활용법

교재의 구성

▶ 적중 MAPPING
출제율 최상위권 문장과 문제 유형을
한눈에 볼 수 있습니다.

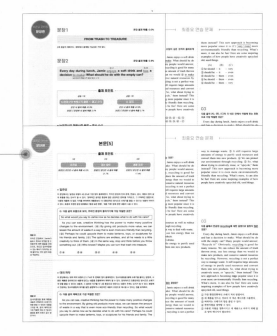

◀ 시간이 없다면! (문장편 / 문단편)

- **최중요 출제 포인트** 각 문장/문단의 출제 확률과 실제 출제될 경우
포인트가 될 수 있는 부분에 대한 통계적 데이터를 참고하여 우선순위
순으로 핵심을 확인할 수 있습니다.

- **최중요 연습 문제** 핵심 출제 포인트 학습을 바탕으로 이해를 점검할
수 있는 문제를 통해, 실제 문제에 포인트가 적용되는 것을 확인하며
이해도를 체크할 수 있습니다.

▶ 100점 맞고 싶다면!

- **기타 연습 문제**
실제 시험에 한 번 이상 출제된 포인트들을 모두 모아
학습하여 빈틈없이 내용을 익힐 수 있습니다.

본문 핵심 분석 ◀
각 지문의 단어, 주제문, 주요 구문 등 출제 가능한 핵심
내용들을 심층 분석한 밀도 있는 자료를 통해 시험 직전
이해를 확인하는 용도로 사용할 수 있습니다.

▶ 시험 문제 미리보기
최중요 출제 포인트를 활용한 시험 문제 2회분을 풀어
보며 자신의 실력을 점검하고 실전 감각을 끌어 올릴 수
있습니다.

목차

리딩
본문[1]

16.8% 확률로 본문[1]에서 출제

FROM TRASH TO TREASURE

Every day during lunch, Jamie enjoys a soft drink and has a decision to make: What should he do with the empty can? Many people would answer, "Recycle it!" Obviously, recycling is good for many reasons. We can reduce the amount of trash thrown away, use less energy than we would to make new products, and conserve natural resources by recycling. However, recycling is not a perfect way to manage waste. It still requires large amounts of energy to purify used resources and convert them into new products. So, what about trying to creatively reuse, or "upcycle," them instead? This new approach is becoming more popular since it is even more environmentally friendly than recycling. What's more, it can also be fun! Here are some inspiring examples of how people have creatively upcycled old, used things.

일관성 〈출제 1위 유형〉

이 문단에서는 재활용의 이점에 대해 언급하다가, 역접의 연결어 However를 사용하여 재활용은 완벽한 방법이 아니라고 말하며 흐름을 전환하는 부분이 문장 삽입 문제로 빈번하게 출제된다. 그 밖에도 올바른 순서로 배열하기나 무관한 문장을 찾는 문제가 출제될 수 있으므로, 이에 대비할 수 있도록 글의 흐름을 명확하게 파악하자.

내용 일치 〈출제 2위 유형〉

내용 일치 유형 문제에서는 글의 세부적인 내용에 유의해야 하는데, 이 문단에서는 쓰레기 처리의 일반적인 방법인 재활용의 장점과 한계점에 대해 이야기한 뒤, 그 대안으로 업사이클링을 제안하며 업사이클링의 장점에 대해 언급한다. 주로 출제되는 포인트인 재활용의 장점과 한계점, 업사이클링의 장점, 그리고 마지막 문장에서 추론할 수 있는 다음에 이어질 내용에 대해 잘 정리해두도록 하자.

지칭 추론 〈출제 3위 유형〉

이 문단에서는 대명사의 지칭이 다양하게 나오므로, 각 대명사가 무엇을 지칭하는지 명확하게 구분할 수 있어야 한다. 문장3의 it은 the empty can을, 문장7의 It은 recycling을, 문장7과 문장8의 them은 used resources를, 문장9의 This new approach와 it, 문장10의 it은 upcycling을 가리킨다. 지칭 추론 문제가 출제될 가능성이 매우 높으므로, 각 대명사가 가리키는 것을 숙지해두자.

출제 1위 문장 ★★★

It still requires large amounts of energy to purify used resources and convert them into new products.

[to부정사 병렬 ― 부사적 용법] 출제 1위 (문장편-문장7 → p.14)
[어휘 convert] 출제 2위 (문장편-문장7 → p.14)

출제 2위 문장 ★★

However, recycling is not a perfect way to manage waste.

[연결어 however] 출제 1위 (문장편-문장6 → p.12)
[to부정사의 형용사적 용법 ― 명사 수식] 출제 2위 (문장편-문장6 → p.13)
[빈칸 recycling is not a perfect way to manage waste] 출제 3위 (문장편-문장6 → p.13)

출제 3위 문장 ★

We can reduce the amount of trash thrown away, use less energy than we would to make new products, and conserve natural resources by recycling.

[과거분사 ― 명사 수식] 출제 1위 (문장편-문장5 → p.9)
[어휘 less] 출제 2위 (문장편-문장5 → p.10)

문장1

FROM TRASH TO TREASURE

2과 본문의 제목이다. 제목에서 출제될 가능성은 거의 없다.

문장2

동사1　　　　　　　　　　　　　　　　동사2
Every day during lunch, Jamie <u>enjoys</u> **a soft drink and** <u>has</u> **a decision** <u>to make</u>**: What should he do with the empty can?**
to부정사의 형용사적 용법 (명사 수식)

┤ **출제 포인트** ├

공동 1위	공동 1위
to부정사의 형용사적 용법 — 명사 수식	**수 일치**
문장 내 출제 확률 42.9%	문장 내 출제 확률 42.9%
본문[1] 문장편 내 출제 확률 2.7%	본문[1] 문장편 내 출제 확률 2.7%

● **to부정사의 형용사적 용법 – 명사 수식**

문장2에서 출제될 가능성은 0.9%이다. 이 문장에서 출제가 된다면, 42.9%의 확률로 to부정사의 형용사적 용법을 묻는 문제가 나올 수 있다. to make는 명사구 a decision을 수식하는 형용사적 용법의 to부정사로, '해야 할 결정'이라는 의미이다. make a decision은 '결정을 하다'라는 의미인 것도 함께 알아두자.

정답 to make

앞의 명사구 a decision을 수식해야 하므로, 형용사적 용법의 to부정사인 to make로 변형한다.

> **Q. 다음 괄호 안의 동사를 알맞은 형태로 고쳐 쓰시오.**
>
> Every day during lunch, Jamie enjoys a soft drink and has a decision _____ (make): What should he do with the empty can?

● **수 일치**

문장2에서 주어와 동사의 수 일치를 묻는 문제도 동일하게 42.9% 비율로 출제된다. 주어(Jamie)가 3인칭 단수이므로, 단수동사 enjoys와 has가 오며, 동사 enjoys와 has는 접속사 and로 병렬 연결되어 있다는 것을 잘 알아두자.

정답 has

주어는 3인칭 단수명사인 Jamie이고 등위접속사 and로 동사 enjoys와 병렬 구조를 이루므로, has가 알맞다.

> **Q. 다음 괄호 안에서 어법상 올바른 것을 고르시오.**
>
> Every day during lunch, Jamie enjoys a soft drink and | has / having | a decision to make: What should he do with the empty can?

출제 포인트 0.6% 정복!

문장3

> **Many people would answer, "Recycle it!"**

문장3에서는 내용 일치와 지칭 추론 유형 외의 문제가 출제될 가능성은 거의 없다. 이 문장에서 it이 앞의 문장의 the empty can을 가리킨다는 것을 기억해 두고, 내용 일치와 지칭 추론 유형은 문단편에서 더 자세히 살펴보도록 하자.

문장4

문장 출제 확률: 0.5%

> **Obviously, recycling is good for many reasons.**

문장4는 출제 빈도가 낮기 때문에 문장편 최중요 포인트에서는 제외된다.

문장5

문장 출제 확률: 2.6%

> 과거분사 – 명사 수식   a. 더 적은
> **We can reduce the amount of trash thrown away, use less energy than we would to make new products, and conserve natural resources by recycling.**

┤ **출제 포인트** ├

1위	2위
과거분사 – 명사 수식	**어휘 less**
문장 내 출제 확률 40.0%	문장 내 출제 확률 15.0%
본문[1] 문장편 내 출제 확률 7.2%	본문[1] 문장편 내 출제 확률 2.7%

● **과거분사 – 명사 수식**

문장5에서 출제될 가능성은 2.6%이다. 이 문장에서 출제가 된다면, 40.0%의 확률로 과거분사의 명사 수식에 대해 물을 수 있다. throw away는 '버리다, 없애다'를 의미하고, trash(쓰레기)는 버려지는 대상이므로, 수동 관계이다. 따라서 과거분사구 thrown away가 뒤에서 명사 trash를 수식한다는 것을 잘 기억해두도록 하자.

> **Q. 다음 괄호 안의 단어를 알맞은 형태로 고쳐 쓰시오.**
>
> We can reduce the amount of trash (A)_____(throw away), use less energy than we would (B)_____(make) new products, and conserve natural resources by recycling.

정답
(A) thrown away
(B) to make

(A) throw away는 '버리다, 없애다'를 의미하고, trash(쓰레기)는 버려지는 대상이므로, 수동의 관계이다. 따라서 과거분사구 thrown away로 올바르게 변형한다.
(B) 'We can use less energy than we would (use)'의 완전한 절에 이어지고, 문맥상 목적의 의미를 나타내야 하므로, to부정사의 부사적 용법 to make가 알맞다.

이 문장에서 두 번째로 출제 확률이 높은 것은 어휘 less이다(15.0%). 재활용이 좋은 이유에 대해 서술하는 부분이므로, 새 제품을 만드는 데 쓰는 것보다 '더 적은(less)' 에너지를 사용할 수 있다는 내용이 제시된다는 것을 잘 알아두자.

Q. 다음 글의 괄호 (A), (B), (C) 안에서 문맥에 맞는 낱말로 가장 적절한 것은?

Every day during lunch, Jamie enjoys a soft drink and has a decision to make: What should he do with the empty can? Many people would answer, "Recycle it!" Obviously, recycling is good for many reasons. We can reduce the amount of trash thrown away, use (A) | more / less | energy than we would to make new products, and (B) | converse / conserve | natural resources by recycling. However, recycling is not a perfect way to manage waste. It still requires large amounts of energy to purify used resources and convert them into new products. So, what about trying to creatively reuse, or "upcycle," them instead? This new approach is becoming more popular since it is even more environmentally (C) | friendly / unfriendly | than recycling. What's more, it can also be fun! Here are some inspiring examples of how people have creatively upcycled old, used things.

	(A)	(B)	(C)
①	less	– converse	– friendly
②	less	– conserve	– unfriendly
③	more	– conserve	– friendly
④	more	– converse	– unfriendly
⑤	less	– conserve	– friendly

정답 ⑤
(A) 재활용이 좋은 이유에 해당하는 부분이므로, 새 제품을 만드는 데 쓰는 것보다 '더 적은(less)' 에너지를 사용할 수 있다고 하는 것이 적절하다.
(B) 재활용이 좋은 이유 중 하나이므로, 재활용을 통해 천연 자원을 '절약할 (conserve)' 수 있다고 하는 것이 알맞다.
converse: ~와 대화를 나누다
(C) 업사이클링이 점점 인기를 얻고 있는 이유에 해당하므로, 업사이클링은 재활용보다 훨씬 더 환경 '친화적 (friendly)'이라는 것을 유추할 수 있다.
unfriendly: 비우호적인

10.0%의 확률로, 조동사 can 뒤에 나오는 동사원형 reduce, use, conserve의 병렬 구조를 파악하고 있는지 묻는 문제가 출제된다. 동사 conserve의 형태를 묻는 문제가 자주 출제되므로 잘 기억해두도록 하자.

Q. 다음 빈칸에 알맞은 것은?

We can reduce the amount of trash thrown away, use less energy than we would to make new products, and _____(conserve) natural resources by recycling.

① conserve   ② to conserve   ③ conserving

④ conserved   ⑤ conserves

정답 ①
조동사 can 뒤에서 접속사 and로 동사원형 reduce, use와 병렬구조를 이루고 있으므로, 동사원형 conserve가 적절하다.

● to부정사 부정사 용법 – 목적

역시 10%의 확률로 목적을 나타내는 부사적 용법의 to부정사에 관해 물을 수 있다. 이 문장에서 to make는 완전한 절에 이어지는 부사적 용법의 to부정사로, 문맥상 '~하기 위해'라는 목적의 의미를 나타낸다. than we would 뒤에는 앞에서 언급된 동사 use가 생략되어 있기 때문에, make가 조동사 would 뒤에 이어져서 동사원형인 make로 쓰일 수 없음에 주의하자.

> **Q. 다음 괄호 안에서 어법상 올바른 것을 고르시오.**
>
> We can reduce the amount of trash thrown away, use less energy than we would | make / to make | new products, and conserve natural resources by recycling.

정답 to make

'We can use less energy than we would (use)'의 완전한 절에 이어지고, 문맥상 목적의 의미를 나타내야 하므로, 부사적 용법의 to부정사 to make가 적절하다. than we would 뒤에는 앞에서 언급된 동사 use가 생략되어 있기 때문에, make가 조동사 would 뒤에 이어지는 것이 아님에 주의한다.

● 어휘 reduce

어휘 reduce 역시 10.0%의 확률로 자주 출제된다. 이 문장은 재활용이 좋은 이유에 대해 서술하는 부분이므로, '줄이다'를 의미하는 어휘 reduce를 사용하여 '재활용을 함으로써 버려지는 쓰레기 양을 줄일 수 있다'는 내용이 제시된다는 것을 잘 알아두자.

> **Q. 다음 글의 (A), (B), (C)의 각 네모 안에서 문맥에 맞는 낱말로 가장 적절한 것은?**
>
> Every day during lunch, Jamie enjoys a soft drink and has a decision to make: What should he do with the empty can? Many people would answer, "Recycle it!" Obviously, recycling is good for many reasons. We can (A) | increase / reduce | the amount of trash thrown away, use less energy than we would to make new products, and conserve natural resources by recycling. However, recycling is not a perfect way to manage waste. It still requires large amounts of energy to (B) | contaminate / purify | used resources and convert them into new products. So, what about trying to creatively reuse, or "upcycle," them instead? This new approach is becoming more (C) | popular / unpopular | since it is even more environmentally friendly than recycling. What's more, it can also be fun! Here are some inspiring examples of how people have creatively upcycled old, used things.
>
> | | (A) | (B) | (C) |
> |---|---|---|---|
> | ① | increase | – contaminate | – popular |
> | ② | reduce | – contaminate | – popular |
> | ③ | reduce | – purify | – unpopular |
> | ④ | reduce | – purify | – popular |
> | ⑤ | increase | – purify | – unpopular |

정답 ④

(A) 재활용이 좋은 이유에 해당하는 부분이므로, 재활용을 함으로써 버려지는 쓰레기 양을 '줄일(reduce)' 수 있다고 하는 것이 적절하다.
increase: 증가시키다
(B) 재활용은 사용된 자원을 '정화시키는(purify)' 데 많은 양의 에너지를 필요로 한다고 하는 것이 자연스럽다.
contaminate: 오염시키다
(C) 업사이클링은 재활용보다 훨씬 더 환경친화적이라고 했으므로, 점점 더 '인기를 얻고 있다(popular)'는 것을 유추할 수 있다.
unpopular: 인기 없는

문장6

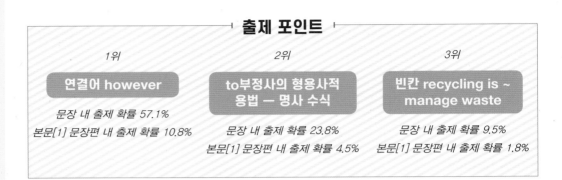

역접의 연결어   빈칸 recycling ~ waste   to부정사 형용사적 용법 (명사 수식)
However, recycling is not a perfect way to manage waste.

⊣ 출제 포인트 ⊢

1위	2위	3위
연결어 however	**to부정사의 형용사적 용법 — 명사 수식**	**빈칸 recycling is ~ manage waste**
문장 내 출제 확률 57.1%	문장 내 출제 확률 23.8%	문장 내 출제 확률 9.5%
본문[1] 문장편 내 출제 확률 10.8%	본문[1] 문장편 내 출제 확률 4.5%	본문[1] 문장편 내 출제 확률 1.8%

● 연결어 however

문장6에서 출제될 가능성은 2.7%이다. 이 문장에서 출제가 된다면 57.1%의 확률로 빈칸에 들어갈 알맞은 연결어를 묻는 문제가 나올 수 있다. 앞에서 재활용이 좋은 이유에 대해 언급하고, 뒤에서는 재활용이 쓰레기를 처리하는 완벽한 방법이 아니라는 내용이 나오므로, 앞의 내용과 반대되는 내용을 연결하는 역접의 연결어 However(그러나, 하지만), Nevertheless(그럼에도 불구하고) 등이 쓰인다는 것을 명심하자.

정답 ⑤

빈칸 앞에서 재활용이 좋은 이유에 대해 언급하고, 빈칸 뒤에서는 재활용이 쓰레기를 처리하는 완벽한 방법이 아니라는 내용이 나오므로, 앞의 내용과 반대되는 내용을 연결하는 역접의 연결어 ⑤ 'However(그러나, 하지만)'가 적절하다.
① 따라서 ② 게다가
③ 대신에 ④ 마찬가지로

Q. 다음 빈칸에 들어갈 말로 가장 적절한 것은?

Every day during lunch, Jamie enjoys a soft drink and has a decision to make: What should he do with the empty can? Many people would answer, "Recycle it!" Obviously, recycling is good for many reasons. We can reduce the amount of trash thrown away, use less energy than we would to make new products, and conserve natural resources by recycling. _____, recycling is not a perfect way to manage waste. It still requires large amounts of energy to purify used resources and convert them into new products. So, what about trying to creatively reuse, or "upcycle," them instead? This new approach is becoming more popular since it is even more environmentally friendly than recycling. What's more, it can also be fun! Here are some inspiring examples of how people have creatively upcycled old, used things.

① Accordingly   ② Besides   ③ Instead   ④ Similarly   ⑤ However

● to부정사의 형용사적 용법 – 명사 수식

이 문장에서 두 번째로 출제 확률이 높은 것은 to부정사의 형용사적 용법이다(23.8%). to manage는 명사구 a perfect way를 수식하는 형용사적 용법의 to부정사로, '쓰레기를 처리하는 완벽한 방법'이라는 의미를 만든다는 것을 기억하자.

> **Q. 다음 글의 밑줄 친 우리말을 〈보기〉의 단어를 사용하여 영작하시오. (단, 필요시 알맞은 형태로 변형할 것)**
>
> > 〈보기〉 a, be, waste, perfect, recycling, not, way, manage
>
> Every day during lunch, Jamie enjoys a soft drink and has a decision to make: What should he do with the empty can? Many people would answer, "Recycle it!" Obviously, recycling is good for many reasons. We can reduce the amount of trash thrown away, use less energy than we would to make new products, and conserve natural resources by recycling. However, 재활용이 쓰레기를 처리하는 완벽한 방법은 아니다. It still requires large amounts of energy to purify used resources and convert them into new products. So, what about trying to creatively reuse, or "upcycle," them instead? This new approach is becoming more popular since it is even more environmentally friendly than recycling. What's more, it can also be fun! Here are some inspiring examples of how people have creatively upcycled old, used things.

정답
recycling is not a perfect way to manage waste

명사구 a perfect way를 수식하여 '쓰레기를 처리하는 완벽한 방법'이라는 의미를 만들어야 하므로, 동사 manage를 형용사적 용법의 to부정사인 to manage로 올바르게 변형한다.

● 빈칸 recycling is not a perfect way to manage waste

9.5%의 확률로, However 뒤에 들어갈 내용을 묻는 문제가 출제될 수 있다. 앞에서 재활용의 장점에 대해 언급하고, 뒤에서는 재활용의 한계점에 대해 제시하므로, 그 사이에는 역접의 연결어 However를 사용하여 '하지만 재활용이 쓰레기를 처리하는 완벽한 방법은 아니다'라는 내용이 제시되어야 한다.

> **Q. 다음 빈칸에 들어갈 말로 가장 적절한 것은?**
>
> Every day during lunch, Jamie enjoys a soft drink and has a decision to make: What should he do with the empty can? Many people would answer, "Recycle it!" Obviously, recycling is good for many reasons. We can reduce the amount of trash thrown away, use less energy than we would to make new products, and conserve natural resources by recycling. However, _____.
> It still requires large amounts of energy to purify used resources and convert them into new products. So, what about trying to creatively reuse, or "upcycle," them instead? This new approach is becoming more popular since it is even more environmentally friendly than recycling. What's more, it can also be fun! Here are some inspiring examples of how people have creatively upcycled old, used things.
>
> ① not many people participate in upcycling
> ② it is more important not to use disposable products than to recycle
> ③ the government must implement a sustainable recycling policy
> ④ we can protect the environment through recycling
> ⑤ recycling is not a perfect way to dispose of waste

정답 ⑤
빈칸 앞의 문장에서 재활용의 장점에 대해 언급하고, 빈칸 뒤의 문장에서는 재활용의 한계점을 제시하므로, '그러나'를 의미하는 역접의 연결어 However 뒤에 이어지는 빈칸에는 ⑤ '재활용이 쓰레기를 처리하는 완벽한 방법은 아니다'라는 내용이 들어가야 한다.
① 업사이클링에 참여하는 사람들은 많지 않다
② 재활용을 하는 것보다 일회용품을 사용하지 않는 것이 더 중요하다
③ 정부는 지속 가능한 재활용 정책을 실시해야 한다
④ 우리는 재활용을 통해 환경을 보호할 수 있다

문장7

to부정사의 부사적 용법 (목적)

It still requires large amounts of energy <u>to purify</u> used resources <u>and convert</u> them into new products.

to부정사의 부사적 용법 (목적)
v. 전환시키다, 개조하다

┤ 출제 포인트 ├

1위	2위
to부정사 병렬 — 부사적 용법	**어휘 convert**
문장 내 출제 확률 36.4%	문장 내 출제 확률 18.2%
본문[1] 문장편 내 출제 확률 4.4%	본문[1] 문장편 내 출제 확률 2.2%

정답 convert

완전한 절(It ~ energy)에 접속사 없이 연결되고 있으므로 부사구의 형태가 되어야 하며, 접속사 and로 to purify와 병렬 구조를 이루고 있으므로 (to) convert가 적절하다. 이때, 병렬 구조로 연결된 두 번째 to부정사구에서 to는 생략될 수 있음에 유의한다.

● to부정사 병렬 – 부사적 용법

이 문장에서는 36.4%의 확률로, to부정사 병렬 구조를 물을 수 있다. to purify와 to convert는 완전한 절(It still requires large amounts of energy)에 이어지는 부사적 용법의 to부정사로, 문맥상 '재활용이 여전히 많은 양의 에너지가 필요한 이유'를 전달하는 목적의 의미를 나타낸다. 완전한 절 뒤에서 to부정사구 to purify와 (to) convert는 접속사 and로 병렬 연결되어 있다. and 다음 to부정사의 to는 생략하는 경우가 많으므로, convert 앞에 to가 생략되어 있음에 유의하자.

> **Q. 다음 괄호 안에서 어법상 올바른 것을 고르시오.**
>
> It still requires large amounts of energy to purify used resources and converts / convert them into new products.

정답
(A) less (B) conserve
(C) convert

(A) 재활용이 좋은 이유에 해당하는 부분이므로, 새 제품을 만드는 데 쓰는 것보다 '더 적은(less)' 에너지를 사용할 수 있다고 하는 것이 적절하다.
(B) 재활용의 이점 중의 하나이므로, 재활용을 함으로써 천연자원을 '절약할 (conserve)' 수 있다고 하는 것이 알맞다.
(C) 재활용의 한계점에 대해 제시하는 부분이므로, 재활용은 여전히 사용된 자원을 새 제품으로 '바꾸기 (convert)' 위해 많은 양의 에너지를 필요로 한다고 하는 것이 적절하다.

● 어휘 convert

이 문장에서 두 번째로 출제 확률이 높은 것은 18.2%의 확률로 나올 수 있는 어휘 convert이다. 재활용은 사용된 자원을 정화하고 새 제품으로 '전환시키는, 개조하는(convert)' 데 많은 양의 에너지를 필요로 한다. convert의 영영풀이도 출제될 수 있으니 아래의 영영풀이도 함께 기억해두자.

convert(개조하다): to change something into a different form(어떤 것을 다른 형태로 바꾸다)

> **Q. 다음 글의 (A), (B), (C)의 각 네모 안에서 문맥에 맞는 낱말로 가장 적절한 것을 고르시오.**
>
> Every day during lunch, Jamie enjoys a soft drink and has a decision to make: What should he do with the empty can? Many people would answer, "Recycle it!" Obviously, recycling is good for many reasons. We can reduce the amount of trash thrown away, use (A) more / less energy than we would to make new products, and (B) convert / conserve natural resources by recycling. However, recycling is not a perfect way to manage waste. It still requires large amounts of energy to purify used resources and (C) convert / conserve them into new products. So, what about trying to creatively reuse, or "upcycle," them instead? This new

approach is becoming more popular since it is even more environmentally friendly than recycling. What's more, it can also be fun! Here are some inspiring examples of how people have creatively upcycled old, used things.

● 어휘 purify

이 문장에서 어휘 purify를 묻는 문제도 9.1%의 확률로 출제될 수 있다. 재활용은 사용된 자원을 '정화시키는(purify)'데 많은 양의 에너지를 필요로 한다. 반의어인 pollute, contaminate(오염시키다)로 바꾸어 출제되거나, 영영풀이를 묻는 문제가 출제될 수 있으니 함께 암기해두자.

purify(정화하다): to remove bad substances from something to make it pure(어떤 것에서 나쁜 물질을 제거하여 그것을 순수[깨끗]하게 만들다)

> **Q. 다음 글의 (A), (B), (C)의 각 네모 안에서 문맥에 맞는 낱말로 가장 적절한 것을 고르시오.**
>
> Every day during lunch, Jamie enjoys a soft drink and has a decision to make: What should he do with the empty can? Many people would answer, "Recycle it!" Obviously, recycling is (A) beneficial / harmful for many reasons. We can reduce the amount of trash thrown away, use less energy than we would to make new products, and conserve natural resources by recycling. However, recycling is not a perfect way to manage waste. It still requires large amounts of energy to (B) pollute / purify used resources and convert them into new products. So, what about trying to creatively reuse, or "upcycle," them instead? This new approach is becoming (C) less / more popular since it is even more environmentally friendly than recycling. What's more, it can also be fun! Here are some inspiring examples of how people have creatively upcycled old, used things.

정답
(A) beneficial (B) purify (C) more

(A) 뒤에 재활용의 장점이 이어지므로, 재활용은 여러 가지 이유에서 '이롭다(beneficial)'고 하는 것이 적절하다.
harmful: 해로운
(B) 재활용은 사용된 자원을 '정화시키는(purify)' 데 많은 양의 에너지가 필요하다고 하는 것이 자연스럽다.
pollute: 오염시키다
(C) 업사이클링은 재활용보다 훨씬 더 환경친화적이라고 했으므로, 점점 '더(more)' 인기를 얻고 있다는 것을 유추할 수 있다.
[원문 변형]
good → beneficial

● 과거분사 – 명사 수식

이 문장에서 출제가 된다면 역시 9.1%의 확률로 과거분사의 명사 수식에 대해 물을 수 있다. resources(자원)는 사용되는 대상이므로, 동사(use)와 명사(resources)는 수동의 관계이다. 따라서 과거분사 used가 명사 resources를 수식한다는 것을 잘 기억해두도록 하자.

> **Q. 다음 괄호 안에서 어법상 올바른 것을 고르시오.**
>
> It still requires large amounts of energy to purify using / used resources and convert them into new products.

정답 used

resources(자원)은 사용되는 대상이므로, 동사(use)와 명사(resources)는 수동의 관계이다. 따라서 과거분사 used가 명사 resources를 수식해야 한다.

● 지칭 them

지칭 them의 쓰임에 대해 묻는 문제 역시 9.1%의 확률로 출제될 수 있다. 앞의 명사 used resources를 가리키므로, 복수형 them이 쓰여야 하며, 단수형인 it으로 쓰지 않음에 주의하자.

> **Q. 다음 글의 밑줄 친 부분 중, 어법상 어색한 것은?**
>
> Every day during lunch, Jamie enjoys a soft drink and has a decision to make: What should he do with the empty can? Many people would answer, "Recycle it!" Obviously, ① recycling is good for many reasons. We can reduce the amount of trash thrown away, use less energy than we would to make new products, and ② conserve natural resources by recycling. However, recycling is not a perfect way to manage waste. It still requires large amounts of energy to purify used resources and ③ convert it into new products. So, what about trying to ④ creatively reuse, or "upcycle," them instead? This new approach is becoming more popular since it is even more environmentally friendly than recycling. What's more, it can also be fun! Here are some ⑤ inspiring examples of how people have creatively upcycled old, used things.

문장8

> 동명사 – 전치사의 목적어
>
> **So, what about <u>trying</u> to creatively reuse, or "upcycle," them instead?**

| 출제 포인트 |

1위

동명사 — 전치사의 목적어

문장 내 출제 확률 28.6%
본문[1] 문장편 내 출제 확률 1.1%

● 동명사 – 전치사의 목적어

이 문장에서는 전치사의 목적어로 쓰인 동명사 trying이 가장 많이 출제되었다(28.6%). 〈What about ~?〉은 '~하는 것은 어때?'라는 제안의 표현으로, 전치사 about 뒤에는 전치사의 목적어 역할을 하는 명사(구) 또는 동명사가 와야 하므로, 동명사 trying이 쓰인다는 것을 기억하도록 하자.

> **Q. 다음 괄호 안의 동사를 알맞은 형태로 고쳐 쓰시오.**
>
> So, what about _____(try) to creatively reuse, or "upcycle," them instead?

문장9

비교급 강조

This new approach is becoming more popular <u>since</u> it is <u>even</u> more <u>environmentally friendly</u> than recycling.

a. 환경친화적인

접속사
(~이기 때문에)

⊣ 출제 포인트 ⊢

1위	공동 2위	공동 2위
어휘 environmentally friendly	**이유 접속사 since**	**비교급 강조**
문장 내 출제 확률 25.0% 본문[1] 문장편 내 출제 확률 2.7%	문장 내 출제 확률 16.7% 본문[1] 문장편 내 출제 확률 1.8%	문장 내 출제 확률 16.7% 본문[1] 문장편 내 출제 확률 1.8%

● 어휘 environmentally friendly

이 문장에서 어휘 environmentally friendly를 묻는 문제는 25.0% 확률로 가장 자주 출제된다. environmentally friendly는 '환경친화적인'이라는 의미로, 유의어인 eco-friendly(비교급: more eco-friendly), green(비교급: greener)과 바꾸어 쓸 수 있다. 형용사를 부사로 만드는 어미인 -ly가 명사 뒤에 오면 명사를 형용사로 만들기 때문에 (environmentally) friendly가 형용사라는 점에 유의하자.

> **Q. 다음 글의 밑줄 친 부분 중, 문맥상 낱말의 쓰임이 적절하지 <u>않은</u> 것은?**
>
> Every day during lunch, Jamie enjoys a soft drink and has a decision to make: What should he do with the empty can? Many people would answer, "Recycle it!" Obviously, recycling is ① <u>good</u> for many reasons. We can reduce the amount of trash thrown away, use ② <u>more</u> energy than we would to make new products, and conserve natural resources by recycling. However, recycling is not a perfect way to manage waste. It still ③ <u>demands</u> large amounts of energy to purify used resources and convert them into new products. So, what about trying to creatively reuse, or "upcycle," them instead? This new approach is becoming more popular since it is even ④ <u>greener</u> than recycling. What's more, it can also be fun! Here are some ⑤ <u>inspirational</u> examples of how people have creatively upcycled old, used things.

정답 ②

재활용이 좋은 이유에 해당하는 부분이므로, 새 제품을 만드는 데 쓰는 것보다 '더 적은' 에너지를 사용할 수 있다고 하는 것이 자연스럽다. 따라서, 'more(더 많은)'을 'less(더 적은)'으로 고쳐야 한다.

[원문 변형]
more environmentally friendly → greener

● 이유 접속사 since

이 문장에서 두 번째로 출제 확률이 높은 것(16.7%)은 접속사 since이다. '업사이클링은 재활용보다 훨씬 더 환경친화적이다'는 업사이클링이 점점 인기를 얻고 있는 이유에 해당하므로, '~ 때문에'를 의미하는 이유를 나타내는 접속사 since가 쓰인다. 접속사 뒤에는 '주어＋동사'가 있는 완전한 절이 오며, 접속사 since가 이유를 나타낼 때는 as, because로 바꿔 쓸 수 있다는 점도 기억하도록 하자.

Q. 다음 글의 빈칸 (A), (B)에 들어갈 말을 〈보기〉에서 골라 쓰시오.

〈보기〉 although / since / furthermore / however / instead

Every day during lunch, Jamie enjoys a soft drink and has a decision to make: What should he do with the empty can? Many people would answer, "Recycle it!" Obviously, recycling is good for many reasons. We can reduce the amount of trash thrown away, use less energy than we would to make new products, and conserve natural resources by recycling. However, recycling is not a perfect way to manage waste. It still requires large amounts of energy to purify used resources and convert them into new products. So, what about trying to creatively reuse, or "upcycle," them instead? This new approach is becoming more popular _____(A)_____ it is even more environmentally friendly than recycling. _____(B)_____, it can also be fun! Here are some inspiring examples of how people have creatively upcycled old, used things.

(A) _____ (B) _____

정답
(A) since
(B) Furthermore

(A) '업사이클링은 재활용보다 훨씬 더 환경친화적이다'는 업사이클링이 점점 인기를 얻고 있는 이유에 해당하므로, '~ 때문에'를 의미하는 이유를 나타내는 접속사 since가 알맞다.
(B) '업사이클링은 재활용보다 훨씬 더 환경친화적이다'라는 장점에 더하여, '업사이클링은 재미있을 수도 있다'는 추가적인 장점을 덧붙이고 있으므로, Furthermore(게다가)가 적절하다.

● 비교급 강조

비교급 강조 표현 역시 16.7% 확률로 자주 출제된다. 비교급 앞에 쓰여 '훨씬'이라는 뜻을 가지는 비교급 강조 표현으로는 much, even, still, a lot, far, by far 등이 있다. very는 원급을 수식하므로, 비교급 앞에 쓰일 수 없다는 점에 유의하자.

Q. 다음 빈칸에 들어갈 말로 적절하지 않은 것은?

This new approach is becoming more popular since it is _____ more environmentally friendly than recycling.

① still   ② a lot   ③ very   ④ far   ⑤ even

정답 ③

비교급 앞에 쓰여 '훨씬'이라는 뜻을 가지는 비교급 강조 표현으로는 much, even, still, a lot, far 등이 있다. very는 원급을 수식하므로, 비교급 앞에 쓰일 수 없다.

● more

어휘나 비교급을 묻는 more 역시 16.7%의 확률로 출제된다. 이 문장은 업사이클링이 점점 인기를 얻고 있는 이유에 해당하는 부분이므로, 업사이클링은 재활용보다 훨씬 '더(more)' 환경친화적이라는 것을 유추할 수 있다. 또한, 비교급을 사용하여 '점점 인기를 얻는다'는 more popular로, '더 환경친화적이다'는 more environmentally friendly로 나타낸다. become은 보어를 필요로 하는데, 부사는 보어가 될 수 없으므로, more popularly로 쓰일 수 없다는 것에도 유의하자.

> **Q. 다음 글의 (A), (B), (C)의 각 네모 안에서 문맥에 맞는 낱말로 가장 적절한 것을 고르시오.**
>
> Every day during lunch, Jamie enjoys a soft drink and has a decision to make: What should he do with the empty can? Many people would answer, "Recycle it!" Obviously, recycling is good for many reasons. We can reduce the amount of trash thrown away, use (A) more / less energy than we would to make new products, and conserve natural resources by recycling. However, recycling is not a perfect way to manage waste. It still requires large amounts of energy to (B) verify / purify used resources and convert them into new products. So, what about trying to creatively reuse, or "upcycle," them instead? This new approach is becoming more popular since it is even (C) more / less environmentally friendly than recycling. What's more, it can also be fun! Here are some inspiring examples of how people have creatively upcycled old, used things.

● 어휘 popular

어휘 popular를 묻는 문제도 역시 16.7% 확률로 출제될 수 있다. 업사이클링은 재활용보다 훨씬 더 환경친화적이라고 했으므로, 점점 더 '인기를 얻고 있다(popular)'는 것을 유추할 수 있다.

> **Q. 다음 글의 (A), (B), (C)의 각 네모 안에서 문맥에 맞는 낱말로 가장 적절한 것을 고르시오.**
>
> Every day during lunch, Jamie enjoys a soft drink and has a decision to make: What should he do with the empty can? Many people would answer, "Recycle it!" Obviously, recycling is (A) good / bad for many reasons. We can reduce the amount of trash thrown away, use less energy than we would to make new products, and conserve natural resources by recycling. However, recycling is not a(n) (B) perfect / imperfect way to manage waste. It still requires large amounts of energy to purify used resources and convert them into new products. So, what about trying to creatively reuse, or "upcycle," them instead? This new approach is becoming more (C) unpopular / popular since it is even more environmentally friendly than recycling. What's more, it can also be fun! Here are some inspiring examples of how people have creatively upcycled old, used things.

출제 포인트 6.8% 정복!

문장10

연결어 '게다가'
What's more, it can also be fun!

┤ **출제 포인트** ├

1위

연결어 what's more

문장 내 출제 확률 100.0%
본문[1] 문장편 내 출제 확률 8.1%

● 연결어 what's more

문장10에서 출제될 가능성은 1.2%이다. 이 문장에서 출제가 된다면 100.0%의 확률로 빈칸에 들어갈 알맞은 연결어를 묻는 문제가 나올 수 있다. '업사이클링은 재활용보다 훨씬 더 환경친화적이다'라는 장점에 더하여, '업사이클링은 재미있을 수도 있다'는 추가적인 장점을 덧붙이고 있으므로, '게다가'를 의미하는 연결어 What's more가 쓰이며, In addition, Additionally, Furthermore, Moreover, Besides 등으로 바꿔 쓸 수 있다는 것을 기억하도록 하자.

> **Q. 다음 빈칸에 들어갈 말로 가장 적절한 것은?**
>
> Every day during lunch, Jamie enjoys a soft drink and has a decision to make: What should he do with the empty can? Many people would answer, "Recycle it!" Obviously, recycling is good for many reasons. We can reduce the amount of trash thrown away, use less energy than we would to make new products, and conserve natural resources by recycling. However, recycling is not a perfect way to manage waste. It still requires large amounts of energy to purify used resources and convert them into new products. So, what about trying to creatively reuse, or "upcycle," them instead? This new approach is becoming more popular since it is even more environmentally friendly than recycling. _____, it can also be fun! Here are some inspiring examples of how people have creatively upcycled old, used things.
>
> ① However
> ② Therefore
> ③ What's more
> ④ Otherwise
> ⑤ For example

정답 ③
'업사이클링은 재활용보다 훨씬 더 환경친화적이다'라는 장점에 더하여, '업사이클링은 재미있을 수도 있다'는 추가적인 장점을 덧붙이고 있으므로, 빈칸에 들어갈 말로는 '게다가'를 의미하는 연결어 What's more가 적절하다.
① 그러나
② 그러므로
④ 그렇지 않으면
⑤ 예를 들어

출제 포인트 7.7% 정복!

현재분사 – 명사 수식
의문사절 – 전치사의 목적어

Here are some <u>inspiring</u> examples of <u>how people have creatively upcycled</u> old, used things.

┤ 출제 포인트 ├

1위	2위
현재분사 – 명사 수식	**의문사절 – 전치사의 목적어**
문장 내 출제 확률 44.4%	문장 내 출제 확률 33.3%
본문[1] 문장편 내 출제 확률 3.6%	본문[1] 문장편 내 출제 확률 2.7%

● 현재분사 – 명사 수식

이 문장에서 출제가 된다면 44.4%의 확률로 현재분사의 명사 수식에 대해 물을 수 있다. examples(예들)은 영감을 주는 것이므로, 동사(inspire: 영감을 주다, 고무시키다)와 명사(examples)는 능동의 관계이다. 따라서, 현재분사 inspiring이 명사 examples를 수식한다는 것을 잘 기억해두도록 하자. 아울러 분사 형용사 inspiring의 영영풀이도 출제될 수 있으니 아래의 영영풀이도 함께 암기해두자.

inspiring(고무하는): exciting and encouraging you to do or feel something(흥미로우며 무언가를 하거나 느끼도록 격려하는)

> **Q. 다음 문장의 밑줄 친 ⓐ~ⓒ 중, 어법상 틀린 것을 찾아 바르게 고치시오.**
>
> Here ⓐ <u>are</u> some ⓑ <u>inspired</u> examples of ⓒ <u>how people have</u> creatively upcycled old, used things.
>
> _____ → _____

정답
ⓑ inspired → inspiring

examples(예들)은 '영감을 주는' 것이므로, 동사(inspire: 영감을 주다, 고무시키다)와 명사(examples)는 능동의 관계이다. 따라서, 현재분사 inspiring이 명사 examples를 수식해야 한다.

● 의문사절 – 전치사의 목적어

이 문장에서 두 번째로 출제 확률이 높은 것은, 33.3%의 비율을 차지하는 전치사 of의 목적어로 쓰인 〈의문사(how)+주어(people)+동사(have creatively upcycled~)〉 어순의 간접의문이다. 간접의문문의 어순과 더불어, 의문사 how 뒤에는 완전한 문장이 온다는 것에 유의하자. 또한, 사람들이 과거에서 현재까지 계속해서 업사이클을 해왔다는 의미를 나타내기 위해 현재완료 시제 have upcycled가 쓰인다는 것도 함께 기억해두자.

> **Q. 주어진 우리말과 같은 뜻이 되도록 〈보기〉의 단어를 사용하여 영작하시오. (단, 필요시 알맞은 형태로 변형할 것)**
>
> 〈보기〉 people, inspire, some, creatively upcycle, how, of, examples, old, used things
>
> 여기 사람들이 오래된 중고 물건들을 어떻게 창의적으로 업사이클해왔는지를 보여주는 몇몇 고무적인 사례들이 있다.
>
> Here are _____.

정답
some inspiring examples of how people have creatively upcycled old, used things

'예들'은 '영감을 주는' 능동의 관계이므로, 현재분사 inspiring이 examples를 수식하도록 올바르게 변형한다. 전치사 of의 목적어로 〈의문사(how)+주어(people)+동사(have creatively upcycled~)〉 어순의 간접의문을 쓴다. '업사이클을 해왔다'는 현재완료 시제 have upcycled로 나타낸다.

출제 포인트 8.3% 정복!

01

다음 글의 밑줄 친 ⓐ~ⓓ 중, 쓰임이 같은 것끼리 올바르게 짝지어진 것은?

Every day during lunch, Jamie enjoys a soft drink and has a decision ⓐ to make: What should he do with the empty can? Many people would answer, "Recycle it!" Obviously, recycling is good for many reasons. We can reduce the amount of trash thrown away, use less energy than we would ⓑ to make new products, and conserve natural resources by recycling. However, recycling is not a perfect way ⓒ to manage waste. It still requires large amounts of energy ⓓ to purify used resources and convert them into new products. So, what about trying to creatively reuse, or "upcycle," them instead? This new approach is becoming more popular since it is even more environmentally friendly than recycling. What's more, it can also be fun! Here are some inspiring examples of how people have creatively upcycled old, used things.

① ⓐ, ⓑ – ⓒ, ⓓ   ② ⓐ, ⓓ – ⓑ, ⓒ
③ ⓐ – ⓑ, ⓒ, ⓓ   ④ ⓐ, ⓑ, ⓓ – ⓒ
⑤ ⓐ, ⓒ – ⓑ, ⓓ

02

다음 글의 (A), (B), (C)의 각 네모 안에서 어법에 맞는 표현으로 가장 적절한 것은?

Every day during lunch, Jamie enjoys a soft drink and has a decision to make: What (A) he should / should he do with the empty can? Many people would answer, "Recycle it!" Obviously, recycling is good for many reasons. We can reduce the amount of trash thrown away, use less energy than we would to make new products, and conserve natural resources by recycling. However, recycling is not a perfect way to manage waste. It still requires large amounts of energy to purify used resources and convert (B) it / them into new products. So, what about trying to creatively reuse, or "upcycle,"

them instead? This new approach is becoming more popular since it is (C) very / even more environmentally friendly than recycling. What's more, it can also be fun! Here are some inspiring examples of how people have creatively upcycled old, used things.

	(A)	(B)	(C)
①	he should	it	very
②	should he	it	even
③	should he	them	even
④	he should	them	even
⑤	should he	them	very

03

다음 글의 (A), (B), (C)의 각 네모 안에서 어법에 맞는 표현으로 가장 적절한 것은?

Every day during lunch, Jamie enjoys a soft drink and has a decision to make: What should he do with the empty can? Many people would answer, "Recycle it!" Obviously, recycling is good for many reasons. We can reduce the amount of trash (A) throwing / thrown away, use less energy than we would to make new products, and conserve natural resources by recycling. However, recycling is not a perfect way to manage waste. It still requires large amounts of energy to purify used resources and (B) converts / convert them into new products. So, what about trying to creatively reuse, or "upcycle," them instead? This new approach is becoming more popular since it is even more environmentally friendly than recycling. What's more, it can also be fun! Here are some (C) inspiring / inspired examples of how people have creatively upcycled old, used things.

	(A)	(B)	(C)
①	thrown	converts	inspiring
②	throwing	converts	inspired
③	throwing	convert	inspiring
④	thrown	convert	inspiring
⑤	thrown	converts	inspired

04

다음 글의 빈칸 (A), (B)에 들어갈 말로 가장 적절한 것은?

Every day during lunch, Jamie enjoys a soft drink and has a decision to make: What should he do with the empty can? Many people would answer, "Recycle it!" Obviously, recycling is good for many reasons. We can reduce the amount of trash thrown away, use less energy than we would to make new products, and conserve natural resources by recycling. ____(A)____, recycling is not a perfect way to manage waste. It still requires large amounts of energy to purify used resources and convert them into new products. So, what about trying to creatively reuse, or "upcycle," them instead? This new approach is becoming more popular since it is even more environmentally friendly than recycling. ____(B)____, it can also be fun! Here are some inspiring examples of how people have creatively upcycled old, used things.

	(A)		(B)
①	Nevertheless	–	Furthermore
②	Nevertheless	–	For instance
③	Therefore	–	For instance
④	Therefore	–	Furthermore
⑤	What's more	–	In contrast

05

다음 글의 밑줄 친 부분 중, 문맥상 낱말의 쓰임이 적절하지 않은 것은?

Every day during lunch, Jamie enjoys a soft drink and has a decision to make: What should he do with the empty can? Many people would answer, "Recycle it!" Obviously, recycling is ① good for many reasons. We can ② reduce the amount of trash thrown away, use ③ less energy than we would to make new products, and conserve natural resources by recycling. However, recycling is not a perfect way to manage waste. It still requires large amounts of energy to purify used resources and ④ convert them into new products. So, what about trying to creatively reuse, or "upcycle," them instead? This new approach is becoming ⑤ less popular since it is even more environmentally friendly than recycling. What's more, it can also be fun! Here are some inspiring examples of how people have creatively upcycled old, used things.

06

다음 글의 (A), (B), (C)의 각 네모 안에서 문맥에 맞는 낱말로 가장 적절한 것은?

Every day during lunch, Jamie enjoys a soft drink and has a decision to make: What should he do with the empty can? Many people would answer, "Recycle it!" Obviously, recycling is good for many reasons. We can (A) increase / decrease the amount of trash thrown away, use less energy than we would to make new products, and conserve natural resources by recycling. However, recycling is not a perfect way to manage waste. It still (B) acquires / requires large amounts of energy to purify used resources and convert them into new products. So, what about trying to creatively reuse, or "upcycle," them instead? This new approach is becoming more popular since it is even (C) more / less environmentally friendly than recycling. What's more, it can also be fun! Here are some inspiring examples of how people have creatively upcycled old, used things.

	(A)		(B)		(C)
①	decrease	–	acquires	–	more
②	increase	–	acquires	–	more
③	decrease	–	requires	–	more
④	decrease	–	requires	–	less
⑤	increase	–	requires	–	less

07

다음 글의 (A), (B), (C)의 각 네모 안에서 어법에 맞는 표현으로 가장 적절한 것은?

Every day during lunch, Jamie enjoys a soft drink and has a decision to make: What should he do with the empty can? Many people would answer, "Recycle it!" Obviously, recycling is good for many reasons. We can reduce the amount of trash thrown away, use less energy than we would to make new products, and (A) conserve / to conserve natural resources by recycling. However, recycling is not a perfect way (B) what / that manages waste. It still requires large amounts of energy to purify used resources and convert them into new products. So, what about trying to creatively reuse, or "upcycle," them instead? This new approach is becoming more popular since it is (C) very / far more environmentally friendly than recycling. What's more, it can also be fun! Here are some inspiring examples of how people have creatively upcycled old, used things.

	(A)	(B)	(C)
①	conserve	– what	– very
②	to conserve	– what	– far
③	conserve	– that	– very
④	to conserve	– that	– far
⑤	conserve	– that	– far

08

다음 글의 밑줄 친 부분 중, 문맥상 낱말의 쓰임이 적절하지 않은 것은?

Every day during lunch, Jamie enjoys a soft drink and has a decision to make: What should he do with the empty can? Many people would answer, "Recycle it!" Obviously, recycling is good for many reasons. We can reduce the amount of trash thrown away, use less energy than we would to make new products, and ① <u>use up</u> natural resources by recycling. However, recycling is not the ② <u>best</u> way to manage waste. It still requires large amounts of energy to ③ <u>purify</u> used resources and convert them into new products. So, what about trying to creatively reuse, or "④ <u>upcycle</u>," them instead? This new approach is becoming more popular since it is even more ⑤ <u>eco-friendly</u> than recycling. What's more, it can also be fun! Here are some inspiring examples of how people have creatively upcycled old, used things.

09

다음 글의 ⓐ~ⓒ에 주어진 단어를 알맞은 형태로 바꿔 쓰시오.

Every day during lunch, Jamie enjoys a soft drink and ⓐ (have) a decision to make: What should he do with the empty can? Many people would answer, "Recycle it!" Obviously, recycling is good for many reasons. We can reduce the amount of trash thrown away, use less energy than we would to make new products, and ⓑ (conserve) natural resources by recycling. However, recycling is not a perfect way ⓒ (manage) waste. It still requires large amounts of energy to purify used resources and convert them into new products. So, what about trying to creatively reuse, or "upcycle," them instead? This new approach is becoming more popular since it is even more environmentally friendly than recycling. What's more, it can also be fun! Here are some inspiring examples of how people have creatively upcycled old, used things.

ⓐ _____ ⓑ _____ ⓒ _____

10

다음 빈칸에 들어갈 말로 가장 적절한 것은?

Every day during lunch, Jamie enjoys a soft drink and has a decision to make: What should he do with the empty can? Many people would answer, "Recycle it!" Obviously, recycling is good for many reasons. We can reduce the amount of trash thrown away, use less energy than we would to make new products, and conserve natural resources by recycling. However, _____ _____. It still requires large amounts of energy to purify used resources and convert them into new products. So, what about trying to creatively reuse, or "upcycle," them instead? This new approach is becoming more popular since it is even more environmentally friendly than recycling. What's more, it can also be fun!

① recycling has limitations as well as advantages
② there are encouraging examples of how people have been recycling
③ people are reluctant to buy recycled products
④ recycling is the best way to manage waste
⑤ people are willing to take many inconveniences to recycle

11

다음 글의 (A), (B), (C)의 각 네모 안에서 어법에 맞는 표현으로 가장 적절한 것은?

Every day during lunch, Jamie enjoys a soft drink and has a decision to make: What should he do with the empty can? Many people would answer, "Recycle it!" Obviously, recycling is good for many reasons. We can reduce the amount of trash (A) throwing away / thrown away , use less energy than we would to make new products, and conserve natural resources by recycling. However, recycling is not a perfect way to manage waste. It still requires large amounts of energy to purify (B) using / used resources and convert them into new products. So, what about trying to creatively reuse, or "upcycle," them instead? This new approach is becoming more popular since it is even more environmentally friendly than recycling. What's more, it can also be fun! Here are some inspiring examples of how (C) have people / people have creatively upcycled old, used things.

	(A)	(B)	(C)
①	thrown away	using	have people
②	throwing away	using	people have
③	throwing away	used	have people
④	thrown away	used	people have
⑤	thrown away	used	have people

12

다음 글의 밑줄 친 부분 중, 문맥상 낱말의 쓰임이 적절하지 <u>않은</u> 것은?

Every day during lunch, Jamie enjoys a soft drink and has a decision to make: What should he do with the empty can? Many people would answer, "Recycle it!" Obviously, recycling is good for many reasons. We can ① <u>decrease</u> the amount of trash thrown away, use ② <u>more</u> energy than we would to make new products, and conserve natural resources by recycling. However, recycling is not a perfect way to ③ <u>handle</u> waste. It still ④ <u>needs</u> large amounts of energy to purify used resources and convert them into new products. So, what about trying to creatively reuse, or "upcycle," them instead? This new approach is becoming ⑤ <u>more</u> popular since it is even more environmentally friendly than recycling. What's more, it can also be fun! Here are some inspiring examples of how people have creatively upcycled old, used things.

13

다음 글의 밑줄 친 부분 중, 어법상 어색한 것의 개수는?

Every day during lunch, Jamie enjoys a soft drink and has a decision ① to make: What should he do with the empty can? Many people would answer, "Recycle it!" Obviously, recycling is good for many reasons. We can reduce the amount of trash thrown away, use less energy than we would ② make new products, and conserve natural resources by recycling. However, recycling is not a perfect way ③ to manage waste. It still requires large amounts of energy ④ purify used resources and convert them into new products. So, what about trying ⑤ to creatively reuse, or "upcycle," them instead? This new approach is becoming more popular since it is even more environmentally friendly than recycling. What's more, it can also be fun! Here are some inspiring examples of how people have creatively upcycled old, used things.

① 1개　　② 2개　　③ 3개　　④ 4개　　⑤ 5개

14

다음 글의 밑줄 친 부분 중, 문맥상 낱말의 쓰임이 적절하지 않은 것은?

Every day during lunch, Jamie enjoys a soft drink and has a decision to make: What should he do with the empty can? Many people would answer, "Recycle it!" ① Clearly, recycling is good for many reasons. We can reduce the amount of trash thrown away, use less energy than we would to ② manufacture new products, and conserve natural resources by recycling. However, recycling is a ③ perfect way to manage waste. It still requires large amounts of energy to ④ purify used resources and convert them into new products. So, what about trying to creatively reuse, or "upcycle," them instead? This new approach is becoming more popular since it is even ⑤ greener than recycling. What's more, it can also be fun! Here are some inspiring examples of how people have creatively upcycled old, used things.

15

다음 글의 빈칸 (A), (B)에 들어갈 말이 바르게 짝지어진 것은?

Every day during lunch, Jamie enjoys a soft drink and has a decision to make: What should he do with the empty can? Many people would answer, "Recycle it!" Obviously, recycling is good for many reasons. We can reduce the amount of trash thrown away, use less energy than we would to make new products, and conserve natural resources by recycling. _____(A)_____, recycling is not a perfect way to manage waste. It still requires large amounts of energy to purify used resources and convert them into new products. So, what about trying to creatively reuse, or "upcycle," them instead? This new approach is becoming more popular _____(B)_____ it is even more environmentally friendly than recycling. What's more, it can also be fun! Here are some inspiring examples of how people have creatively upcycled old, used things.

	(A)	(B)
①	However	if
②	Therefore	if
③	Therefore	because
④	However	as
⑤	Similarly	while

16

다음 글의 밑줄 친 부분 중, 문맥상 낱말의 쓰임이 적절하지 않은 것은?

Every day during lunch, Jamie enjoys a soft drink and has a decision to make: What should he do with the empty can? Many people would answer, "Recycle it!" Obviously, recycling is good for many reasons. We can ① lessen the amount of trash thrown away, use ② less energy than we would to make new products, and ③ conserve natural resources by recycling. However, recycling is not a perfect way to manage waste. It still requires ④ small amounts of energy to purify used resources and convert them into new products. So, what about trying to creatively reuse, or "upcycle," them instead? This new approach is becoming more ⑤ popular since it is even more environmentally friendly than recycling. What's more, it can also be fun! Here are some inspiring examples of how people have creatively upcycled old, used things.

17

다음 글의 (A), (B), (C)의 각 네모 안에서 어법에 맞는 표현으로 가장 적절한 것은?

Every day during lunch, Jamie enjoys a soft drink and has a decision to make: What should he do with the empty can? Many people would answer, "Recycle it!" Obviously, recycling is good for many reasons. We can reduce the amount of trash thrown away, use less energy than we would (A) make / to make new products, and conserve natural resources by recycling. However, recycling is not a perfect way to manage waste. It still requires large amounts of energy to purify used resources and

(B) converts / convert them into new products. So, what about trying to creatively reuse, or "upcycle," them instead? This new approach is becoming more popular since it is (C) a lot / very more environmentally friendly than recycling. What's more, it can also be fun! Here are some inspiring examples of how people have creatively upcycled old, used things.

	(A)	(B)	(C)
①	make	– converts	– very
②	to make	– converts	– a lot
③	to make	– convert	– a lot
④	to make	– convert	– very
⑤	make	– convert	– a lot

18

다음 글의 밑줄 친 부분 중, 문맥상 낱말의 쓰임이 적절하지 않은 것은?

Every day during lunch, Jamie enjoys a soft drink and has a decision to make: What should he do with the empty can? Many people would answer, "Recycle it!" ① Undoubtedly, recycling is good for many reasons. We can reduce the amount of trash thrown away, use ② less energy than we would to make new products, and ③ deplete natural resources by recycling. However, recycling is not a perfect way to ④ dispose of waste. It still requires large amounts of energy to purify used resources and convert them into new products. So, what about trying to creatively reuse, or "upcycle," them instead? This new approach is becoming more popular since it is even more ⑤ environmentally friendly than recycling. What's more, it can also be fun! Here are some inspiring examples of how people have creatively upcycled old, used things.

19

다음 글의 빈칸 (A), (B)에 들어갈 말로 가장 적절한 것은?

Every day during lunch, Jamie enjoys a soft drink and has a decision to make: What should he do with the empty can? Many people would answer, "Recycle it!" Obviously, recycling is good for many reasons. We can reduce the amount of trash thrown away, use less energy than we would to make new products, and conserve natural resources by recycling. _____(A)_____ these advantages, recycling is not a perfect way to manage waste. It still requires large amounts of energy to purify used resources and convert them into new products. So, what about trying to creatively reuse, or "upcycle," them instead? This new approach is becoming more popular since it is even more environmentally friendly than recycling. _____(B)_____, it can also be fun! Here are some inspiring examples of how people have creatively upcycled old, used things.

	(A)	(B)
①	In spite of	Furthermore
②	Due to	In addition
③	In addition to	However
④	Despite	Therefore
⑤	Because of	Nevertheless

20

다음 글의 밑줄 친 문장 중, 어법상 틀린 부분을 포함하고 있는 것은?

Every day during lunch, Jamie enjoys a soft drink and has a decision to make: What should he do with the empty can? Many people would answer, "Recycle it!" Obviously, recycling is good for many reasons. ① We can reduce the amount of trash thrown away, use less energy than we would to make new products, and conserve natural resources by recycling. However, recycling is not a perfect way to manage waste. ② It still requires large amounts of energy to purify used resources and convert them into new products. ③ So, what about trying to creatively reuse, or "upcycle," them instead? ④ This new approach is becoming more popular since it is even more environmentally friendly than recycling. What's more, it can also be fun! ⑤ Here are some inspired examples of how people have creatively upcycled old, used things.

21

〈보기〉에 있는 뜻에 해당하는 단어를 다음 글에서 찾아 한 단어로 쓰시오.

〈보기〉 encouraging or motivating you to feel or do something

Every day during lunch, Jamie enjoys a soft drink and has a decision to make: What should he do with the empty can? Many people would answer, "Recycle it!" Obviously, recycling is good for many reasons. We can reduce the amount of trash thrown away, use less energy than we would to make new products, and conserve natural resources by recycling. However, recycling is not a perfect way to manage waste. It still requires large amounts of energy to purify used resources and convert them into new products. So, what about trying to creatively reuse, or "upcycle," them instead? This new approach is becoming more popular since it is even more environmentally friendly than recycling. What's more, it can also be fun! Here are some inspiring examples of how people have creatively upcycled old, used things.

22

다음 글의 밑줄 친 부분 중, 어법상 어색한 것은?

Every day during lunch, Jamie enjoys a soft drink and has a decision ① making: What should he do with the empty can? Many people would answer, "Recycle it!" Obviously, recycling is good for many reasons. We can reduce the amount of trash ② thrown away, use less energy than we would to make new products, and ③ conserve natural resources by recycling. However, recycling is not a perfect way to manage waste. It still requires large amounts of energy to purify used resources and ④ convert them into new products. So, what about trying to creatively reuse, or "upcycle," them instead? This new approach is becoming more popular since it is even more environmentally friendly than recycling. What's more, it can also be fun! Here are some ⑤ inspiring examples of how people have creatively upcycled old, used things.

23

다음 글의 (A), (B), (C)의 각 네모 안에서 어법에 맞는 표현으로 가장 적절한 것은?

Every day during lunch, Jamie enjoys a soft drink and has a decision to make: What should he do with the empty can? Many people would answer, "Recycle it!" Obviously, recycling is good for many reasons. We can reduce the amount of trash thrown away, use less energy than we would to make new products, and (A) conserve / conserves natural resources by recycling. However, recycling is not a perfect way to manage waste. It still requires large amounts of energy to purify used resources and (B) converts / convert them into new products. So, what about trying to creatively reuse, or "upcycle,"

them instead? This new approach is becoming more popular since it is even more environmentally friendly than recycling. What's more, it can also be fun! Here are some inspiring examples of how (C) people have / have people creatively upcycled old, used things.

	(A)	(B)	(C)
①	conserve	converts	people have
②	conserves	convert	have people
③	conserve	convert	people have
④	conserves	converts	people have
⑤	conserve	convert	have people

24

다음 글의 (A), (B), (C)의 각 네모 안에서 어법상 알맞은 말을 고르시오.

Every day during lunch, (A) enjoying / enjoyed a soft drink, Jamie has a decision to make: What should he do with the empty can? Many people would answer, "Recycle it!" Obviously, recycling is good for many reasons. We can reduce the amount of trash (B) throwing / thrown away, use less energy than we would to make new products, and conserve natural resources by recycling. However, recycling is not a perfect way to manage waste. It still requires large amounts of energy to purify used resources and convert them into new products. So, what about (C) to try / trying to creatively reuse, or "upcycle," them instead? This new approach is becoming more popular since it is even more environmentally friendly than recycling. What's more, it can also be fun! Here are some inspiring examples of how people have creatively upcycled old, used things.

	(A)	(B)	(C)
①	enjoying	throwing	to try
②	enjoyed	throwing	trying
③	enjoying	thrown	trying
④	enjoyed	thrown	trying
⑤	enjoying	thrown	to try

25

다음 글의 밑줄 친 ⓐ~ⓔ 중, 어법상 바르게 고쳐 쓰지 않은 것은?

Every day during lunch, Jamie enjoys a soft drink and ⓐ <u>have</u> a decision to make: What should he do with the empty can? Many people would answer, "Recycle it!" Obviously, recycling is good for many reasons. We can reduce the amount of trash ⓑ <u>throw</u> away, use less energy than we would to make new products, and conserve natural resources by recycling. However, recycling is not a perfect way to manage waste. It still requires large amounts of energy to purify used resources and convert ⓒ <u>it</u> into new products. So, what about ⓓ <u>to try</u> to creatively reuse, or "upcycle," them instead? This new approach is becoming more ⓔ <u>popularly</u> since it is even more environmentally friendly than recycling. What's more, it can also be fun! Here are some inspiring examples of how people have creatively upcycled old, used things.

① ⓐ → has
② ⓑ → throwing
③ ⓒ → them
④ ⓓ → trying
⑤ ⓔ → popular

본문[1]

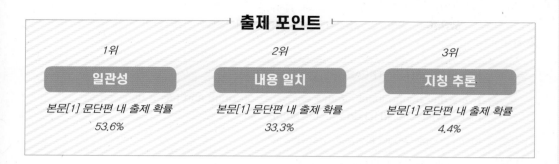

출제 포인트

1위	2위	3위
일관성	내용 일치	지칭 추론
본문[1] 문단편 내 출제 확률 53.6%	본문[1] 문단편 내 출제 확률 33.3%	본문[1] 문단편 내 출제 확률 4.4%

● 일관성

본문[1]에서 출제가 된다면, 53.6%의 확률로 일관성 문제가 나올 수 있다. 재활용의 이점에 대해 언급하다가, 역접의 연결어 However를 사용하여 재활용이 완벽한 방법이 아니라고 말하면서 글의 흐름을 전환하는 부분이 중요하다. 또한, 앞 문장의 recycling을 이어지는 문장에서 대명사 It으로 받아 재활용의 한계점에 대해 서술하는 내용의 흐름도 중요하다. 본문이 일부 생략되어 나올 수 있으므로, 주어진 글과 문장에서 연결어와 대명사로 글의 흐름의 단서를 찾을 수 있다는 점을 참고하자.

Q. 다음 글의 흐름으로 보아, 주어진 문장이 들어가기에 가장 적절한 곳은?

> However, recycling is not a perfect way to manage waste.

Every day during lunch, Jamie enjoys a soft drink and has a decision to make: What should he do with the empty can? Many people would answer, "Recycle it!" Obviously, recycling is good for many reasons. (A) We can reduce the amount of trash thrown away, use less energy than we would to make new products, and conserve natural resources by recycling. (B) It still requires large amounts of energy to purify used resources and convert them into new products. (C) So, what about trying to creatively reuse, or "upcycle," them instead? (D) This new approach is becoming more popular since it is even more environmentally friendly than recycling. (E) What's more, it can also be fun! Here are some inspiring examples of how people have creatively upcycled old, used things.

① (A)　　　　② (B)　　　　③ (C)　　　　④ (D)　　　　⑤ (E)

정답 ②

앞문장에서 재활용의 장점에 대해 언급하고, 뒷문장에서는 재활용의 한계점에 대해 제시하고 있다. 따라서, '그러나'를 의미하는 역접의 연결어 However를 문두에 두어 '재활용이 쓰레기를 처리하는 완벽한 방법은 아니다'라는 내용을 담고 있는 주어진 문장이 들어가기에 가장 적절한 곳은 (B)이다.

● 내용 일치

이 문단에서 출제가 된다면, 33.3%의 확률로 내용 일치 문제가 나올 수 있다. 쓰레기를 처리하는 일반적인 방법인 재활용의 장점과 한계점에 대해 이야기한 뒤, 그 대안으로 업사이클링을 제안하면서 업사이클링의 장점에 대해 언급한다. 해당 문단에서 주로 출제되는 포인트인 재활용의 장점과 한계점, 업사이클링의 장점에 대한 내용을 확실하게 파악하도록 하자.

문장1	FROM TRASH TO TREASURE	0%
문장2	Every day during lunch, Jamie enjoys a soft drink and has a decision to make: What should he do with the empty can?	1.9%
문장3	Many people would answer, "Recycle it!"	1.9%
문장4	Obviously, recycling is good for many reasons.	0%
문장5	We can reduce the amount of trash thrown away, use less energy than we would to make new products, and conserve natural resources by recycling.	22.2%
문장6	However, recycling is not a perfect way to manage waste.	14.8%
문장7	It still requires large amounts of energy to purify used resources and convert them into new products.	16.7%
문장8	So, what about trying to creatively reuse, or "upcycle," them instead?	9.3%
문장9	This new approach is becoming more popular since it is even more environmentally friendly than recycling.	27.8%
문장10	What's more, it can also be fun!	3.7%
문장11	Here are some inspiring examples of how people have creatively upcycled old, used things.	1.9%

Q. 글의 내용과 일치하면 T, 일치하지 않으면 F에 표시하시오.

(1) 업사이클링이 재활용보다 훨씬 더 환경친화적이라는 사실은 업사이클링이 인기를 얻고 있는 이유이다. (T / F)

(2) 재활용을 하는 데는 새 제품을 만드는 데 쓰는 것보다 더 많은 에너지가 든다. (T / F)

(3) 재활용은 쓰레기를 처리하는 완벽한 방법은 아니다. (T / F)

(4) 글쓴이는 재활용보다 업사이클링을 시도해볼 것을 제안하고 있다. (T / F)

(5) 우리는 업사이클링을 하면서 재미를 느낄 수도 있다. (T / F)

(6) 재활용은 사람들에게 널리 알려진 쓰레기 처리 방법이 아니다. (T / F)

(7) 글쓴이는 이어서 재활용의 몇몇 고무적인 사례들에 대해 이야기할 것이다. (T / F)

(8) 재활용은 분명히 여러 가지 이유에서 이롭다. (T / F)

(9) Recycling is the most environmentally friendly way to handle waste. (T / F)

(10) We can contribute to reducing the amount of trash thrown away by recycling. (T / F)

(11) Purifying used resources and converting them into new products takes little energy. (T / F)

(12) It takes a huge amount of energy to purify used resources. (T / F)

(13) Upcycling means creatively reusing used resources. (T / F)

(14) Recycling is the only way to manage waste. (T / F)

(15) Upcycling can have interesting elements. (T / F)

(16) Jamie has a habit of drinking soft drinks when he has lunch. (T / F)

(17) Jamie rarely drinks soft drinks. (T / F)

(18) Most people consider recycling to be a common way to dispose of waste. (T / F)

(19) The writer will talk about some creative upcycling cases next. (T / F)

(20) The benefits of recycling are unclear. (T / F)

정답

1	T	2	F	3	T
4	T	5	T	6	F
7	F	8	T	9	F
10	T	11	F	12	T
13	T	14	F	15	T
16	T	17	F	18	T
19	T	20	F		

(9) 재활용은 쓰레기를 처리하는 가장 환경친화적인 방식이다.

(10) 우리는 재활용을 함으로써 버려진 쓰레기의 양을 줄이는 데 기여할 수 있다.

(11) 사용된 자원을 정화하여 새로운 제품으로 바꾸는 것은 에너지가 거의 들지 않는다.

(12) 사용된 자원을 정화하는 데 많은 양의 에너지가 든다.

(13) 업사이클링은 사용된 자원을 창의적으로 재사용하는 것을 의미한다.

(14) 재활용은 쓰레기를 처리하는 유일한 방식이다.

(15) 업사이클링은 재미있는 요소를 가질 수 있다.

(16) Jamie는 점심 먹을 때 탄산 음료를 마시는 습관을 가지고 있다.

(17) Jamie는 탄산 음료를 거의 마시지 않는다.

(18) 대부분의 사람들은 재활용을 쓰레기를 처리하는 흔한 방식으로 생각한다.

(19) 글쓴이는 창의적인 업사이클링의 사례에 대해 이어서 이야기할 것이다.

(20) 재활용의 이점은 분명하지 않다.

● 지칭 추론

이 문단에서 문제가 출제된다면, 4.4%의 확률로 지칭 추론 문제가 나올 수 있다. 대명사의 지칭이 다양하게 나타나는데, Many로 시작한 문장에서 it은 the empty can을 가리키며, It still로 시작하는 문장과 So로 시작하는 문장에서 them은 모두 used resources를 가리킨다. 또한, This new로 시작하는 문장과 What's more로 시작하는 문장에서 it은 모두 upcycling을 가리킨다. 각 대명사가 가리키는 것이 무엇인지 정확히 파악하도록 하자.

> **Q. 다음 글의 밑줄 친 ⓐ~ⓕ 중, 가리키는 대상이 같은 것끼리 묶인 것은?**
>
> Every day during lunch, Jamie enjoys a soft drink and has a decision to make: What should he do with the empty can? Many people would answer, "Recycle ⓐ it!" Obviously, ⓑ it is good for many reasons. We can reduce the amount of trash thrown away, use less energy than we would to make new products, and conserve natural resources by recycling. However, ⓒ it is not a perfect way to manage waste. ⓓ It still requires large amounts of energy to purify used resources and convert them into new products. So, what about trying to creatively reuse, or "upcycle," them instead? This new approach is becoming more popular since ⓔ it is even more environmentally friendly than recycling. What's more, ⓕ it can also be fun! Here are some inspiring examples of how people have creatively upcycled old, used things.
>
> ① ⓐ, ⓑ, ⓒ, ⓓ   ② ⓑ, ⓒ, ⓓ   ③ ⓒ, ⓓ, ⓔ   ④ ⓑ, ⓔ, ⓕ   ⑤ ⓐ, ⓔ

정답 ②

ⓐ는 the empty can을, ⓑ, ⓒ, ⓓ는 recycling을 가리키며, ⓔ, ⓕ는 upcycling을 가리킨다.

● 제목

이 문단에서 출제된다면, 4.4%의 확률로 제목 문제가 나올 수 있다. 재활용은 사용된 자원을 정화하여 새 제품으로 바꾸는 데 에너지 소모가 큰 반면, 업사이클링은 더 환경친화적인 접근 방식이기 때문에, 업사이클링이 쓰레기를 처리하는 데 더 나은 대안이 될 수 있다는 것이 글쓴이의 시각이다.

> **Q. 다음 글의 제목으로 가장 적절한 것은?**
>
> Every day during lunch, Jamie enjoys a soft drink and has a decision to make: What should he do with the empty can? Many people would answer, "Recycle it!" Obviously, recycling is good for many reasons. We can reduce the amount of trash thrown away, use less energy than we would to make new products, and conserve natural resources by recycling. However, recycling is not a perfect way to manage waste. It still requires large amounts of energy to purify used resources and convert them into new products. So, what about trying to creatively reuse, or "upcycle," them instead? This new approach is becoming more popular since it is even more environmentally friendly than recycling. What's more, it can also be fun! Here are some inspiring examples of how people have creatively upcycled old, used things.
>
> ① The Best Way to Dispose of Trash: Just Bury Them All!
> ② Use the Recyclables a Few More Times before Throwing Them Away
> ③ A Better Way to Use Wastes than Recycling
> ④ What Limits Does Upcycling Have?
> ⑤ Advantages of Recycling Used Resources

정답 ③

재활용이 장점뿐만 아니라 한계점도 가지고 있기 때문에, 그 대안으로 업사이클링을 제안하는 내용의 글이다. 따라서, 글의 제목으로 가장 적절한 것은 ③ '재활용보다 쓰레기를 활용하는 더 나은 방법'이다.
① 쓰레기를 처리하는 가장 좋은 방법: 그냥 모두 묻어라!
② 재활용 가능한 것을 버리기 전에 몇 번 더 사용하라
④ 업사이클링의 한계는 무엇인가?
⑤ 사용된 자원을 재활용하는 이점

01

다음 글의 내용과 일치하지 <u>않는</u> 것은?

Every day during lunch, Jamie enjoys a soft drink and has a decision to make: What should he do with the empty can? Many people would answer, "Recycle it!" Obviously, recycling is good for many reasons. We can reduce the amount of trash thrown away, use less energy than we would to make new products, and conserve natural resources by recycling. However, recycling is not a perfect way to manage waste. It still requires large amounts of energy to purify used resources and convert them into new products. So, what about trying to creatively reuse, or "upcycle," them instead? This new approach is becoming more popular since it is even more environmentally friendly than recycling. What's more, it can also be fun! Here are some inspiring examples of how people have creatively upcycled old, used things.

① We can save natural resources as well as reduce the amount of trash through recycling.
② Recycling is not the best way to deal with waste.
③ By recycling, we can use less energy than we would to make new products.
④ Jamie likes to drink soft drinks.
⑤ Recycling requires little energy to purify used resources and convert them into new products.

02

다음 글에서 전체 흐름과 관계 <u>없는</u> 문장은?

Every day during lunch, Jamie enjoys a soft drink and has a decision to make: What should he do with the empty can? Many people would answer, "Recycle it!" Obviously, recycling is good for many reasons. ① We can reduce the amount of trash thrown away, use less energy than we would to make new products, and conserve natural resources by recycling. ② However, recycling is not a perfect

way to manage waste. ③ It still requires large amounts of energy to purify used resources and convert them into new products. ④ We can protect our environment through recycling. ⑤ So, what about trying to creatively reuse, or "upcycle," them instead? This new approach is becoming more popular since it is even more environmentally friendly than recycling. What's more, it can also be fun! Here are some inspiring examples of how people have creatively upcycled old, used things.

03

다음 글에서 언급된 <u>recycling</u>에 대한 설명으로 알맞지 <u>않은</u> 것은?

Every day during lunch, Jamie enjoys a soft drink and has a decision to make: What should he do with the empty can? Many people would answer, "Recycle it!" Obviously, <u>recycling</u> is good for many reasons. We can reduce the amount of trash thrown away, use less energy than we would to make new products, and conserve natural resources by recycling. However, recycling is not a perfect way to manage waste. It still requires large amounts of energy to purify used resources and convert them into new products. So, what about trying to creatively reuse, or "upcycle," them instead? This new approach is becoming more popular since it is even more environmentally friendly than recycling. What's more, it can also be fun! Here are some inspiring examples of how people have creatively upcycled old, used things.

① 가장 환경친화적인 쓰레기 처리 방법이다.
② 새 제품을 만드는 것보다 더 적은 에너지를 사용한다.
③ 버려지는 쓰레기의 양을 줄일 수 있다.
④ 천연자원을 절약할 수 있다.
⑤ 사용된 자원을 정화시키고 새 제품으로 바꾸기 위해 많은 양의 에너지가 필요하다.

04

다음 글에서 전체 흐름과 관계 없는 문장은?

Every day during lunch, Jamie enjoys a soft drink and has a decision to make: What should he do with the empty can? Many people would answer, "Recycle it!" Obviously, recycling is good for many reasons. We can reduce the amount of trash thrown away, use less energy than we would to make new products, and conserve natural resources by recycling. ① However, recycling is not a perfect way to manage waste. ② It still requires large amounts of energy to purify used resources and convert them into new products. ③ Recycling turns old or used items into their basic raw materials. ④ So, what about trying to creatively reuse, or "upcycle," them instead? ⑤ This new approach is becoming more popular since it is even more environmentally friendly than recycling. What's more, it can also be fun! Here are some inspiring examples of how people have creatively upcycled old, used things.

05

다음 글의 흐름으로 보아, 주어진 문장이 들어가기에 가장 적절한 곳은?

It still requires large amounts of energy to purify used resources and convert them into new products.

Every day during lunch, Jamie enjoys a soft drink and has a decision to make: What should he do with the empty can? Many people would answer, "Recycle it!" Obviously, recycling is good for many reasons. (①) We can reduce the amount of trash thrown away, use less energy than we would to make new products, and conserve natural resources by recycling. (②) However, recycling is not a

perfect way to manage waste. (③) So, what about trying to creatively reuse, or "upcycle," them instead? (④) This new approach is becoming more popular since it is even more environmentally friendly than recycling. (⑤) What's more, it can also be fun! Here are some inspiring examples of how people have creatively upcycled old, used things.

06

다음 글의 내용과 일치하지 않는 것은?

Every day during lunch, Jamie enjoys a soft drink and has a decision to make: What should he do with the empty can? Many people would answer, "Recycle it!" Obviously, recycling is good for many reasons. We can reduce the amount of trash thrown away, use less energy than we would to make new products, and conserve natural resources by recycling. However, recycling is not a perfect way to manage waste. It still requires large amounts of energy to purify used resources and convert them into new products. So, what about trying to creatively reuse, or "upcycle," them instead? This new approach is becoming more popular since it is even more environmentally friendly than recycling. What's more, it can also be fun! Here are some inspiring examples of how people have creatively upcycled old, used things.

① 재활용은 버려지는 쓰레기 양을 줄인다.
② 재활용은 사용된 자원을 정화하는 데 많은 에너지를 필요로 한다.
③ 사용된 자원을 새 제품으로 바꾸는 데에는 많은 양의 에너지가 필요하다.
④ 업사이클링은 재활용보다 더 환경친화적이다.
⑤ 재활용을 하면서 재미도 느낄 수 있다.

07

다음 글을 읽고 답할 수 없는 것은?

Every day during lunch, Jamie enjoys a soft drink and has a decision to make: What should he do with the empty can? Many people would answer, "Recycle it!" Obviously, recycling is good for many reasons. We can reduce the amount of trash thrown away, use less energy than we would to make new products, and conserve natural resources by recycling. However, recycling is not a perfect way to manage waste. It still requires large amounts of energy to purify used resources and convert them into new products. So, what about trying to creatively reuse, or "upcycle," them instead? This new approach is becoming more popular since it is even more environmentally friendly than recycling. What's more, it can also be fun! Here are some inspiring examples of how people have creatively upcycled old, used things.

① Why is recycling not the perfect way to manage waste?
② What will the writer tell next?
③ What are the advantages of recycling?
④ What are the disadvantages of upcycling?
⑤ Why is upcycling becoming more popular?

08

다음 글의 흐름으로 보아, 주어진 문장이 들어가기에 가장 적절한 곳은?

So, what about trying to creatively reuse, or "upcycle," them instead?

Every day during lunch, Jamie enjoys a soft drink and has a decision to make: What should he do with the empty can? Many people would answer, "Recycle it!" Obviously, recycling is good for many reasons. (①) We can reduce the amount of trash thrown away, use less energy than we would to make new products, and conserve natural resources by recycling. (②) However, recycling is not a perfect way to manage waste. (③) It still requires large amounts of energy to purify used resources and convert them into new products. (④) This new approach is becoming more popular since it is even more environmentally friendly than recycling. (⑤) What's more, it can also be fun! Here are some inspiring examples of how people have creatively upcycled old, used things.

09

다음 글에서 전체 흐름과 관계 없는 문장은?

Every day during lunch, Jamie enjoys a soft drink and has a decision to make: What should he do with the empty can? Many people would answer, "Recycle it!" Obviously, recycling is good for many reasons. ① Some environmental activists are concerned that recycling may not be of great help to the environment. ② We can reduce the amount of trash thrown away, use less energy than we would to make new products, and conserve natural resources by recycling. ③ However, recycling is not a perfect way to manage waste. ④ It still requires large amounts of energy to purify used resources and convert them into new products. ⑤ So, what about trying to creatively reuse, or "upcycle," them instead? This new approach is becoming more popular since it is even more environmentally friendly than recycling. What's more, it can also be fun! Here are some inspiring examples of how people have creatively upcycled old, used things.

10

다음 글의 흐름으로 보아, 주어진 문장이 들어가기에 가장 적절한 곳은?

> This new approach is becoming more popular since it is even more environmentally friendly than recycling.

Every day during lunch, Jamie enjoys a soft drink and has a decision to make: What should he do with the empty can? (①) Many people would answer, "Recycle it!" Obviously, recycling is good for many reasons. (②) We can reduce the amount of trash thrown away, use less energy than we would to make new products, and conserve natural resources by recycling. (③) However, recycling is not a perfect way to manage waste. It still requires large amounts of energy to purify used resources and convert them into new products. (④) So, what about trying to creatively reuse, or "upcycle," them instead? (⑤) What's more, it can also be fun! Here are some inspiring examples of how people have creatively upcycled old, used things.

11

주어진 글 다음에 이어질 글의 순서로 가장 적절한 것은?

> Every day during lunch, Jamie enjoys a soft drink and has a decision to make: What should he do with the empty can?

(A) What's more, it can also be fun! Here are some inspiring examples of how people have creatively upcycled old, used things.

(B) Many people would answer, "Recycle it!" Obviously, recycling is good for many reasons.

(C) We can reduce the amount of trash thrown away, use less energy than we would to make new products, and conserve natural resources by recycling.

(D) However, recycling is not a perfect way to manage waste. It still requires large amounts of energy to purify used resources and convert them into new products.

(E) So, what about trying to creatively reuse, or "upcycle," them instead? This new approach is becoming more popular since it is even more environmentally friendly than recycling.

① (B) – (A) – (E) – (C) – (D)
② (B) – (C) – (D) – (E) – (A)
③ (C) – (B) – (D) – (E) – (A)
④ (C) – (D) – (A) – (B) – (E)
⑤ (D) – (E) – (A) – (B) – (C)

12

다음 글의 밑줄 친 ⓐ~ⓔ가 가리키는 대상으로 옳지 않은 것은?

Every day during lunch, Jamie enjoys a soft drink and has a decision to make: What should he do with the empty can? Many people would answer, "Recycle ⓐ it!" Obviously, recycling is good for many reasons. We can reduce the amount of trash thrown away, use less energy than we would to make new products, and conserve natural resources by recycling. However, ⓑ it is not a perfect way to manage waste. It still requires large amounts of energy to purify used resources and convert ⓒ them into new products. So, what about trying to creatively reuse, or "upcycle," ⓓ them instead? This new approach is becoming more popular since it is even more environmentally friendly than recycling. What's more, ⓔ it can also be fun! Here are some inspiring examples of how people have creatively upcycled old, used things.

① ⓐ: the empty can
② ⓑ: recycling
③ ⓒ: used resources
④ ⓓ: new products
⑤ ⓔ: upcycling

13

다음 글의 흐름으로 보아, 주어진 문장이 들어가기에 가장 적절한 곳은?

> We can reduce the amount of trash thrown away, use less energy than we would to make new products, and conserve natural resources by recycling.

Every day during lunch, Jamie enjoys a soft drink and has a decision to make: What should he do with the empty can? Many people would answer, "Recycle it!" Obviously, recycling is good for many reasons. (①) However, recycling is not a perfect way to manage waste. (②) It still requires large amounts of energy to purify used resources and convert them into new products. (③) So, what about trying to creatively reuse, or "upcycle," them instead? (④) This new approach is becoming more popular since it is even more environmentally friendly than recycling. (⑤) What's more, it can also be fun! Here are some inspiring examples of how people have creatively upcycled old, used things.

14

주어진 글 다음에 이어질 글의 순서로 가장 적절한 것은?

> Every day during lunch, Jamie enjoys a soft drink and has a decision to make: What should he do with the empty can? Many people would answer, "Recycle it!" Obviously, recycling is good for many reasons. We can reduce the amount of trash thrown away, use less energy than we would to make new products, and conserve natural resources by recycling.

(A) So, what about trying to creatively reuse, or "upcycle," them instead? This new approach is becoming more popular since it is even more environmentally friendly than recycling.

(B) What's more, it can also be fun! Here are some inspiring examples of how people have creatively upcycled old, used things.

(C) However, recycling is not a perfect way to manage waste. It still requires large amounts of energy to purify used resources and convert them into new products.

① (A) – (C) – (B) ② (B) – (A) – (C)
③ (B) – (C) – (A) ④ (C) – (A) – (B)
⑤ (C) – (B) – (A)

15

주어진 글 다음에 이어질 글의 순서로 가장 적절한 것은?

Every day during lunch, Jamie enjoys a soft drink and has a decision to make: What should he do with the empty can?

(A) However, recycling is not a perfect way to manage waste.

(B) What's more, it can also be fun! Here are some inspiring examples of how people have creatively upcycled old, used things.

(C) It still requires large amounts of energy to purify used resources and convert them into new products. So, what about trying to creatively reuse, or "upcycle," them instead? This new approach is becoming more popular since it is even more environmentally friendly than recycling.

(D) Many people would answer, "Recycle it!" Obviously, recycling is good for many reasons. We can reduce the amount of trash thrown away, use less energy than we would to make new products, and conserve natural resources by recycling.

① (A) – (C) – (B) – (D)
② (B) – (A) – (D) – (C)
③ (C) – (D) – (A) – (B)
④ (D) – (A) – (C) – (B)
⑤ (D) – (B) – (A) – (C)

16

주어진 글 다음에 이어질 글의 순서로 가장 적절한 것은?

Every day during lunch, Jamie enjoys a soft drink and has a decision to make: What should he do with the empty can? Many people would answer, "Recycle it!" Obviously, recycling is good for many reasons.

(A) However, recycling is not a perfect way to manage waste. It still requires large amounts of energy to purify used resources and convert them into new products. So, what about trying to creatively reuse, or "upcycle," them instead? This new approach is becoming more popular since it is even more environmentally friendly than recycling.

(B) We can reduce the amount of trash thrown away, use less energy than we would to make new products, and conserve natural resources by recycling.

(C) What's more, it can also be fun! Here are some inspiring examples of how people have creatively upcycled old, used things.

① (A) – (C) – (B)   ② (B) – (A) – (C)
③ (B) – (C) – (A)   ④ (C) – (A) – (B)
⑤ (C) – (B) – (A)

1회 등장 포인트

● 어휘 Obviously, good, reason

> Obviously, recycling is good for many reasons.

● 어휘 amount, make

> We can reduce the amount of trash thrown away, use less energy than we would to make new products, and conserve natural resources by recycling.

● 어휘 perfect, manage

> However, recycling is not a perfect way to manage waste.

● 어휘 require, large

> It still requires large amounts of energy to purify used resources and convert them into new products.

● 어휘 creatively, upcycle

> So, what about trying to creatively reuse, or "upcycle," them instead?

● 어휘 recycling

> This new approach is becoming more popular since it is even more environmentally friendly than recycling.

01

다음 글의 밑줄 친 ⓐ~ⓔ의 영영풀이로 옳지 않은 것은?

Every day during lunch, Jamie enjoys a soft drink and has a decision to make: What should he do with the empty can? Many people would answer, "Recycle it!" Obviously, recycling is good for many ⓐ reasons. We can reduce the ⓑ amount of trash thrown away, use less energy than we would to make new products, and conserve natural resources by recycling. However, recycling is not a perfect way to ⓒ manage waste. It still requires large amounts of energy to purify used resources and convert them into new products. So, what about trying to creatively reuse, or "ⓓ upcycle," them instead? This new approach is becoming more popular since it is even more environmentally friendly than ⓔ recycling. What's more, it can also be fun! Here are some inspiring examples of how people have creatively upcycled old, used things.

① ⓐ: a cause or justification for an action or event
② ⓑ: the total quantity or volume of something
③ ⓒ: to control, handle, or oversee
④ ⓓ: to take discarded or used materials and transform them into something of higher value or quality
⑤ ⓔ: waste material, garbage, or discarded objects

02

다음 글의 (A), (B), (C)의 각 네모 안에서 문맥에 맞는 낱말로 가장 적절한 것은?

Every day during lunch, Jamie enjoys a soft drink and has a decision to make: What should he do with the empty can? Many people would answer, "Recycle it!" Obviously, recycling is (A) [good / bad] for many reasons. We can reduce the amount of trash thrown away, use less energy than we would to make new products, and conserve natural resources by recycling. However, recycling is not a (B) [poor / perfect] way to manage waste. It still (C) [acquires / requires] large amounts of energy to purify used resources and convert them into new products. So, what about trying to creatively reuse, or "upcycle," them instead? This new approach

40

is becoming more popular since it is even more environmentally friendly than recycling. What's more, it can also be fun! Here are some inspiring examples of how people have creatively upcycled old, used things.

	(A)	(B)	(C)
①	good	– poor	– acquires
②	bad	– poor	– acquires
③	good	– perfect	– requires
④	bad	– perfect	– requires
⑤	good	– perfect	– acquires

03

다음 글의 밑줄 친 부분 중, 문맥상 낱말의 쓰임이 적절하지 않은 것은?

Every day during lunch, Jamie enjoys a soft drink and has a decision to make: What should he do with the empty can? Many people would answer, "Recycle it!" ① <u>Clearly</u>, recycling is good for many reasons. We can ② <u>decrease</u> the amount of trash thrown away, use less energy than we would to ③ <u>manufacture</u> new products, and conserve natural resources by recycling. However, recycling is not a perfect way to manage waste. It still requires ④ <u>small</u> amounts of energy to purify used resources and convert them into new products. So, what about trying to creatively reuse, or "upcycle," them instead? This new approach is becoming more popular since it is even more environmentally friendly than recycling. What's more, it can also be fun! Here are some inspiring examples of how people have ⑤ <u>creatively</u> upcycled old, used things.

● 목적

04

다음 글의 목적으로 가장 적절한 것은?

Every day during lunch, Jamie enjoys a soft drink and has a decision to make: What should he do with the empty can? Many people would answer, "Recycle it!" Obviously, recycling is good for many reasons. We can reduce the amount of trash thrown away, use less energy than we would to make new products, and conserve natural resources

by recycling. However, recycling is not a perfect way to manage waste. It still requires large amounts of energy to purify used resources and convert them into new products. So, what about trying to creatively reuse, or "upcycle," them instead? This new approach is becoming more popular since it is even more environmentally friendly than recycling. What's more, it can also be fun! Here are some inspiring examples of how people have creatively upcycled old, used things.

① to persuade readers to actively participate in recycling
② to introduce a creative way of reusing used resources
③ to show how to recycle properly
④ to point out the disadvantages of recycling
⑤ to compare the pros and cons of upcycling

● 문장 변형

> We can reduce the amount of trash thrown away, use less energy than we would to make new products, and conserve natural resources by recycling.

재활용이 좋은 세 가지 이유를 제시한 위의 문장을, 두 문장으로 나누어, 그 사이에 들어갈 올바른 연결어를 묻는 문제로 변형되어 출제될 수 있다. 재활용이 좋은 이유를 추가하는 것이므로, '게다가'를 의미하는 연결어 What's more, In addition, Furthermore, Moreover, Besides 등이 들어갈 수 있다는 것을 알아두자.

● 연결어 So

> So, what about trying to creatively reuse, or "upcycle," them instead?

05

다음 글의 빈칸 (A), (B)에 들어갈 말로 가장 적절한 것은?

Every day during lunch, Jamie enjoys a soft drink and has a decision to make: What should he do with the empty can? Many people would answer, "Recycle it!" Obviously, recycling is good for many reasons. By recycling, we can reduce the amount of trash thrown away and use less energy than we would to make new products. _____(A)_____, we can conserve natural resources through recycling. However, recycling is not a perfect way to manage waste. It still requires large amounts of energy to purify used resources and convert them into new products. _____(B)_____, what about trying to creatively reuse, or "upcycle," them instead? This new approach is becoming more popular since it is even more environmentally friendly than recycling. What's more, it can also be fun! Here are some inspiring examples of how people have creatively upcycled old, used things.

	(A)		(B)
①	In addition	–	For example
②	Instead	–	So
③	What's more	–	So
④	However	–	Furthermore
⑤	Therefore	–	However

● 빈칸 **how people have creatively upcycled old, used things**

> Here are some inspiring examples of how people have creatively upcycled old, used things.

06

다음 글의 빈칸에 들어갈 내용으로 가장 적절한 것은?

Every day during lunch, Jamie enjoys a soft drink and has a decision to make: What should he do with the empty can? Many people would answer, "Recycle it!" Obviously, recycling is good for many reasons. We can reduce the amount of trash thrown away, use less energy than we would to make new products, and conserve natural resources by recycling. However, recycling is not a perfect

way to manage waste. It still requires large amounts of energy to purify used resources and convert them into new products. So, what about trying to creatively reuse, or "upcycle," them instead? This new approach is becoming more popular since it is even more environmentally friendly than recycling. What's more, it can also be fun! Here are some inspiring examples of _____.

① why we should be educated about recycling from an early age
② how people have creatively upcycled old, used things
③ why recycling can help protect the environment
④ how people can reduce the amount of trash thrown away through recycling
⑤ how people have developed sustainable energy

● 부사 **creatively**

> So, what about trying to creatively reuse, or "upcycle," them instead?

07

다음 문장의 밑줄 친 ⓐ~ⓒ 중, 어법상 틀린 것을 찾아 바르게 고치시오.

> So, what about ⓐ trying to ⓑ creative reuse, or "upcycle," them ⓒ instead?

_____ → _____

● 조동사 **should** 의문문

> Every day during lunch, Jamie enjoys a soft drink and has a decision to make: What should he do with the empty can?

● **them** 지칭 추론

> So, what about trying to creatively reuse, or "upcycle," them instead?

08

다음 글의 밑줄 친 부분 중, 어법상 **틀린** 것은?

Every day during lunch, Jamie enjoys a soft drink and has a decision to make: ① <u>What should he do</u> with the empty can? Many people would answer, "Recycle it!" Obviously, recycling is good for many reasons. We can reduce the amount of trash thrown away, use less energy than we would ② <u>to make new products</u>, and conserve natural resources by recycling. However, recycling is not a perfect way to manage waste. It still requires large amounts of energy ③ <u>to purify used resources</u> and convert them into new products. So, what about trying to creatively reuse, ④ <u>or "upcycle," it</u> instead? This new approach is becoming more popular since it is even more environmentally friendly than recycling. What's more, it can also be fun! Here are some inspiring examples of ⑤ <u>how people have creatively upcycled</u> old, used things.

● 능동태

> It still requires large amounts of energy to purify used resources and convert them into new products.

09

다음 문장의 밑줄 친 ⓐ~ⓒ 중, 어법상 **틀린** 것을 찾아 바르게 고치시오.

> It ⓐ <u>is still required</u> large amounts of energy to purify ⓑ <u>used</u> resources and ⓒ <u>convert</u> them into new products.

_____ → _____

● 동명사 주어 수 일치

> Obviously, recycling is good for many reasons.

● 수 일치

> **Here** are some inspiring examples of how people have creatively upcycled old, used things.

Here는 뒤에 〈동사＋주어〉의 어순으로 쓰므로, 3인칭 복수인 주어 some inspiring examples의 수에 일치시켜 복수형 동사 are을 썼다는 것에 주의하자.

10

다음 글의 밑줄 친 부분 중, 어법상 **틀린** 것을 **모두** 고르시오.

Every day during lunch, Jamie enjoys a soft drink and has a decision to make: What should he do with the empty can? Many people would answer, "Recycle it!" Obviously, ① <u>recycling are</u> good for many reasons. We can reduce the amount of trash thrown away, use less energy than we would to make new products, and conserve natural resources by recycling. However, recycling is not a perfect way to manage waste. It still requires large amounts of energy to purify ② <u>used</u> resources and convert them into new products. So, what about trying ③ <u>to creatively reuse</u>, or "upcycle," them instead? This new approach is becoming ④ <u>more popularly</u> since it is even more environmentally friendly than recycling. What's more, it can also be fun! Here ⑤ <u>is</u> some inspiring examples of how people have creatively upcycled old, used things.

출제 포인트 16.9% 정복!

리딩
본문[2]

25.8% 확률로 본문[2]에서 출제

Through upcycling, a seemingly useless object can be transformed into something completely different that is useful for everyday life. What do you think can be done with old truck tarps, car seat belts, and bicycle inner tubes? Individually, these things look like trash, but with a little imagination the Freitag brothers, Markus and Daniel, repurpose them for something totally new: very strong bags. These bags are perfect for bicyclists going to work every day in all kinds of weather. Similarly, a man named Kyle Parsons and his partners have been creatively reusing old motorcycle tires from Bali, Indonesia. A shocking number of tires get thrown away there every year, and they are a serious environmental problem since they cannot decompose or be recycled. To solve this problem, Parsons and his team are turning them into sandal bottoms. They then use canvas and natural materials to make the other sandal parts. What a great reuse of resources!

일관성 〈출제 1위 유형〉

일관성 문제를 풀기 위해서는 내용 흐름을 숙지해야 한다. 해당 본문의 내용 흐름은 다음과 같다. 〈업사이클링을 통해 쓸모없는 물건이 유용한 것으로 바뀔 수 있음 → 예시1(Freitag 형제가 폐품들로 가방을 만듦) → 예시2(Kyle Parsons와 그의 팀이 낡은 오토바이 타이어로 샌들 밑창을, 그리고 캔버스와 천연 재료로 샌들의 다른 부분을 만듦) 대명사나 관사, Similarly 등의 연결어로 힌트를 얻을 수 있다.

내용 일치 〈출제 2위 유형〉

- Freitag 형제는 '자전거 타이어 안쪽 튜브, 트럭 방수포, 자동차 안전벨트'로 튼튼한 가방을 만듦
- Freitag 형제가 만든 가방은 어떤 날씨에도 통근하는 자전거 이용자들에게 완벽함
- 오래된 오토바이 타이어는 분해되거나 재활용되지 않으므로 심각한 환경 문제를 야기함
- Kyle Parsons와 그의 팀은 오래된 '오토바이 타이어'로 '샌들 밑창'을 만듦
- 샌들 밑창 이외의 샌들의 다른 부분은 캔버스와 천연 재료로 만들어짐

지칭 추론 〈출제 3위 유형〉

대명사 they, them이 많이 쓰였으므로 각 대명사가 무엇을 지칭하는지 정확히 구분할 줄 알아야 한다. 특히, Parsons의 예시 부분의 them과 they가 old motorcycle tires와 Parsons and his team 둘 중 무엇을 지칭하는지 묻는 문제가 자주 출제되므로 유의하자.

출제 1위 문장 ★★★

A shocking number of tires get thrown away there every year, and they are a serious environmental problem since they cannot decompose or be recycled.

[a number of + 복수명사 + 복수동사] 출제 공동 1위 (문장편-문장6 → p.56)
[어휘 decompose] 출제 공동 1위 (문장편-문장6 → p.56)
[조동사 수동태] 출제 3위 (문장편-문장6 → p.56)

출제 2위 문장 ★★

Through upcycling, a seemingly useless object can be transformed into something completely different that is useful for everday life.

[주격관계대명사 that] 출제 1위 (문장편-문장1 → p.46)
[어휘 useless / useful] 출제 2위 (문장편-문장1 → p.46)
[조동사 수동태] 출제 3위 (문장편-문장1 → p.47)

출제 3위 문장 ★

Individually, these things look like trash, but with a little imagination the Freitag brothers, Markus and Daniel, repurpose them for something totally new: very strong bags.

[어휘 repurpose A for B] 출제 1위 (문장편-문장3 → p.49)
[어휘 individually] 출제 공동 2위 (문장편-문장3 → p.50)
[어휘 trash] 출제 공동 2위 (문장편-문장3 → p.50)

문장1 문장 출제 확률: 5.2% (총 771개의 출제 포인트 중40회 출현, 46개 문장 중 3위)

> 쓸모없는   조동사 수동태 can be p.p.
> **Through upcycling, a seemingly <u>useless</u> object <u>can be</u> <u>transformed</u> into something completely different <u>that</u> is <u>useful</u> for everyday life.**
> 주격관계대명사 that   유용한

┤ 출제 포인트 ├

1위	2위	3위
주격관계대명사 that	**어휘 useless / useful**	**조동사 수동태**
문장 내 출제 확률 42.5%	문장 내 출제 확률 20.0%	문장 내 출제 확률 12.5%
본문[2] 문장편 내 출제 확률 8.5%	본문[2] 문장편 내 출제 확률 4.0%	본문[2] 문장편 내 출제 확률 2.5%

● 주격관계대명사 that

문장1에서 출제될 가능성은 5.2%이다. 이 문장에서 출제가 된다면, 42.5%의 확률로 관계대명사 that과 what을 비교하는 문제와 주격관계대명사절 동사의 수일치 문제가 나올 수 있다. 이 문장의 that은 선행사 something을 수식하는 주격관계대명사로, 뒤에 주어가 빠진 불완전한 절이 오며, that 바로 뒤에는 선행사 something에 수일치한 단수 be동사 is가 온다. 관계대명사 that은 선행사를 수식하므로 앞에 선행사가 있는 반면, 관계대명사 what은 선행사를 포함하므로 앞에 선행사가 없다는 점과 주격관계대명사절의 동사는 선행사에 수일치 한다는 점을 명심하자.

> **Q. 다음 문장의 괄호 안에 들어갈 말로 어법상 적절한 것을 고르시오.**
>
> Through upcycling, a seemingly useless object can be transformed into something completely different (what / that) is useful for everyday life.

● 어휘 useless / useful

이 문장에서 20%의 확률로 어휘 useless나 useful과 관련된 문제가 나올 수 있다. 뒷부분에 폐품으로 만든 새로운 가방과 오토바이 타이어로 샌들을 만드는 업사이클링의 예시가 나오므로, 해당 문장에는 예시처럼 겉보기에 '쓸모없는' 물건이 일상생활에서 완전히 다른 '유용한' 것으로 변할 수 있다는 내용의 문장이 나오는 것이 흐름상 자연스럽다. 이러한 내용의 흐름을 잘 숙지하고 어휘 useless(쓸모없는), useful(유용한)이 각각 해당 문장의 어느 위치에 쓰였는지 꼭 알아 두자. 또한, useless는 valueless와 worthless로, useful은 valuable, invaluable, helpful 등으로 바꿔 쓸 수 있다는 것을 기억하자.

> **Q. 다음 글의 (A), (B)에 들어갈 말로 적절한 것을 각각 고르시오.**
>
>   Through upcycling, a seemingly (A) useless / useful object can be transformed into something completely different that is (B) valuable / worthless for everyday life. What do you think can be done with old truck tarps, car seat belts, and bicycle inner tubes? Individually, these things look like trash, but with a little imagination the Freitag brothers, Markus and Daniel, repurpose them for something totally new: very strong bags.

● 조동사 수동태

이 문장에서 조동사 수동태 can be transformed의 형태를 묻는 문제 또한 12.5%의 확률로 나올 수 있다. 문맥상 해당 문장의 주어 a seemingly useless object가 '변형되는' 것이므로 주어와 동사 transform은 수동 관계이다. 따라서, 동사 transform은 앞에 있는 조동사 can과 함께 조동사 can의 수동태 〈can be p.p.〉 형태로 쓰였다는 것을 명심하자. 또한, 능동태 문장 We can transform a seemingly useless object into ~.로 변형되어 출제되는 경우도 있으므로, 문제를 풀 때 주어가 무엇인지부터 꼭 확인하도록 하자.

> **Q. 다음 괄호 안의 동사를 어법상 알맞은 형태로 고쳐 쓰시오.**
>
> Through upcycling, a seemingly useless object can _____ (transform) into something completely different that is useful for everyday life.

정답 be transformed

문맥상 주어 a seemingly useless object가 '변형되는' 것이므로 주어와 동사 transform이 수동 관계이며, 앞에 조동사 can과 함께 쓰이기 때문에 동사 부분인 빈칸은 조동사 can의 수동태 〈can be p.p.〉 형태로 쓰여야 한다. 따라서 답은 be transformed이다.

● something＋부사(completely)＋형용사(different)

〈something＋부사＋형용사〉의 어순을 묻는 문제도 10%의 확률로 나올 수 있다. 명사 something은 형용사의 후치 수식을 받는 명사이므로 something different의 어순이며, 중간에 부사 completely가 형용사 different를 수식하기 위해 쓰였다. 〈something＋형용사〉 어순을 기억하고, 형용사는 부사만이 수식할 수 있으므로 부사 completely를 형용사 complete로 바꿔 쓸 수 없음에 유의하자.

> **Q. 다음 문장에서 어법상 틀린 부분을 찾아 문장 전체를 바르게 고쳐 쓰시오.**
>
> Through upcycling, a seemingly useless object can be transformed into completely different something that is useful for everyday life.
> (업사이클링을 통해, 겉보기에는 쓸모없는 물건도 일상 생활에 유용한 완전히 다른 것으로 탈바꿈될 수 있다.)
> _____

정답
Through upcycling, a seemingly useless object can be transformed into something completely different that is useful for everyday life.
(completely different something → something completely different)

명사 something은 형용사가 뒤에서 수식해야 하므로 something different의 어순으로 쓰고, 중간에 형용사 different를 수식하는 부사 completely가 들어가야 한다.

● 전치사 through

전치사 through와 〈전치사＋명사〉 형태를 아는지 묻는 문제도 5%의 확률로 나올 수 있다. 문맥상 '업사이클링을 통해'라는 의미이고, 뒤에 명사 upcycling이 오므로 '~을 통해'라는 뜻의 전치사 through가 알맞다. 철자가 비슷한 접속사 though, although 등과 혼동하지 않도록 유의하자. 그리고 전치사 뒤에는 명사(구)만 올 수 있으므로, 전치사 through 뒤에 upcycle, upcycled 등의 동사가 올 수 없음에 유의하자.

> **Q. 다음 문장의 (A), (B)에 알맞은 것을 고르시오.**
>
> (A) Although / Through (B) upcycling / upcycle , a seemingly useless object can be transformed into something completely different that is useful for everyday life.

정답 (A) Through
　　　 (B) upcycling

(A) 문맥상 '업사이클링을 통해'라는 의미가 되어야 하므로 '~을 통해'라는 뜻의 전치사 through가 들어가는 것이 적절하다. Although는 '비록 ~일지라도'라는 뜻의 접속사이므로 해당 자리에 올 수 없다.
(B) 전치사 뒤에는 명사(구)만 올 수 있으므로, 전치사 through 뒤에 명사 upcycling(업사이클링)이 알맞다.

● 어휘 transform A into B

〈transform A into B〉에 대해 묻는 문제도 5%의 확률로 나올 수 있다. 뒤에 '쓸모없는 물건들이 새로운 가방과 샌들 밑창으로 탈바꿈되는' 예시가 나온다. 따라서, 'A를 B로 변형시키다'라는 뜻의 〈transform A into B〉가 쓰였다. 〈transform A into B〉는 〈turn A into B〉, 〈convert A into B〉, 〈change A into B〉 등으로 바꿔 쓸 수 있다는 것을 기억하자. 또한, transform의 영영풀이 to change (something) into another form((무언가를) 다른 형태로 바꾸다)도 기억해두자.

> **Q. 다음 빈칸에 들어갈 말로 적절하지 <u>않은</u> 것은?**
>
> Through upcycling, a seemingly useless object can be _____ something completely different that is useful for everyday life. What do you think can be done with old truck tarps, car seat belts, and bicycle inner tubes? Individually, these things look like trash, but with a little imagination the Freitag brothers, Markus and Daniel, repurpose them for something totally new: very strong bags.
>
> ① transformed into   ② converted into   ③ changed into
> ④ preserved from   ⑤ turned into

문장2

조동사 수동태 can be p.p.

What do you think <u>can be done</u> with old truck tarps, car seat belts, and bicycle inner tubes?

─┤ **출제 포인트** ├─

1위

조동사 수동태

문장 내 출제 확률 100.0%
본문[2] 문장편 내 출제 확률 1.5%

● 조동사 수동태

문장2에서 출제될 가능성은 0.4%이다. 이 문장에서 출제가 된다면, 100%의 확률로 문장의 태에 관련하여 can be done과 can do 중 무엇이 들어가야 하는지 묻는 문제가 나올 수 있다. 문맥상 무엇이 '되어질 수 있는지' 묻는 문장이며 do 뒤에 목적어가 없으므로 수동태를 써야 하는데, 앞에 조동사 can이 있으므로 〈can be p.p.〉 형태인 can be done이 되어야 한다.

정답 be done

문맥상 무엇이 '되어질 수 있
는지'의 의미이므로 동사 do
의 수동태를 써야 한다. 단,
앞에 조동사 can이 있으므
로, 조동사 can의 수동태
〈can be p.p.〉 형태인 can
be done으로 쓰여야 한다.

Q. 다음 괄호 안에 들어갈 말로 적절한 것을 고르시오.

What do you think can (be done / do) with old truck tarps, car seat belts, and bicycle inner tubes?

출제 포인트 20.7% 정복!

문장3　　문장 출제 확률: 4.9% (총 771개의 출제 포인트 중 38회 출현, 46개 문장 중 5위)

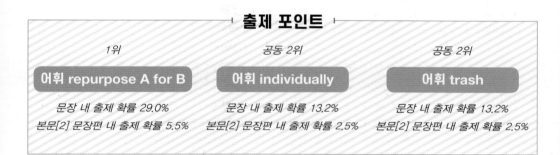

개별적으로　　　　　　　　　　　　　　　　　　　　　　쓰레기
Individually, these things look like trash, but with a little imagination the Freitag brothers, Markus and Daniel, repurpose them for something totally new: very strong bags. repurpose A for B: A를 B로 바꾸다[용도 변경하다]

┤ 출제 포인트 ├

1위	*공동 2위*	*공동 2위*
어휘 repurpose A for B	**어휘 individually**	**어휘 trash**
문장 내 출제 확률 29.0%	*문장 내 출제 확률 13.2%*	*문장 내 출제 확률 13.2%*
본문[2] 문장편 내 출제 확률 5.5%	*본문[2] 문장편 내 출제 확률 2.5%*	*본문[2] 문장편 내 출제 확률 2.5%*

● 어휘 repurpose A for B

문장3에서 출제될 가능성은 4.9%이다. 이 문장에서 출제가 된다면, 29.0%의 확률로 〈repurpose A for B〉에 관한 문제가 나올 수 있다. 업사이클링의 예시로 Freitag 형제가 폐품을 새로운 가방으로 '바꾸었다'는 내용으로, 'A를 B로 바꾸다(용도 변경하다)'라는 뜻의 〈repurpose A for B〉가 쓰였다. 비슷한 표현인 〈transform A into B〉, 〈turn A into B〉와, 영영풀이 to apply or adapt something for a different purpose or use(무언가를 다른 목적이나 용도를 위해 조정하다)를 기억해두자.

Q. 다음 글의 밑줄 친 우리말을 영작한 것으로 옳지 <u>않은</u> 것을 <u>모두</u> 고르면?

　　Through upcycling, a seemingly useless object can be transformed into something completely different that is useful for everyday life. What do you think can be done with old truck tarps, car seat belts, and bicycle inner tubes? Individually, these things look like trash, but with a little imagination the Freitag brothers, Markus and Daniel, <u>이것들을 완전히 새로운 것으로 바꾼다</u>: very strong bags.

① purpose them for something totally new
② change them into something totally new
③ reduce them into something totally new
④ transform them into something totally new
⑤ turn them into something totally new

정답 ①, ③

①의 purpose는 '~을 의도
하다', ③의 reduce는 '줄
이다'라는 뜻으로 밑줄 친
우리말과 뜻이 다르다. 'A
를 B로 바꾸다'라는 뜻의
표현으로 〈change A into
B〉, 〈transform A into B〉,
〈turn A into B〉가 모두 쓰
일 수 있다.

● 어휘 individually

어휘 individually 빈칸 문제도 13.2%의 확률로 나올 수 있다. 주어 these things(old truck tarps, car seat belts, and bicycle inner tubes)는 '개별적으로'는 쓰레기처럼 보이지만 Freitag 형제들이 이것들로 가방을 만들었다는 해당 문장의 내용 흐름상 '개별적으로'라는 뜻의 단어 Individually가 쓰였다는 것을 알아두자. 또한, individually의 유의어인 separately, respectively와, individually의 영영풀이 separately, rather than as a set(하나의 집합으로가 아니라 따로따로)를 함께 기억해두자.

> **Q. 다음 빈칸에 들어갈 말로 적절한 것을 <u>모두</u> 고르시오.**
>
> What do you think can be done with old truck tarps, car seat belts, and bicycle inner tubes? _____, these things look like trash, but with a little imagination the Freitag brothers, Markus and Daniel, repurpose them for something totally new: very strong bags.
>
> ① Unfortunately   ② In addition   ③ Individually
> ④ Accordingly   ⑤ Separately

● 어휘 trash

trash를 다른 어휘와 비교하는 문제도 13.2%의 확률로 나올 수 있다. 문맥상 주어 these things(old truck tarps, car seat belts, and bicycle inner tubes)가 쓸모없는 것, 즉 '쓰레기(trash)'처럼 보이지만, Freitag 형제가 그것들을 새로운 가방으로 바꿨다는 의미이므로, 어휘 trash가 쓰였다. trash의 유의어 junk, garbage, waste를 꼭 기억해두고, 어휘 treasure(보물)와 비교하는 문제가 자주 출제된다는 점을 명심하자.

> **Q. 다음 괄호 안에 들어갈 말로 적절한 것을 고르시오.**
>
> Through upcycling, a seemingly useless object can be transformed into something completely different that is useful for everyday life. What do you think can be done with old truck tarps, car seat belts, and bicycle inner tubes? Individually, these things look like (treasure / trash), but with a little imagination the Freitag brothers, Markus and Daniel, repurpose them for something totally new: very strong bags.

● a little

a little을 little, a few, few와 비교하는 문제도 10.5%의 확률로 나올 수 있다. 문맥상 '약간의'라는 뜻의 표현이 적절하며, 뒤에 불가산명사 imagination이 오므로 a little이 쓰였다. little은 뒤에 불가산명사가 오지만 '거의 없는'이라는 뜻이므로 쓰일 수 없으며, a few(약간의)와 few(거의 없는)는 뒤에 가산명사가 와야 하므로 쓰일 수 없다는 것을 명심하자.

> **Q. 다음 괄호 안에 들어갈 말로 가장 적절한 것을 고르시오.**
>
> Individually, these things look like trash, but with (a few / few / a little / little) imagination the Freitag brothers, Markus and Daniel, repurpose them for something totally new: very strong bags.
> (개별적으로 보면 이것들은 쓰레기처럼 보일 수 있지만, Markus와 Daniel이라는 Freitag 형제는 약간의 상상력으로 이것들을 완전히 새로운 것으로 바꾸었다: 매우 튼튼한 가방이 바로 그것이다.)

정답 a little

문맥상 '약간의'라는 뜻의 표현이 들어가야 하며, 뒤에 불가산명사 imagination이 오므로, 빈칸에는 'a little'이 들어가야 한다. little은 뒤에 불가산명사가 오지만 '거의 없는' 이라는 뜻이므로 문맥상 해당 문장에 쓰일 수 없으며, a few(약간의)와 few(거의 없는)는 뒤에 가산명사가 와야 하므로 해당 빈칸에 들어갈 수 없다.

● 대명사 them

대명사 them을 대명사 it과 비교하는 문제도 7.9%의 확률로 나올 수 있다. 이 문장에서 them은 앞 문장에서 언급된 복수명사 these things(old truck tarps, car seat belts, and bicycle inner tubes)를 대신하는 것으로, 단수명사를 대신하는 it으로 바꿔 쓸 수 없다. 대명사 them은 앞의 복수명사를 가리키고, it은 단수명사를 가리킨다는 점을 구분해서 기억해두자.

> **Q. 다음 괄호 안에서 어법상 올바른 것을 고르시오.**
>
> What do you think can be done with old truck tarps, car seat belts, and bicycle inner tubes? Individually, these things look like trash, but with a little imagination the Freitag brothers, Markus and Daniel, repurpose (it / them) for something totally new: very strong bags.

정답 them

복수명사 these things(old truck tarps, car seat belts, and bicycle inner tubes)를 대신하는 대명사 them이 들어가는 것이 적절하다. it은 단수명사를 가리키는 대명사로, 해당 자리에 들어갈 수 없다.

● 본동사 찾기

본동사 repurpose의 형태를 묻는 문제도 7.9%의 확률로 나올 수 있다. 이 문장의 repurpose는 주어 the Freitag brothers, Markus and Daniel 뒤에 오는 본동사이므로, 복수명사인 주어에 수일치하여 복수형으로 쓰인 것이다. 이 자리에는 to repurpose, repurposing을 쓸 수 없다는 것을 꼭 기억하고, 주어를 imagination으로 혼동하여 단수형 repurposes로 쓰지 않도록 유의하자.

> **Q. 다음 빈칸에 들어갈 말로 가장 적절한 것은?**
>
> Individually, these things look like trash, but with a little imagination the Freitag brothers, Markus and Daniel, _____ them for something totally new: very strong bags.
>
> ⓐ repurpose   ⓑ repurposes   ⓒ repurposing   ⓓ to repurpose

정답 ⓐ

빈칸은 주어 the Freitag brothers, Markus and Daniel 뒤에 오는 본동사 자리이므로, 복수명사인 주어에 수일치하여 일반동사 repurpose의 복수형인 repurpose로 써야 한다.

● look like + 명사

look like 뒤에 어떤 품사가 와야 하는지 묻는 문제도 5.3%의 확률로 나올 수 있다. look like 뒤에는 명사가 와야한다는 점과 함께 look 뒤에는 형용사가 와야 한다는 점을 구분하여 기억해두자. 또한, 해당 문장에 쓰인 look like trash(〈look like + 명사〉)가 비슷한 의미인 look useless(〈look + 형용사〉) 등으로 변형되어 출제되는 경우가 종종 있으니, 두 형태 모두 알아두자.

> **Q. 다음 괄호 안에 들어갈 말로 적절한 것을 고르시오.**
>
> Individually, these things (look / look like) trash, but with a little imagination the Freitag brothers, Markus and Daniel, repurpose them for something totally new: very strong bags.

● something + 부사(totally) + 형용사(new)

〈something + 부사 + 형용사〉의 어순을 묻는 문제도 5.3%의 확률로 나올 수 있다. something은 형용사의 후치 수식을 받는 명사이므로 something new의 어순이며, 부사 totally는 형용사 new를 수식하기 위해 중간에 쓰였다. 〈something + 형용사〉 어순을 꼭 기억하고, 형용사는 부사만이 수식할 수 있으므로 부사 totally를 형용사 total로 바꿔 쓸 수 없음에 유의하자.

> **Q. 다음 문장에서 틀린 부분을 찾아 바르게 고치시오.**
>
> Individually, these things look like trash, but with a little imagination the Freitag brothers, Markus and Daniel, repurpose them for totally new something: very strong bags.
>
> _____ → _____

문장4

문장 출제 확률: 2.5%

완벽한   현재분사 – 명사 수식

These bags are <u>perfect</u> for bicyclists <u>going</u> to work every day in all kinds of weather.

┤ 출제 포인트 ├

1위	2위
현재분사 — 명사 수식	**어휘 perfect**
문장 내 출제 확률 79.0%	문장 내 출제 확률 10.5%
본문[2] 문장편 내 출제 확률 7.5%	본문[2] 문장편 내 출제 확률 1.0%

● 현재분사 – 명사 수식

문장4에서 출제될 가능성은 2.5%이다. 이 문장에서 출제가 된다면, 79.0%의 확률로 현재분사 going에 관한 문제가 나올 수 있다. 문맥상 수식을 받는 명사 bicyclists가 일하러 '가는' 것이므로 능동 의미인 현재분사 going으로 수식하는 것이 적절하다. 과거분사 gone은 수동의 의미이므로 쓰일 수 없으며, 동사 go는 명사를 수식하는 해당 자리에 쓰일 수 없다는 점을 명심하자. 또한 현재분사구(going to work)가 관계대명사절(who[that] are going to work)로 변형되어 출제될 수 있으므로, 명사 bicyclists를 수식하는 현재분사구, 관계대명사절 형태 모두 기억해두자.

> **Q. 다음 괄호 안에 들어갈 말로 적절한 것을 고르시오.**
>
> These bags are perfect for bicyclists (go / going / gone) to work every day in all kinds of weather.

정답 going

문맥상 수식을 받는 명사 bicyclists가 일하러 '가는' 것이므로 능동의 의미인 현재분사 going으로 수식하는 것이 적절하다. 과거분사 gone은 수동의 의미이므로 문맥상 해당 자리에 쓰일 수 없으며, 동사 go는 이미 문장에 동사 are이 있으며, 해당 자리가 명사를 수식하는 자리이므로 어법상 쓰일 수 없다.

● 어휘 perfect

perfect에 관한 문제도 10.5%의 확률로 나올 수 있다. 앞 문장에서 Freitag 형제가 쓰레기처럼 보이는 낡은 방수포, 자동차 벨트, 자전거 타이어의 안쪽 튜브를 완전히 새로운 '매우 튼튼한 가방'으로 바꿨다고 했으므로, 이 튼튼한 가방은 어떤 날씨에도 매일 일하러 가는 자전거 이용자들에게 '완벽하다(perfect)'는 것을 유추할 수 있다. perfect는 suitable(적합한), adequate(적절한) 등의 유의어로 바꿔서 출제될 수 있으니 함께 기억해두자.

> **Q. 다음 빈칸에 들어갈 단어로 적절한 것을 모두 고르시오.**
>
> What do you think can be done with old truck tarps, car seat belts, and bicycle inner tubes? Individually, these things look like trash, but with a little imagination the Freitag brothers, Markus and Daniel, repurpose them for something totally new: very strong bags. These bags are _____ for bicyclists going to work every day in all kinds of weather.
>
> ① perfect   ② inadequate   ③ suitable
> ④ adequate   ⑤ unsuitable

정답 ①, ③, ④

앞 문장에서 Freitag 형제가 쓰레기처럼 보이는 낡은 방수포, 자동차 벨트, 자전거 타이어의 안쪽 튜브를 완전히 새로운 '매우 튼튼한 가방'으로 바꿨다고 했으므로, 이 튼튼한 가방은 어떤 날씨에도 매일 일하러 가는 자전거 이용자들에게 적절하고, 완벽하다는 것을 유추할 수 있다. 따라서, 빈칸에 ① perfect(완벽한), ③ suitable(적합한), ④ adequate(적절한)이 들어갈 수 있다.
② 부적절한
⑤ 적합하지 않은

출제 포인트 25.6% 정복!

문장5   문장 출제 확률: 4.3% (총 771개의 출제 포인트 중 33회 출현, 46개 문장 중 7위)

연결어 similarly   과거분사 – 명사 수식   현재완료 진행 have been v-ing

Similarly, a man named Kyle Parsons and his partners have been creatively reusing old motorcycle tires from Bali, Indonesia.

1위	2위	3위
과거분사 – 명사 수식	**현재완료 진행**	**연결어 similarly**
문장 내 출제 확률 33.3%	문장 내 출제 확률 30.3%	문장 내 출제 확률 27.3%
본문[2] 문장편 내 출제 확률 5.5%	본문[2] 문장편 내 출제 확률 5.0%	본문[2] 문장편 내 출제 확률 4.5%

● 과거분사 – 명사 수식

문장5에서 출제될 가능성은 4.3%이며, 이 문장에서 출제된다면 33.3%의 확률로 과거분사 named에 관한 문제가 나올 수 있다. 수식하는 명사 a man이 Kyle Parsons라고 '이름 지어진' 것이므로 동사 name(이름을 지어주다)과 수동 관계이다. 따라서, 과거분사 named의 형태로 명사 a man을 수식해야 한다는 점을 기억하자.

> **Q. 다음 괄호 안에 들어갈 말로 적절한 것을 고르시오.**
>
> Similarly, a man (naming / named) Kyle Parsons and his partners have been creatively reusing old motorcycle tires from Bali, Indonesia.

정답 named

a man(남자)이 Kyle Parsons라고 이름 지어진 것이므로, 동사 name(이름을 지어주다)과 수동 관계이다. 따라서, 과거분사 named의 형태로 명사 a man을 수식해야 한다.

● 현재완료 진행

이 문장에서 30.3%의 확률로 현재완료 진행시제에 대한 문제도 나올 수 있다. 현재완료 진행시제는 〈have[has] been v-ing〉의 형태로, 과거부터 현재까지 계속 진행 중인 일을 나타낼 때 사용하며 '~해오고 있다' 라고 해석한다. 해당 문장에서는 문맥상 Kyle Parsons와 동업자들이 오토바이 타이어를 (과거부터 현재까지 계속) '재사용해오고 있는' 것이므로 현재완료 진행시제가 쓰였다는 것을 기억하자. 또한, 주어 Kyle Parsons and his partners가 복수명사이므로, 주어에 수일치하여 has가 아닌 have가 쓰였다는 점도 주목하자.

> **Q. 다음 문장의 (A), (B)에 들어갈 말로 적절한 것을 고르시오.**
>
> Similarly, a man named Kyle Parsons and his partners (A) has / have been creatively (B) reusing / reused old motorcycle tires from Bali, Indonesia.

정답

(A) have (B) reusing

(A) 복수명사인 주어 Kyle Parsons and his partners에 수일치하여 복수형인 have가 들어가는 것이 적절하다. (B) 뒤에 목적어 old motorcycle tires가 있으므로 수동태 문장이 될 수 없으며, 문맥상으로도 주어인 Kyle Parsons와 그의 동업자들이 타이어를 계속해서 '재사용해오고 있는 것'이므로 '~해오고 있다'는 능동 의미인 현재완료 진행 〈have been v-ing〉 형태가 들어가야 한다. 따라서, (B)에는 reusing이 들어가는 것이 적절하다.

● 연결어 similarly

연결어 similarly에 대한 문제도 27.3%의 확률로 나올 수 있다. 문장5 앞에는 업사이클링에 대한 첫 번째 예시로서 Freitag 형제의 사례가 나오고, 문장5부터 두 번째 예시인 Kyle Parsons와 그의 동업자들의 사례가 나온다. 따라서, 이 두 예시를 연결하는 부분에는 유사한 내용을 연결하는 연결어 Similarly(유사하게), Likewise(마찬가지로), In the same manner(마찬가지로) 등이 쓰여야 한다는 것을 기억해두자.

> **Q. 다음 글의 흐름에 맞도록 빈칸에 주어진 글자로 시작하는 적절한 단어를 쓰시오.**
>
> Through upcycling, a seemingly useless object can be transformed into something completely different that is useful for everyday life. What do you think can be done with old truck tarps, car seat belts, and bicycle inner tubes?

Individually, these things look like trash, but with a little imagination the Freitag brothers, Markus and Daniel, repurpose them for something totally new: very strong bags. These bags are perfect for bicyclists going to work every day in all kinds of weather. S_____, a man named Kyle Parsons and his partners have been creatively reusing old motorcycle tires from Bali, Indonesia. A shocking number of tires get thrown away there every year, and they are a serious environmental problem since they cannot decompose or be recycled. To solve this problem, Parsons and his team are turning them into sandal bottoms. They then use canvas and natural materials to make the other sandal parts. What a great reuse of resources!

_____

정답 Similarly

업사이클링에 대한 첫 번째 예시인 Freitag 형제의 사례에 이어서 Kyle Parsons와 그의 동업자들의 사례가 업사이클링에 대한 두 번째 예시로 설명되고 있으므로, 이 두 유사한 내용을 연결하는 연결어이면서 S로 시작하는 Similarly가 들어가야 한다.

● 부사 creatively

부사 creatively와 형용사 creative를 비교하는 문제도 9.1%의 확률로 나올 수 있다. 문맥상 '창의적으로' 재사용해 오고 있는 것이므로, 동사 have been reusing(재사용해오고 있다)을 수식하기 위해 부사 creatively가 쓰인 것이다. 동사는 부사만이 수식할 수 있으므로, 형용사 creative는 쓸 수 없다는 점을 명심하자.

> Q. 다음 괄호 안에 들어갈 말로 적절한 것을 고르시오.
>
> Similarly, a man named Kyle Parsons and his partners have been (creative / creatively) reusing old motorcycle tires from Bali, Indonesia.

정답 creatively

동사 have been reusing (재사용해오고 있다)을 수식하는 자리이므로, 부사 creatively가 들어가는 것이 적절하다. 부사는 동사, 형용사, 부사, 그리고 문장 전체를 수식할 수 있는 반면, 형용사는 명사만을 수식할 수 있다는 점에 유의한다.

출제 포인트 28.7% 정복!

문장6   문장 출제 확률: 5.6% (총 771개의 출제 포인트 중 43회 출현, 46개의 문장 중 1위)

a number of + 복수명사 + 복수동사
A shocking <u>number of tires get</u> thrown away there every year, and they are a serious environmental problem since they <u>cannot decompose</u> or <u>be recycled</u>.
조동사 수동태 cannot be p.p.
decompose: 분해되다

출제 포인트

공동 1위	공동 1위	3위
a number of + 복수명사 + 복수동사	**어휘 decompose**	**조동사 수동태**
	문장 내 출제 확률 25.6%	문장 내 출제 확률 14.0%
문장 내 출제 확률 25.6%	본문[2] 문장편 내 출제 확률 5.5%	본문[2] 문장편 내 출제 확률 3.0%
본문[2] 문장편 내 출제 확률 5.5%		

● a number of＋복수명사＋복수동사

문장6에서 출제될 가능성은 5.6%이며, 이 문장에서 출제가 된다면, 25.6%의 확률로 〈a number of＋복수명사＋복수동사〉의 형태를 아는지 묻는 문제가 나올 수 있다. 〈a number of＋복수명사〉는 '많은 ~들'이라는 뜻으로, 뒤에 복수동사가 온다는 것을 명심하자. 이와 비슷하게 생긴 '~의 수'라는 뜻의 〈the number of＋복수명사〉는 뒤에 단수동사가 온다는 것도 함께 기억해두자.

> **Q. 다음 문장에서 어법상 틀린 부분 2개를 찾아 고쳐 쓰시오.**
>
> The shocking number of tires gets thrown away there every year, and they are a serious environmental problem since they cannot decompose or be recycled.
>
> _____ → _____ / _____ → _____

● 어휘 decompose

decompose에 대한 문제도 25.6%의 확률로 나올 수 있다. decompose는 매년 버려지는 타이어들이 '분해되거나' 재활용되지 않기 때문에 심각한 환경 문제라는 내용에 쓰였다. decompose의 뜻 '분해되다'를 꼭 기억하고, 비슷하게 생긴 compose(구성하다), propose(제안하다) 등과 같은 어휘들과 혼동하지 않도록 유의하자. 그리고 decompose의 영영풀이 to break down or separate into smaller parts or simpler substances, often through natural processes of decay(주로 자연적인 부패 과정을 통해 더 작은 부분이나 더 단순한 물질로 쪼개지거나 분리되다)도 함께 기억해두자.

> **Q. 다음 글의 흐름에 맞도록 빈칸에 주어진 글자로 시작하는 적절한 단어를 쓰시오.**
>
>   A man named Kyle Parsons and his partners have been creatively reusing old motorcycle tires from Bali, Indonesia. A shocking number of tires get thrown away there every year, and they are a serious environmental problem since they cannot _____ or be recycled. To solve this problem, Parsons and his team are turning them into sandal bottoms. They then use canvas and natural materials to make the other sandal parts. What a great reuse of resources!
>
>   d_____

● 조동사 수동태

이 문장에 쓰인 조동사 수동태 cannot be recycled와 능동태 cannot recycle을 비교하는 어법 문제도 14.0%의 확률로 나올 수 있다. a shocking number of tires(엄청난 수의 타이어들)를 가리키는 주어 they는 '재활용될 수 없는' 것이므로, 동사 recycle(재활용하다)과 수동 관계이다. 따라서, 동사 recycle은 앞의 조동사 cannot과 함께 쓰여 조동사 수동태 〈cannot be p.p.〉 형태로 쓰였다. 능동태 cannot decompose와 수동태 cannot be recycled가 or로 병렬 연결된 형태라는 점도 기억해두자.

Q. 주어진 동사를 빈칸에 맞게 2단어로 바꿔 쓰시오.

A shocking number of tires get thrown away there every year, and they are a serious environmental problem since they cannot decompose or _____ (recycle).

● 자동사 decompose

동사 decompose의 형태에 대해 묻는 문제도 11.6%의 확률로 나올 수 있다. 여기서 decompose는 '분해되다, 부패하다'는 의미인 자동사로 쓰였다. 수동의 의미로 생각해서 cannot decompose를 틀린 표현으로 생각하지 않도록 유의하자.

Q. 다음 글의 밑줄 친 (A), (B), (C)가 어법상 옳으면 O, 틀리면 X에 표시하시오.

　　Similarly, a man named Kyle Parsons and his partners (A) <u>have been creatively reused</u> old motorcycle tires from Bali, Indonesia. A shocking number of tires get thrown away there every year, and they are a serious environmental problem since they (B) <u>cannot decompose</u> or be recycled. To solve this problem, Parsons and his team (C) <u>is turning</u> them into sandal bottoms.

(A) (O / X)　　　　　　(B) (O / X)　　　　　　(C) (O / X)

정답
(A) X (B) O (C) X
(A) 주어 a man ~ his partners가 재사용'되는' 것이 아니라 그들이 낡은 오토바이 타이어를 재사용'하는' 것이므로 능동태 현재완료진행 have been creatively reusing이 알맞다.
(B) '분해되다, 부패하다'의 의미인 자동사 decompose가 옳게 쓰였다.
(C) 주어가 Parsons and his team으로 3인칭 복수형이므로, is turning을 are turning으로 고치는 것이 적절하다.

● get p.p.

〈get p.p.〉 형태로 쓰인 동사 get thrown away에 대한 어법 문제도 11.6%의 확률로 나올 수 있다. 주어 A shocking number of tires(엄청난 수의 타이어들)는 사람에 의해 '버려지는' 것이므로, 수동의 의미를 나타내는 과거분사 thrown away가 쓰였다. 〈get p.p.〉는 동작의 변화나 과정을 강조하는 표현임을 기억해두자.

Q. 우리말 뜻에 맞게 다음 문장의 밑줄 친 부분을 고쳐 쓰시오.

A shocking number of tires <u>get throw away</u> there every year, and they are a serious environmental problem since they cannot decompose or be recycled.
(그곳에서 매년 엄청난 수의 타이어들이 버려지고, 그것들은 분해되거나 재활용될 수 없기 때문에 심각한 환경 문제이다.)

_____

정답 get thrown away
'버려지다'라는 의미로 〈get p.p.〉 표현을 사용한 것으로, get 뒤에는 과거분사 형태를 써야 한다.

어휘 throw away에 대한 문제도 4.7%의 확률로 나올 수 있다. 타이어들이 매년 인도네시아 발리에 '버려지고' 이 타이어들이 분해되거나 재활용되지 않아 심각한 환경 문제라는 내용의 흐름상 어휘 throw away가 쓰였다. 비슷한 의미인 throw out, dump, abandon 등도 함께 암기해두자.

Q. 다음 글의 밑줄 친 부분 중, 문맥상 낱말의 쓰임이 적절하지 <u>않은</u> 것은?

Through upcycling, a seemingly ① valueless object can be transformed into something completely different that is useful for everyday life. What do you think can be done with old truck tarps, car seat belts, and bicycle inner tubes? Individually, these things look like ② garbage, but with a little imagination the Freitag brothers, Markus and Daniel, repurpose them for something totally new: very strong bags. These bags are ③ appropriate for bicyclists going to work every day in all kinds of weather. Similarly, a man named Kyle Parsons and his partners have been creatively reusing old motorcycle tires from Bali, Indonesia. A shocking number of tires get ④ upcycled there every year, and they are a serious environmental problem since they cannot decompose or be recycled. To ⑤ <u>deal with</u> this problem, Parsons and his team are turning them into sandal bottoms. They then use canvas and natural materials to make the other sandal parts. What a great reuse of resources!

정답 ④

분해되거나 재활용되지 않는 타이어들이 심각한 환경 문제라는 내용이 뒤에 이어진 것은, 이 타이어들이 매년 인도네시아 발리에서 업사이클 되어서가 아니라 '버려지기' 때문이라는 흐름이 자연스럽다. 따라서 throw away 등의 표현이 적절한데, 앞에 get이 있으므로 수동의 의미인 과거분사 형태를 써야 한다.
[원문 변형]
① useless → valueless
② trash → garbage
③ perfect → appropriate
⑤ solve → deal with

출제 포인트 32.5% 정복!

문장7

문장 출제 확률: 1.7%

this problem = a serious environmental problem   현재진행

To solve <u>this problem</u>, Parsons and his team <u>are turning</u> them into sandal bottoms.

┤ 출제 포인트 ├

1위	2위
현재진행	**this problem의 의미**
문장 내 출제 확률 38.5%	문장 내 출제 확률 23.1%
본문[2] 문장편 내 출제 확률 2.5%	본문[2] 문장편 내 출제 확률 1.5%

● 현재진행

문장7에서 출제될 가능성은 1.7%이며, 이 문장에서 출제된다면 38.5%의 확률로 현재진행 시제에 대한 문제가 나올 수 있다. 문맥상 Parsons와 그의 팀이 오토바이 타이어를 샌들 밑창으로 '계속 탈바꿈시키고 있는' 것이므로, 'A를 B로 바꾸다'라는 뜻의 표현 〈turn A into B〉가 현재에도 계속 진행 중임을 나타내는 현재진행형 〈are/is/am v-ing〉 형태로 쓰였다. 주어가 복수명사인 Parsons and his team이므로 복수형 be동사 are이 쓰인 것도 주목하자. 뒤에 목적어 them이 있으므로, 수동태 are turned가 쓰일 수 없음을 명심하자.

> **Q. 다음 괄호에 어법상 적절한 것을 고르시오.**
>
> To solve this problem, Parsons and his team are (turning / turned) them into sandal bottoms.

정답 turning

뒤에 'a shocking number of tires(엄청난 수의 타이어들)'를 가리키는 대명사 them을 목적어로 취하고 있으므로, 수동태 are turned는 들어갈 수 없다. 능동과 진행의 의미를 나타내는 현재진행 시제 are turning이 들어가는 것이 적절하다.

● this problem의 의미

this problem이 의미하는 바가 무엇인지 묻는 문제도 23.1%의 확률로 나올 수 있다. this problem은 앞 문장에 나온 a serious environmental problem, 즉 '매년 버려지는 많은 타이어가 분해되거나 재활용되지 않아 발생하는 심각한 환경 문제'를 의미한다. 지칭이나 밑줄 의미 유형으로 출제될 수 있으니 정확한 내용을 기억해두자.

> **Q. 다음 글의 밑줄 친 this problem이 의미하는 바를 40자 이내의 우리말로 쓰시오.**
>
> Similarly, a man named Kyle Parsons and his partners have been creatively reusing old motorcycle tires from Bali, Indonesia. A shocking number of tires get thrown away there every year, and they are a serious environmental problem since they cannot decompose or be recycled. To solve this problem, Parsons and his team are turning them into sandal bottoms. They then use canvas and natural materials to make the other sandal parts. What a great reuse of resources!

정답

매년 버려지는 많은 타이어가 분해되거나 재활용되지 않아 발생하는 심각한 환경 문제

this problem이 가리키는 것은 앞 문장의 a serious environmental problem이다. 40자 이내로 쓰라고 했으므로, 인도네시아 발리라는 장소나, 오토바이 타이어라는 구체적인 내용은 생략하여 쓰도록 한다.

● to부정사의 부사적 용법 – 목적

To solve의 용법을 묻는 문제도 15.4%의 확률로 나올 수 있다. 해당 문장은 Parsons와 그의 팀이 버려지는 타이어들을 샌들 밑창으로 탈바꿈시키는 목적을 나타내는 내용으로, To solve는 to부정사의 부사적 용법으로 쓰여 '해결하기 위해'라는 목적을 나타낸다. In order to solve나 In order that they solve 등 목적을 나타내는 다양한 표현으로 바꿔 쓸 수 있다는 것도 함께 알아두자.

> **Q. 다음 글의 밑줄 친 (A)에 주어진 동사를 어법에 맞게 변형하여 2단어로 쓰시오.**
>
> Similarly, a man named Kyle Parsons and his partners have been creatively reusing old motorcycle tires from Bali, Indonesia. A shocking number of tires get thrown away there every year, and they are a serious environmental problem since they cannot decompose or be recycled. (A) solve this problem, Parsons and his team are turning them into sandal bottoms. They then use canvas and natural materials to make the other sandal parts. What a great reuse of resources!

정답 To solve

'이 문제를 해결하기 위해'라고 해석되며 Parsons와 그의 팀이 타이어를 샌들 밑창으로 탈바꿈시킨 목적을 나타내야 한다. 문제에서 2단어로 쓰라고 했으므로, 목적을 나타내는 부사적 용법의 to부정사 형태인 To solve로 변형하는 것이 적절하다.

● 어휘 solve

어휘 solve에 대한 문제도 15.4%의 확률로 나올 수 있다. 목적어 this problem이 가리키는 것은 버려지는 타이어들이 분해되거나 재활용될 수 없어 발생하는 심각한 환경 문제로, Parsons와 그의 팀이 폐타이어로 샌들 밑창을 만든 것은 이 문제를 '해결하기' 위한 행동이다. 이러한 문맥에 따라 어휘 solve가 쓰였다는 것을 알아 두고, 유의어 resolve, handle, deal with 등도 함께 기억해두자.

> **Q. 다음 글의 흐름에 맞도록 빈칸 (A)에 주어진 글자로 시작하는 적절한 2단어를 쓰시오.**
>
> Similarly, a man named Kyle Parsons and his partners have been creatively reusing old motorcycle tires from Bali, Indonesia. A shocking number of tires get thrown away there every year, and they are a serious environmental problem since they cannot decompose or be recycled. To (A) d_____ _____ this problem, Parsons and his team are turning them into sandal bottoms. They then use canvas and natural materials to make the other sandal parts. What a great reuse of resources!
>
> _____

출제 포인트 33.6% 정복!

문장8

문장 출제 확률: 0.4%

to부정사의 부사적 용법 – 목적
They then use canvas and natural materials <u>to make</u> the other sandal parts.

┤ 출제 포인트 ├

1위

to부정사의 부사적 용법 — 목적

문장 내 출제 확률 66.7%
본문[2] 문장편 내 출제 확률 1.0%

● to부정사의 부사적 용법 – 목적

문장8에서 출제될 가능성은 0.4%이며, 이 문장에서 출제된다면 해당 문장에 쓰인 to make의 용법을 묻는 문제가 66.7%의 확률로 나올 수 있다. to make는 '만들기 위해'라고 해석되며, Parsons와 그의 팀이 캔버스와 천연 재료를 활용하는 목적을 나타내고 있다. to make가 목적을 나타내는 to부정사의 부사적 용법으로 쓰였음을 기억하고, in order to make, in order that they make, so that they make 등 목적을 나타내는 다양한 표현으로 바꿔 쓸 수 있다는 것을 유념하자.

출제 포인트 33.8% 정복!

문장9

문장 출제 확률: 0.9%

What 감탄문   재사용
What a great reuse of resources!

┤ 출제 포인트 ├

1위	2위
What 감탄문	**어휘 reuse**
문장 내 출제 확률 57.1%	문장 내 출제 확률 28.6%
본문[2] 문장편 내 출제 확률 2.0%	본문[2] 문장편 내 출제 확률 1.0%

● What 감탄문

문장9에서 출제될 가능성은 0.9%이며, 이 문장에서 출제된다면 What 감탄문에 대한 문제가 57.1%의 확률로 나올 수 있다. Freitag 형제와 Parsons 팀의 업사이클링이 자원을 재사용한 매우 훌륭한 사례임을 감탄하기 위해 '얼마나 ~한 …인가'의 의미인 What 감탄문이 쓰였다. What 감탄문 〈What+(a/an)+형용사+명사(+주어+동사)〉와 How 감탄문 〈How+형용사/부사(+주어+동사)〉의 형태를 구분하여 기억해두자.

> **Q. 다음 문장에서 어법상 어색한 것을 고쳐 쓰시오.**
>
> How a great reuse of resources!
>
> _____ → _____

● 어휘 reuse

어휘 reuse에 대한 문제도 28.6%의 확률로 나올 수 있다. 앞에서 나온 방수포, 안전 벨트 등으로 가방을 만든 Freitag 형제와 타이어, 캔버스 등으로 샌들을 만든 Parsons의 팀의 사례가 모두 훌륭하게 자원을 '재사용'(reuse)한 사례임을 감탄하는 내용에서 reuse가 쓰였다.

Q. 다음 글의 빈칸 (A)에 들어갈 문맥상 적절한 말을 본문에서 찾아 〈조건〉에 맞게 쓰시오.

〈조건〉 1. 주어진 철자로 시작하는 한 단어를 쓸 것
2. 필요한 경우 단어를 변형할 것

A man named Kyle Parsons and his partners have been creatively reusing old motorcycle tires from Bali, Indonesia. A shocking number of tires get thrown away there every year, and they are a serious environmental problem since they cannot decompose. To solve this problem, Parsons and his team are turning them into sandal bottoms. They then use canvas and natural materials to make the other sandal parts. What a great (A) r_____ of resources!

_____

01

다음 글의 밑줄 친 부분 중, 어법상 틀린 것은?

Through upcycling, a ① seemingly useless object can be transformed into something completely different that is useful for everyday life. What do you think can be done with old truck tarps, car seat belts, and bicycle inner tubes? Individually, these things look like trash, but with a little imagination the Freitag brothers, Markus and Daniel, ② repurpose them for something totally new: very strong bags. These bags are perfect for bicyclists going to work every day in all kinds of weather. ③ Similarly, a man named Kyle Parsons and his partners have been creatively reusing old motorcycle tires from Bali, Indonesia. ④ The shocking number of tires get thrown away there every year, and they are a serious environmental problem since they cannot decompose or be recycled. To solve this problem, Parsons and his team are turning them into sandal bottoms. They then use canvas and natural materials to make the other sandal parts. What a great ⑤ reuse of resources!

02

다음 글의 (A), (B), (C)의 각 네모 안에서 어법상 가장 적절한 것은?

Through upcycling, a seemingly useless object can be transformed into something completely different that is useful for everyday life. What do you think can be done with old truck tarps, car seat belts, and bicycle inner tubes? Individually, these things look like trash, but with a (A) few / little imagination the Freitag brothers, Markus and Daniel, repurpose them for something totally new: very strong bags. These bags are perfect for bicyclists going to work every day in all kinds of weather. Similarly, a man named Kyle Parsons and his partners have been creatively (B) reusing / reused old motorcycle tires from Bali, Indonesia. A shocking number of tires get thrown away there every year, and they are a serious environmental problem since they cannot decompose or (C) recycle / be recycled. To solve this problem, Parsons and his team are turning them into sandal bottoms. They then use canvas and natural materials to make the other sandal parts. What a great reuse of resources!

	(A)	(B)	(C)
①	few	reusing	recycle
②	little	reusing	recycle
③	little	reusing	be recycled
④	little	reused	be recycled
⑤	few	reused	be recycled

03

다음 글의 빈칸 (A), (B)에 들어갈 말로 가장 적절한 것은?

Through upcycling, a seemingly useless object can be transformed into something completely different that is useful for everyday life. What do you think can be done with old truck tarps, car seat belts, and bicycle inner tubes? Individually, these things look like trash, but with a little imagination the Freitag brothers, Markus and Daniel,   (A)   them for something totally new: very strong bags. These bags are perfect for bicyclists going to work every day in all kinds of weather. Similarly, a man named Kyle Parsons and his partners have been creatively reusing old motorcycle tires from Bali, Indonesia. A shocking number of tires get thrown away there every year, and they are a serious environmental problem since they cannot   (B)   or be recycled. To solve this problem, Parsons and his team are turning them into sandal bottoms. They then use canvas and natural materials to make the other sandal parts. What a great reuse of resources!

	(A)	(B)
①	repurpose	decompose
②	recover	purpose
③	repurpose	purpose
④	recover	decompose
⑤	purpose	compose

04

다음 글의 밑줄 친 부분 중, 어법상 틀린 것은?

Through upcycling, a seemingly useless object can be transformed into something completely different ① that is useful for everyday life. What do you think ② can be done with old truck tarps, car seat belts, and bicycle inner tubes? Individually, these things look like trash, but with a little imagination the Freitag brothers, Markus and Daniel, repurpose them for ③ totally new something: very strong bags. These bags are perfect for bicyclists ④ going to work every day in all kinds of weather. Similarly, a man named Kyle Parsons and his partners have been creatively reusing old motorcycle tires from Bali, Indonesia. A shocking number of tires get thrown away there every year, and they are a serious environmental problem since they cannot ⑤ decompose or be recycled. To solve this problem, Parsons and his team are turning them into sandal bottoms. They then use canvas and natural materials to make the other sandal parts. What a great reuse of resources!

05

다음 글의 밑줄 친 부분 중, 어법상 틀린 것은?

Through upcycling, a seemingly useless object can be transformed into something ① completely different that is useful for everyday life. What do you think can be done with old truck tarps, car seat belts, and bicycle inner tubes? Individually, these things look like trash, but with ② a little imagination the Freitag brothers, Markus and Daniel, repurpose them for something totally new: very strong bags. These bags are perfect for bicyclists going to work every day in all kinds of weather. Similarly, a man ③ named Kyle Parsons and his partners have been creatively reusing old motorcycle tires from Bali, Indonesia. A shocking number of tires ④ thrown away there every year, and they are a serious environmental problem since they cannot decompose or be recycled. To solve this problem, Parsons and his team are turning them ⑤ into sandal bottoms. They then use canvas and natural materials to make the other sandal parts. What a great reuse of resources!

06

다음 글의 밑줄 친 부분 중, 문맥상 낱말의 쓰임이 적절하지 않은 것은?

Through upcycling, a seemingly ① valueless object can be transformed into something completely different that is ② useless for everyday life. What do you think can be done with old truck tarps, car seat belts, and bicycle inner tubes? Individually, these things look like ③ trash, but with a little imagination the Freitag brothers, Markus and Daniel, ④ repurpose them for something totally new: very strong bags. These bags are ⑤ perfect for bicyclists going to work every day in all kinds of weather.

07

다음 글의 밑줄 친 (A) that과 쓰임이 같은 that을 포함한 문장을 모두 고르시오.

> Through upcycling, a seemingly useless object can be transformed into something completely different (A) that is useful for everyday life.

① This park proves that it's possible to preserve the heritage of a place.
② They insisted that science was the most important thing.
③ He always reminds us that everyone is important to a team's success.
④ There is also an artist that shows even disposable cups can be reused as artistic material.
⑤ Your home is a special place that protects you and your family from everything.

08

다음 글의 밑줄 친 ⓐ~ⓔ의 영영풀이로 옳지 <u>않은</u> 것은?

Through upcycling, a seemingly ⓐ <u>useless</u> object can be ⓑ <u>transformed</u> into something completely different that is useful for everyday life. What do you think can be done with old truck tarps, car seat belts, and bicycle inner tubes? Individually, these things look like trash, but with a little ⓒ <u>imagination</u> the Freitag brothers, Markus and Daniel, ⓓ <u>repurpose</u> them for something totally new: very ⓔ <u>strong</u> bags. These bags are perfect for bicyclists going to work every day in all kinds of weather.

① ⓐ: not serving a purpose, or lacking practical value
② ⓑ: to remain in a certain state or condition
③ ⓒ: the ability or capacity to form mental images or concepts of things that are not present
④ ⓓ: to use something for a new purpose or function
⑤ ⓔ: not easily damaged or broken

09

다음 밑줄 친 ⓐ~ⓔ를 어법상 바르게 고치지 <u>않은</u> 것은?

Through upcycling, a seemingly useless object ⓐ <u>can transform</u> into ⓑ <u>complete different something</u> that is useful for everyday life. What do you think can be done with old truck tarps, car seat belts, and bicycle inner tubes? Individually, these things ⓒ <u>look trash</u>, but with ⓓ <u>a few</u> imagination the Freitag brothers, Markus and Daniel, repurpose them for something totally new: very strong bags. These bags are perfect for bicyclists ⓔ <u>go</u> to work every day in all kinds of weather.

① ⓐ: can be transformed
② ⓑ: something complete different
③ ⓒ: look like trash
④ ⓓ: a little
⑤ ⓔ: going

10

다음 글의 밑줄 친 ⓐ~ⓔ의 영영풀이로 옳지 <u>않은</u> 것은?

Through upcycling, a seemingly useless object can be transformed into something completely different that is ⓐ <u>useful</u> for everyday life. What do you think can be done with old truck tarps, car seat belts, and bicycle inner tubes? ⓑ <u>Individually</u>, these things look like trash, but with a little imagination the Freitag brothers, Markus and Daniel, ⓒ <u>repurpose</u> them for something totally new: very strong bags. These bags are perfect for bicyclists going to work every day in all kinds of weather. Similarly, a man named Kyle Parsons and his partners have been creatively reusing old motorcycle tires from Bali, Indonesia. A shocking number of tires get thrown away there every year, and they are a serious environmental problem since they cannot ⓓ <u>decompose</u> or be recycled. To solve this problem, Parsons and his team are turning them into sandal bottoms. They then use canvas and ⓔ <u>natural</u> materials to make the other sandal parts.

① ⓐ: providing help or benefit in a particular task or situation
② ⓑ as a group
③ ⓒ: to modify or alter for a different objective or function
④ ⓓ: to be destroyed slowly by nature process
⑤ ⓔ: not made or caused by humans

11

다음 글의 밑줄 친 부분 중, 어법상 틀린 것은?

Through upcycling, we can ① be transformed a seemingly useless object into something completely different that is useful for everyday life. What do you think can ② be done with old truck tarps, car seat belts, and bicycle inner tubes? Individually, these things look like trash, but with a little imagination the Freitag brothers, Markus and Daniel, repurpose them for something totally new: very strong bags. These bags are perfect for bicyclists ③ going to work every day in all kinds of weather. Similarly, a man named Kyle Parsons and his partners have been creatively reusing old motorcycle tires from Bali, Indonesia. A shocking number of tires ④ get thrown away there every year, and they are a serious environmental problem since they cannot decompose or be recycled. To solve this problem, Parsons and his team are turning them into sandal bottoms. They then use canvas and natural materials ⑤ to make the other sandal parts. What a great reuse of resources!

12

다음 글의 밑줄 친 @~@를 바르게 고치지 않은 것은?

Through upcycling, a seemingly useless object can be transformed into something @ complete different that is useful for everyday life. What do you think can be done with old truck tarps, car seat belts, and bicycle inner tubes? Individually, these things look like trash, but with ⓑ a few imagination the Freitag brothers, Markus and Daniel, repurpose them for totally new something: very strong bags. These bags are perfect for bicyclists going to work every day in all kinds of weather. Similarly, a man named Kyle Parsons and his partners have been creatively

ⓒ reused old motorcycle tires from Bali, Indonesia. A shocking number of tires get thrown away there every year, and they are a serious environmental problem since they cannot decompose or ⓓ recycled. To solve this problem, Parsons and his team are ⓔ turned them into sandal bottoms. They then use canvas and natural materials to make the other sandal parts. What a great reuse of resources!

① @ → completely
② ⓑ → few
③ ⓒ → reusing
④ ⓓ → be recycled
⑤ ⓔ → turning

13

다음 글의 밑줄 친 부분 중, 어법상 틀린 것은?

Through upcycling, a seemingly useless object can be ① transformed into something completely different that is useful for everyday life. What do you think can be done with old truck tarps, car seat belts, and bicycle inner tubes? Individually, these things ② look like useless, but with a little imagination the Freitag brothers, Markus and Daniel, repurpose ③ them for something totally new: very strong bags. These bags are perfect for bicyclists ④ going to work every day in all kinds of weather. Similarly, a man named Kyle Parsons and his partners have been creatively reusing old motorcycle tires from Bali, Indonesia. A shocking number of tires ⑤ get thrown away there every year, and they are a serious environmental problem since they cannot decompose or be recycled. To solve this problem, Parsons and his team are turning them into sandal bottoms. They then use canvas and natural materials to make the other sandal parts. What a great reuse of resources!

14

다음 글의 빈칸 (A), (B)에 들어갈 말로 가장 적절한 것은?

Through upcycling, a seemingly useless object can be transformed into something completely different that is useful for everyday life. What do you think can be done with old truck tarps, car seat belts, and bicycle inner tubes? Individually, these things look like _____(A)_____, but with a little imagination the Freitag brothers, Markus and Daniel, repurpose them for something totally _____(B)_____: very strong bags. These bags are perfect for bicyclists going to work every day in all kinds of weather.

(A)	(B)
① garbage	– worthless
② junk	– useful
③ waste	– useless
④ treasure	– new
⑤ trash	– valueless

15

다음 밑줄 친 부분 중, 문맥상 낱말의 쓰임이 적절하지 않은 것은?

Through upcycling, a seemingly ① valueless object can be transformed into something completely different that is useful for everyday life. What do you think can be done with old truck tarps, car seat belts, and bicycle inner tubes? Individually, these things look like ② junk, but with a little imagination the Freitag brothers, Markus and Daniel, ③ purpose them for something totally new: very strong bags. These bags are perfect for bicyclists going to work every day in all kinds of weather. Similarly, a man named Kyle Parsons and his partners have

been creatively reusing old motorcycle tires from Bali, Indonesia. A shocking number of tires get thrown away there every year, and they are a serious environmental problem since they cannot decompose or be recycled. To ④ solve this problem, Parsons and his team are turning them into sandal bottoms. They then use canvas and natural materials to make the other sandal parts. What a ⑤ great reuse of resources!

16

다음 글의 밑줄 친 ⓐ~ⓖ 중, 어법상 쓰임이 적절하지 않은 것을 두 개 골라 바르게 고치시오.

What do you think can be done with old truck tarps, car seat belts, and bicycle inner tubes? Individually, these things look ⓐ like trash, but with a little imagination the Freitag brothers, Markus and Daniel, repurpose ⓑ it for something totally new: very strong bags. These bags are perfect for bicyclists ⓒ go to work every day in all kinds of weather. Similarly, a man named Kyle Parsons and his partners ⓓ have been creatively reusing old motorcycle tires from Bali, Indonesia. A shocking number of tires ⓔ get thrown away there every year, and they are a serious environmental problem since they cannot ⓕ decompose or be recycled. To solve this problem, Parsons and his team are turning them into sandal bottoms. They then use canvas and natural materials ⓖ to make the other sandal parts.

_____ : _____ → _____

_____ : _____ → _____

17

다음 글의 밑줄 친 ⓐ~ⓔ의 영영풀이로 옳지 <u>않은</u> 것은?

Through upcycling, a seemingly useless object can be ⓐ <u>transformed</u> into something completely different that is useful for everyday life. What do you think can be done with old truck tarps, car seat belts, and bicycle inner tubes? Individually, these things look like trash, but with a little imagination the Freitag brothers, Markus and Daniel, ⓑ <u>repurpose</u> them for something totally new: very strong bags. These bags are perfect for bicyclists going to work every day in all kinds of weather. Similarly, a man named Kyle Parsons and his partners have been creatively reusing old motorcycle tires from Bali, Indonesia. A shocking number of tires get thrown away there every year, and they are a serious environmental problem since they cannot decompose or be ⓒ <u>recycled</u>. To solve this problem, Parsons and his team are ⓓ <u>turning</u> them into sandal bottoms. They then use canvas and natural materials to make the other sandal parts. What a great reuse of ⓔ <u>resources</u>!

① ⓐ: to change (something) into another form
② ⓑ: to keep something in its original state or condition
③ ⓒ: to collect and treat waste materials so that they can be used again
④ ⓓ: to switch or change something into different form
⑤ ⓔ: a natural or human-made material or asset that is used to create wealth or perform a certain function

18

다음 빈칸에 들어갈 말로 가장 적절한 것은?

Through upcycling, a seemingly useless object can be transformed into something completely different that is useful for everyday life. What do you think can be done with old truck tarps, car seat belts, and bicycle inner tubes? Individually, these things look like trash, but with a little imagination the Freitag brothers, Markus and Daniel, repurpose them for something totally new: very strong bags. These bags are perfect for bicyclists going to work every day in all kinds of weather. _____, a man named Kyle Parsons and his partners have been creatively reusing old motorcycle tires from Bali, Indonesia. A shocking number of tires get thrown away there every year, and they are a serious environmental problem since they cannot decompose or be recycled. To solve this problem, Parsons and his team are turning them into sandal bottoms. They then use canvas and natural materials to make the other sandal parts. What a great reuse of resources!

① Similarly　　　　② Consequently
③ In other words　④ Conversely
⑤ Nevertheless

19

다음 글의 밑줄 친 부분 중, 어법상 틀린 것은?

Through upcycling, a seemingly useless object ① can be transformed into something completely different that is useful for everyday life. What do you think can be done with old truck tarps, car seat belts, and bicycle inner tubes? Individually, these things look ② like trash, but with a little imagination the Freitag brothers, Markus and Daniel, repurpose them for something totally new: very strong bags. These bags are perfect for bicyclists going to work every day in all kinds of weather. Similarly, a man ③ naming Kyle Parsons and his partners have been creatively reusing old motorcycle tires from Bali, Indonesia. A shocking number of tires ④ get thrown away there every year, and they are a serious environmental problem since they cannot decompose or ⑤ be recycled. To solve this problem, Parsons and his team are turning them into sandal bottoms. They then use canvas and natural materials to make the other sandal parts. What a great reuse of resources!

20

다음 글의 (A), (B), (C)의 각 네모 안에서 문맥에 맞는 표현으로 바르게 짝지어진 것은?

Through upcycling, a seemingly useless object can be (A) transformed into / transferred to something completely different that is useful for everyday life. What do you think can be done with old truck tarps, car seat belts, and bicycle inner tubes? Individually, these things look like trash, but with a little imagination the Freitag brothers, Markus and Daniel, repurpose them for something totally new: very strong bags. These bags are perfect for bicyclists going to work every day in all kinds of weather. Similarly, a man named Kyle Parsons and his partners have been (B) typically / creatively reusing old motorcycle tires from Bali, Indonesia. A shocking number of tires get thrown away there every year, and they are a serious environmental problem since they cannot (C) constitute / decompose or be recycled. To solve this problem, Parsons and his team are turning them into sandal bottoms. They then use canvas and natural materials to make the other sandal parts. What a great reuse of resources!

	(A)	(B)	(C)
①	transformed into	typically	constitute
②	transferred to	typically	decompose
③	transformed into	creatively	constitute
④	transferred to	creatively	decompose
⑤	transformed into	creatively	decompose

21

다음 글의 밑줄 친 부분 중, 어법상 틀린 것은?

Through upcycling, a seemingly useless object can ① be transformed into something completely different that is useful for everyday life. What do you think can be done ② with old truck tarps, car seat belts, and bicycle inner tubes? ③ Individually, these things look like trash, but with a little imagination the Freitag brothers, Markus and Daniel, repurpose them for something totally new: very strong bags. These bags are perfect for bicyclists going to work every day in all kinds of weather. Similarly, a man named Kyle Parsons and his partners ④ has been creatively reusing old motorcycle tires from Bali, Indonesia. A shocking number of tires get thrown away there every year, and they are a serious environmental problem since they cannot ⑤ decompose or be recycled. To solve this problem, Parsons and his team are turning them into sandal bottoms. They then use canvas and natural materials to make the other sandal parts. What a great reuse of resources!

22

다음 글의 (A), (B), (C)의 각 네모 안에서 어법에 맞는 표현으로 바르게 짝지어진 것은?

Through upcycling, a seemingly useless object can be transformed into something completely different (A) what / that is useful for everyday life. What do you think can be done with old truck tarps, car seat belts, and bicycle inner tubes? Individually, these things look like trash, but with a little imagination the Freitag brothers, Markus and Daniel, repurpose them for something totally new: very strong bags. These bags are perfect for bicyclists (B) go / going to work every day in all kinds of weather. Similarly, a man named Kyle Parsons and his partners have been creatively (C) reused / reusing old motorcycle tires from Bali, Indonesia. A shocking number of tires get thrown away there every year, and they are a serious environmental problem since they cannot decompose or be recycled. To solve this problem, Parsons and his team are turning them into sandal bottoms. They then use canvas and natural materials to make the other sandal parts. What a great reuse of resources!

	(A)		(B)		(C)
①	what	–	go	–	reused
②	what	–	going	–	reusing
③	that	–	go	–	reused
④	that	–	going	–	reusing
⑤	that	–	going	–	reused

23

다음 글의 (A), (B), (C)의 각 네모 안에서 문맥에 맞는 표현으로 바르게 짝지어진 것은?

Through upcycling, a seemingly useless object can be transformed into something completely different that is useful for everyday life. What do you think can be done with old truck tarps, car seat belts, and bicycle inner tubes? Individually, these things look like (A) trash / treasure , but with a little imagination the Freitag brothers, Markus and Daniel, repurpose them for something totally new: very strong bags. These bags are (B) suitable / inadequate for bicyclists going to work every day in all kinds of weather. Similarly, a man named Kyle Parsons and his partners have been creatively reusing old motorcycle tires from Bali, Indonesia. A shocking number of tires get thrown away there every year, and they are a serious environmental problem since they cannot (C) decompose / compose or be recycled. To solve this problem, Parsons and his team are turning them into sandal bottoms. They then use canvas and natural materials to make the other sandal parts. What a great reuse of resources!

	(A)		(B)		(C)
①	trash	–	suitable	–	decompose
②	treasure	–	suitable	–	decompose
③	trash	–	suitable	–	compose
④	treasure	–	inadequate	–	compose
⑤	trash	–	inadequate	–	compose

24

다음 빈칸에 들어갈 말로 가장 적절한 것은?

Through upcycling, a seemingly useless object can be transformed into something completely different that is useful for everyday life. What do you think can be done with old truck tarps, car seat belts, and bicycle inner tubes? Individually, these things look like trash, but with a little imagination the Freitag brothers, Markus and Daniel, _____ _____ : very strong bags. These bags are perfect for bicyclists going to work every day in all kinds of weather.

① transform them into something unfamiliar
② change them into related items
③ turn them into worthless products
④ repurpose them for something totally new
⑤ replace them with cheap objects

25

다음 글의 밑줄 친 ⓐ~ⓔ 중, 쓰임이 같은 것끼리 짝지어진 것은?

Every day during lunch, Jamie enjoys a soft drink and has a decision ⓐ to make: What should he do with the empty can? Many people would answer, "Recycle it!" Obviously, recycling is good for many reasons. We can reduce the amount of trash thrown away, use less energy than we would ⓑ to make new products, and conserve natural resources by recycling. However, recycling is not a perfect way to manage waste. It still requires large amounts of energy ⓒ to purify used resources and convert them into new products. So, what about trying ⓓ to creatively reuse, or "upcycle," them instead? This new approach is becoming more popular since it is even more environmentally friendly than recycling. What's more, it can also be fun! Here are some inspiring examples of how people have creatively upcycled old, used things.

Through upcycling, a seemingly useless object can be transformed into something completely different that is useful for everyday life. What do you think can be done with old truck tarps, car seat belts, and bicycle inner tubes? Individually, these things look like trash, but with a little imagination the Freitag brothers, Markus and Daniel, repurpose them for something totally new: very strong bags. These bags are perfect for bicyclists going to work every day in all kinds of weather. Similarly, a man named Kyle Parsons and his partners have been creatively reusing old motorcycle tires from Bali, Indonesia. A shocking number of tires get thrown away there every year, and they are a serious environmental problem since they cannot decompose or be recycled. ⓔ To solve this problem, Parsons and his team are turning them into sandal bottoms. They then use canvas and natural materials to make the other sandal parts. What a great reuse of resources!

① ⓐ, ⓓ   ② ⓐ, ⓑ, ⓔ
③ ⓑ, ⓔ   ④ ⓑ, ⓒ, ⓔ
⑤ ⓒ, ⓓ

26

다음 밑줄 친 우리말을 〈조건〉에 맞게 영작하시오.

〈조건〉 1. 아래 〈보기〉의 단어를 모두 사용하여 영작할 것
         (필요시 단어 변형 및 추가 가능)
       2. 총 6 단어로 영작할 것
       3. 현재진행 시제를 사용할 것

〈보기〉 turn, into, sandal bottoms

To solve this problem, Parsons and his team 그것들을 샌들 밑창으로 바꾸고 있다.

_____

27

다음 글의 (A), (B), (C)의 각 네모 안에서 문맥에 맞는 표현으로 바르게 짝지어진 것은?

Through upcycling, a seemingly (A) useless / priceless object can be transformed into something completely different that is useful for everyday life. What do you think can be done with old truck tarps, car seat belts, and bicycle inner tubes? Individually, these things look like trash, but with a little imagination the Freitag brothers, Markus and Daniel, repurpose them for something totally new: very strong bags. These bags are (B) proper / imperfect for bicyclists going to work every day in all kinds of weather. Similarly, a man named Kyle Parsons and his partners have been creatively reusing old motorcycle tires from Bali, Indonesia. A shocking number of tires get thrown away there every year, and they are a serious environmental problem since they cannot decompose or be recycled. To (C) overlook / resolve this problem, Parsons and his team are turning them into sandal bottoms. They then use canvas and natural materials to make the other sandal parts. What a great reuse of resources!

	(A)		(B)		(C)
①	useless	–	proper	–	overlook
②	priceless	–	proper	–	overlook
③	useless	–	proper	–	resolve
④	priceless	–	imperfect	–	resolve
⑤	useless	–	imperfect	–	resolve

28

다음 우리말을 〈조건〉에 맞게 영작하시오.

> 〈조건〉 1. 아래 〈보기〉의 단어를 모두 사용하여 영작할 것
>   (필요시 변형 및 단어 추가 가능)
>   2. 감탄문을 사용할 것
>   3. 총 6단어로 영작할 것

> 〈보기〉 great, a, of, resources, reuse

얼마나 훌륭한 자원의 재사용인가!

29

다음 글의 밑줄 친 부분 중, 어법상 틀린 것은?

Through upcycling, a seemingly useless object ① can be transformed into something completely different that is useful for everyday life. What do you think ② can do with old truck tarps, car seat belts, and bicycle inner tubes? Individually, these things ③ look like trash, but with a little imagination the Freitag brothers, Markus and Daniel, ④ repurpose them for something totally new: very strong bags. These bags are perfect for bicyclists ⑤ going to work every day in all kinds of weather.

30

다음 중, 밑줄 친 (A)와 쓰임이 같은 것은?

> They then use canvas and natural materials (A) to make the other sandal parts.

① She decided to take a break from work and travel for a while.
② My plan to start a business was hindered by a lack of funding.
③ The doctor recommended her to eat a balanced diet regularly.
④ He went to the nearby store to buy some groceries for dinner.
⑤ We are pleased to hear the news of our friends' engagement.

본문[2]

출제 포인트

1위	2위
일관성	내용 일치
본문[2] 문단편 내 출제 확률 29.5%	본문[2] 문단편 내 출제 확률 23.1%

● **일관성**

이 문단에서는 일관성을 확인하는 문제들이 29.5%로 가장 많이 출제되었다. 순서, 문장 삽입, 무관한 문장 찾기 유형의 문제가 자주 출제되고 있으므로 내용 흐름을 숙지해야 한다. 특히, 순서나 문장 삽입 유형 문제의 경우, 대명사나 관사, 그리고 연결어 Similarly가 단서가 될 수 있다는 점을 유의하자.

Q. 주어진 문장이 들어갈 곳으로 가장 적절한 것은?

To solve this problem, Parsons and his team are turning them into sandal bottoms.

 Through upcycling, a seemingly useless object can be transformed into something completely different that is useful for everyday life. What do you think can be done with old truck tarps, car seat belts, and bicycle inner tubes? Individually, these things look like trash, but with a little imagination the Freitag brothers, Markus and Daniel, repurpose them for something totally new: very strong bags. (①) These bags are perfect for bicyclists going to work every day in all kinds of weather. (②) Similarly, a man named Kyle Parsons and his partners have been creatively reusing old motorcycle tires from Bali, Indonesia. (③) A shocking number of tires get thrown away there every year, and they are a serious environmental problem since they cannot decompose or be recycled. (④) They then use canvas and natural materials to make the other sandal parts. (⑤) What a great reuse of resources!

정답 ④

주어진 문장의 this problem은 문맥상 낡은 오토바이 타이어가 분해되거나 재활용될 수 없기 때문에 생기는 환경 문제, 즉 ④ 앞 문장의 a serious environmental problem을 가리키며, 그다음에 샌들 밑창 이외의 부분들(the other sandal parts)을 만든다는 내용이 ④의 뒷문장에 이어진다. 따라서, '이 문제를 해결하기 위해 Parsons와 그의 팀은 타이어를 샌들 밑창으로 탈바꿈시키고 있다'는 내용의 주어진 문장은 ④에 들어가는 것이 적절하다.

● 내용 일치

이 문단에서 내용 일치 유형은 23.1%로 두 번째로 많이 출제되었다. 이 유형에 대비하기 위해서는, 시험 전에 본문의 모든 내용을 숙지하고, 시험 문제에서 본문과 다른 부분이 없는지 확인해야 한다. 본문에서 언급된 업사이클링 제품에 대한 소개와 만든 사람, 제품을 만드는 데 사용한 재료들에 대한 정보를 충분히 숙지하도록 하자.

문장1	Through upcycling, a seemingly useless object can be transformed into something completely different that is useful for everyday life.	2.6%
문장2	What do you think can be done with old truck tarps, car seat belts, and bicycle inner tubes?	7.9%
문장3	Individually, these things look like trash, but with a little imagination the Freitag brothers, Markus and Daniel, repurpose them for something totally new: very strong bags.	18.4%
문장4	These bags are perfect for bicyclists going to work every day in all kinds of weather.	13.2%
문장5	Similarly, a man named Kyle Parsons and his partners have been creatively reusing old motorcycle tires from Bali, Indonesia.	13.2%
문장6	A shocking number of tires get thrown away there every year, and they are a serious environmental problem since they cannot decompose or be recycled.	21.1%
문장7	To solve this problem, Parsons and his team are turning them into sandal bottoms.	15.8%
문장8	They then use canvas and natural materials to make the other sandal parts.	7.9%
문장9	What a great reuse of resources!	0%

정답

1	F	2	T	3	F
4	T	5	T	6	F
7	T	8	F	9	T
10	F	11	F	12	T

(7) 재활용되지 않는 타이어를 업사이클하면 환경문제를 예방할 수 있다.
(8) 오래된 트럭 방수포와 낡은 자전거 타이어와 같은 쓸모없는 물건들을 사용하여, Freitag 형제는 튼튼한 가방을 만든다.
(9) 오래된 오토바이 타이어를 샌들 바닥으로 바꿈으로써 Parsons와 그의 팀은 심각한 환경 문제를 해결하는 것을 돕는다.
(10) Freitag 형제가 만든 가방은 비가 오는 날에만 사용할 수 있다.
(11) Kyle과 그의 파트너들은 창의적으로 낡은 자전거 타이어를 재사용한다.
(12) 샌들의 모든 부분이 폐타이어로 만들어진 것은 아니다.

Q. 글의 내용과 일치하면 T, 일치하지 않으면 F에 표시하시오.

(1) 너무 많은 타이어가 버려지고 분해되어서 심각한 환경 문제가 발생한다. (T / F)
(2) 자전거의 안쪽 튜브, 낡은 트럭 방수포, 자동차 안전벨트를 가지고 가방을 만들 수 있다. (T / F)
(3) Kyle Parsons와 그의 팀은 샌들 밑창을 재사용해서 타이어를 만든다. (T / F)
(4) Freitag 형제가 만든 가방은 튼튼해서 날씨와 상관없이 이용할 수 있다. (T / F)
(5) Kyle과 그의 팀은 오래된 오토바이 타이어를 재사용할 방법을 찾았다. (T / F)
(6) 샌들 밑창을 만드는 데 캔버스와 천연 재료들이 활용된다. (T / F)
(7) Upcycling non-recyclable tires can prevent an environmental problem. (T / F)
(8) Using useless objects, such as old truck tarps and old bicycle tires, the Freitag brothers make strong bags. (T / F)
(9) By turning old motorcycle tires into sandal bottoms, Parsons and his team help solve a serious environmental problem. (T / F)
(10) The bag created by Freitag brothers only can be used on a rainy day. (T / F)
(11) Kyle and his partners creatively reuse old bicycle tires. (T / F)
(12) Not all parts of sandals are made of waste tires. (T / F)

● 지칭 추론

이 문단에서는 지칭 추론 유형이 19.2%로 공동 3위로 출제되었다. 특히, 대명사 them과 they가 각 문장 내에서 old motorcycle tires와 Kyle parsons and his team 중 무엇을 지칭하는지 확실하게 구분할 수 있어야 한다. 또한, 지시대명사를 활용한 변형 문제로 출제되는 확률도 높으니 이 점을 주의하도록 하자.

Q. 다음 글의 밑줄 친 (A), (B), (C), (D)가 가리키는 말을 본문에서 찾아 영어로 쓰시오.

Through upcycling, a seemingly useless object can be transformed into something completely different that is useful for everyday life. What do you think can be done with old truck tarps, car seat belts, and bicycle inner tubes? Individually, these things look like trash, but with a little imagination the Freitag brothers, Markus and Daniel, repurpose (A) them for something totally new: very strong bags. These bags are perfect for bicyclists going to work every day in all kinds of weather. Similarly, a man named Kyle Parsons and his partners have been creatively reusing old motorcycle tires from Bali, Indonesia. A shocking number of tires get thrown away there every year, and (B) they are a serious environmental problem since they cannot decompose or be recycled. To solve this problem, Parsons and his team are turning (C) them into sandal bottoms. (D) They then use canvas and natural materials to make the other sandal parts. What a great reuse of resources!

(A) _____   (B) _____

(C) _____   (D) _____

정답
(A) old truck tarps, car seat belts, and bicycle inner tubes
(B) old motorcycle tires (from Bali, Indonesia)
(C) old motorcycle tires (from Bali, Indonesia)
(D) (Kyle) Parsons and his team [partners]

● 대의 파악

이 문단에서는 대의 파악 유형이 공동 3위로 19.2% 출제되었다. 주제 문제에서는 '업사이클링 사례'에 관한 선지를, 제목 문제에서는 '업사이클링에 대한 설명'과 비슷한 내용을 담은 선지를 답으로 골라야 한다. 주제, 제목, 주장, 요지 문제 모두 글의 전체적인 내용을 포괄해야 하므로, 본문의 일부 내용만을 다루는 선지를 고르지 않도록 주의하자.

Q. 다음 글의 제목으로 가장 적절한 것은?

Through upcycling, a seemingly useless object can be transformed into something completely different that is useful for everyday life. What do you think can be done with old truck tarps, car seat belts, and bicycle inner tubes? Individually, these things look like trash, but with a little imagination the Freitag brothers, Markus and Daniel, repurpose them for something totally new: very strong bags. These bags are perfect for bicyclists going to work every day in all kinds of weather. Similarly, a man named Kyle Parsons and his partners have been creatively reusing old motorcycle tires from Bali, Indonesia. A shocking number of tires get thrown away there every year, and they are a serious environmental problem since they cannot decompose or be recycled. To solve this problem, Parsons and his team are turning them into sandal bottoms. They then use canvas and natural materials to make the other sandal parts. What a great reuse of resources!

정답 ③

Freitag 형제가 낡은 트럭 방수포 등으로 만든 가방과 Kyle Parsons와 그의 동업자들이 오래된 오토바이 타이어로 만든 샌들 밑창처럼, 업사이클링을 통해 겉보기에 쓰레기처럼 보이는 물건들이 일상 생활에 완전히 다른 유용한 것으로 탈바꿈될 수 있다는 내용의 글이다. 따라서 글의 제목으로 ③ '업사이클링: 쓸모없는 물건을 유용하게 만드는 방법'이 가장 적절하다.

① 친환경적인 물건들을 사용하여 친환경적이 되어라!
② 업사이클링과 재활용 – 어떤 것이 더 나은가?
④ Kyle Parsons: 오토바이 타이어의 아버지
⑤ 업사이클링: 환경 문제를 해결하는 유일한 방법

① Go Green by Using Eco-friendly Products!
② Upcycle vs Recycle – Which One Is Better?
③ Upcycling: A Way to Make Useless Items Valuable
④ Kyle Parsons: The Father of Motorcycle Tires
⑤ Upcycling: The Only Way to Solve Environmental Problems

● 요약

이 문단에서는 요약 유형이 7.7% 출제되었으며, 본문의 첫 번째 문장인 'Through upcycling, a seemingly useless object can be transformed into something completely different that is useful for everyday life.'가 변형되어 요약문으로 나오는 경우가 많았다. '쓸모없어 보이는 물건들이 업사이클링을 통해 완전히 새롭고 유용한 것으로 바뀔 수 있다'는 내용을 담은 문장이 요약문으로 적절하다는 것을 기억하도록 하자.

Q. 다음 글의 내용을 한 문장으로 요약하고자 한다. 빈칸 (A), (B)에 들어갈 말로 적절한 것끼리 짝지은 것은?

What do you think can be done with old truck tarps, car seat belts, and bicycle inner tubes? Individually, these things look like trash, but with a little imagination the Freitag brothers, Markus and Daniel, repurpose them for something totally new: very strong bags. These bags are perfect for bicyclists going to work every day in all kinds of weather. Similarly, a man named Kyle Parsons and his partners have been creatively reusing old motorcycle tires from Bali, Indonesia. A shocking number of tires get thrown away there every year, and they are a serious environmental problem since they cannot decompose or be recycled. To solve this problem, Parsons and his team are turning them into sandal bottoms. They then use canvas and natural materials to make the other sandal parts. What a great reuse of resources!

Objects which look _____(A)_____ can be changed into something totally _____(B)_____ through upcycling.

   (A)   (B)
① useful   – old and useless
② useless   – new and useful
③ worthless – similar and eco-friendly
④ valuable – creative and useful
⑤ creative – private and new

01

다음 글의 밑줄 친 ⓐ~ⓖ 중에서 가리키는 대상이 같은 것끼리 묶인 것은?

　Through upcycling, a seemingly useless object can be transformed into something completely different that is useful for everyday life. What do you think can be done with old truck tarps, car seat belts, and bicycle inner tubes? Individually, ⓐ <u>these things</u> look like trash, but with a little imagination the Freitag brothers, Markus and Daniel, repurpose ⓑ <u>them</u> for something totally new: very strong bags. ⓒ <u>These</u> are perfect for bicyclists going to work every day in all kinds of weather. Similarly, a man named Kyle Parsons and his partners have been creatively reusing old motorcycle tires from Bali, Indonesia. A shocking number of ⓓ <u>them</u> get thrown away there every year, and ⓔ <u>they</u> are a serious environmental problem since ⓕ <u>they</u> cannot decompose or be recycled. To solve this problem, Parsons and his team are turning them into sandal bottoms. ⓖ <u>They</u> then use canvas and natural materials to make the other sandal parts. What a great reuse of resources!

① ⓐ, ⓑ, ⓓ 　 ② ⓐ, ⓒ, ⓔ 　 ③ ⓒ, ⓓ, ⓖ
④ ⓓ, ⓔ, ⓕ 　 ⑤ ⓓ, ⓔ, ⓖ

02

다음 글의 흐름으로 보아, 주어진 문장이 들어가기에 가장 적절한 곳은?

> Individually, these things look like trash, but with a little imagination the Freitag brothers, Markus and Daniel, repurpose them for something totally new: very strong bags.

　Through upcycling, a seemingly useless object can be transformed into something completely different that is useful for everyday life. (①) What do you think can be done with old truck tarps, car seat belts, and bicycle inner tubes? (②) These bags are perfect for bicyclists going to work every day in all kinds of weather. (③) Similarly, a man named Kyle Parsons and his partners have been creatively reusing old motorcycle tires from Bali, Indonesia. (④) A shocking number of tires get thrown away there every year, and they are a serious environmental problem since they cannot decompose or be recycled. (⑤) To solve this problem, Parsons and his team are turning them into sandal bottoms. They then use canvas and natural materials to make the other sandal parts. What a great reuse of resources!

03

다음 글에서 전체 흐름과 관계 <u>없는</u> 문장은?

　Through upcycling, a seemingly useless object can be transformed into something completely different that is useful for everyday life. What do you think can be done with old truck tarps, car seat belts, and bicycle inner tubes? Individually, these things look like trash. ① <u>However, with a little imagination the Freitag brothers, Markus and Daniel, repurpose them for something totally new: very strong bags.</u> ② <u>These face a strong backlash from many bicyclists because of the price.</u> ③ <u>These bags are perfect for bicyclists going to work every day in all kinds of weather.</u> Similarly, a man named Kyle Parsons and his partners have been creatively reusing old motorcycle tires from Bali, Indonesia. ④ <u>A shocking number of tires get thrown away there every year, and they are a serious environmental problem since they cannot decompose or be recycled.</u> To solve this problem, Parsons and his team are turning them into sandal bottoms. ⑤ <u>They then use canvas and natural materials to make the other sandal parts.</u> What a great reuse of resources!

04

주어진 글 다음에 이어질 글의 순서로 가장 적절한 것은?

Through upcycling, a seemingly useless object can be transformed into something completely different that is useful for everyday life. What do you think can be done with old truck tarps, car seat belts, and bicycle inner tubes? Individually, these things look like trash.

(A) A shocking number of tires get thrown away there every year, and they are a serious environmental problem since they cannot decompose or be recycled.

(B) However, with a little imagination the Freitag brothers, Markus and Daniel, repurpose them for something totally new: very strong bags.

(C) These bags are perfect for bicyclists going to work every day in all kinds of weather. Similarly, a man named Kyle Parsons and his partners have been creatively reusing old motorcycle tires from Bali, Indonesia.

(D) To solve this problem, Parsons and his team are turning them into sandal bottoms. They then use canvas and natural materials to make the other sandal parts.

① (A) – (C) – (B) – (D)
② (B) – (A) – (C) – (D)
③ (B) – (C) – (A) – (D)
④ (C) – (A) – (D) – (B)
⑤ (C) – (D) – (A) – (B)

05

다음 글의 밑줄 친 ⓐ~ⓔ가 다음 글에서 의미하는 바로 적절하지 않은 것을 모두 고르시오.

Through upcycling, a seemingly useless object can be transformed into something completely different that is useful for everyday life. What do you think can be done with old truck tarps, car seat belts, and bicycle inner tubes? Individually, ⓐ these things look like trash, but with a little imagination the Freitag brothers, Markus and Daniel, repurpose ⓑ them for something totally new: very strong bags. These bags are perfect for bicyclists going to work every day in all kinds of weather. Similarly, a man named Kyle Parsons and his partners have been creatively reusing old motorcycle tires from Bali, Indonesia. A shocking number of ⓒ them get thrown away there every year, and they are a serious environmental problem since they cannot decompose or be recycled. To solve ⓓ it, Parsons and his team are turning them into sandal bottoms. ⓔ They then use canvas and natural materials to make the other sandal parts. What a great reuse of resources!

① ⓐ: old truck tarps, car seat belts, and old motorcycle tires
② ⓑ: strong bags
③ ⓒ: old motorcycle tires
④ ⓓ: the environmental problem
⑤ ⓔ: Parsons and his team

06

다음 글의 내용을 한 문장으로 요약하고자 한다. 빈칸 (A)와 (B)에 들어갈 말로 가장 적절한 것은?

What do you think can be done with old truck tarps, car seat belts, and bicycle inner tubes? Individually, these things look like trash, but with a little imagination the Freitag brothers, Markus and Daniel, repurpose them for something totally new: very strong bags. These bags are perfect for bicyclists going to work every day in all kinds of weather. Similarly, a man named Kyle Parsons and his partners have been creatively reusing old motorcycle tires from Bali, Indonesia. A shocking number of tires get thrown away there every year, and they are a serious environmental problem since they cannot decompose or be recycled. To solve this problem, Parsons and his team are turning them into sandal bottoms. They then use canvas and natural materials to make the other sandal parts. What a great reuse of resources!

> We can bring life into _____(A)_____ objects using a little _____(B)_____ .

	(A)		(B)
①	useless	–	imitation
②	worthless	–	creativity
③	useful	–	inspiration
④	valuable	–	imagination
⑤	usable	–	originality

07

주어진 글 다음에 이어질 글의 순서로 가장 적절한 것은?

> What do you think can be done with old truck tarps, car seat belts, and bicycle inner tubes?

(A) Similarly, a man named Kyle Parsons and his partners have been creatively reusing old motorcycle tires from Bali, Indonesia. A shocking number of tires get thrown away there every year, and they are a serious environmental problem since they cannot decompose or be recycled.

(B) Individually, these things look like trash, but with a little imagination the Freitag brothers, Markus and Daniel, repurpose them for something totally new: very strong bags. These bags are perfect for bicyclists going to work every day in all kinds of weather.

(C) To solve this problem, Parsons and his team are turning them into sandal bottoms. They then use canvas and natural materials to make the other sandal parts.

① (A) – (C) – (B) ② (B) – (A) – (C)
③ (B) – (C) – (A) ④ (C) – (A) – (B)
⑤ (C) – (B) – (A)

[08~10]

다음 글을 읽고, 물음에 답하시오.

Through upcycling, a seemingly useless object can be transformed into something completely different that is useful for everyday life. What do you think can be done with old truck tarps, car seat belts, and bicycle inner tubes? Individually, these things look like trash, but with a little imagination the Freitag brothers, Markus and Daniel, repurpose them for something totally new: very strong bags. These bags are perfect for bicyclists going to work every day in all kinds of weather. Similarly, a man named Kyle Parsons and his partners have been creatively reusing old motorcycle tires from Bali, Indonesia. A shocking number of tires get thrown away there every year, and they are a serious environmental problem since they cannot decompose or be recycled. To solve this problem, Parsons and his team are turning them into sandal bottoms. Then canvas and natural materials are used to make the other sandal parts by them. What a great reuse of resources!

08

윗글의 제목으로 가장 적절한 것은?

① How to Make Sandals from Old Tires
② Upcycling: From Garbage to Treasure
③ The Side Effects of Upcycling on the Environment
④ Recycling: The Only Way to Protect Our Environment
⑤ Difference between Recycling and Upcycling

09

윗글의 내용과 일치하지 않는 것을 모두 고르시오.

① 자전거의 안쪽 튜브, 낡은 트럭 방수포, 자동차 안전벨트는 업사이클될 수 있다.
② Freitag 형제가 만든 가방은 자전거로 통근하는 사람들에게 유용하다.
③ 낡은 오토바이 타이어로 샌들의 모든 부분을 만든다.
④ Kyle Parsons와 그의 동업자들은 낡은 오토바이 타이어를 업사이클해오고 있다.
⑤ 많은 낡은 오토바이 타이어들이 버려지고 분해됨에 따라 심각한 환경 문제가 야기된다.

10

윗글을 읽고 대답할 수 없는 질문을 모두 고르시오.

① Why did the Freitag brothers decide to make bags using old and useless objects?
② What kind of useless objects did the Freitag brothers use to make strong bags?
③ Why do used tires thrown away cause a serious environmental problem?
④ Why can't old motorcycle tires decompose or be recycled?
⑤ What can be made out of old motorcycle tires?

다음 글을 읽고, 물음에 답하시오.

Through upcycling, a seemingly useless object can be transformed into something completely different that is useful for everyday life. What do you think can be done with old truck tarps, car seat belts, and bicycle inner tubes? Individually, these things look like trash, but with a little imagination the Freitag brothers, Markus and Daniel, repurpose them for something totally new: very strong bags. These bags are perfect for bicyclists going to work every day in all kinds of weather. Similarly, a man named Kyle Parsons and his partners have been creatively reusing old motorcycle tires from Bali, Indonesia. A shocking number of tires get thrown away there every year, and they are a serious environmental problem since they cannot decompose or be recycled. To solve this problem, Parsons and his team are turning them into sandal bottoms. Then canvas and natural materials are used to make the other sandal parts by them. What a great reuse of resources!

11

윗글의 주제로 가장 적절한 것은?

① ways to recycle effectively
② importance of thinking creatively
③ the difficulty of reusing useless things
④ examples of repurposing worthless objects
⑤ the similarity between upcycling and recycling

12

윗글의 내용과 일치하지 <u>않는</u> 것을 <u>모두</u> 고르시오.

① The Freitag brothers invented strong bags using old truck tarps, motorcycle tires, and bicycle inner tubes.
② The bags the Freitag brothers made are useful for bicyclists as they are tough.
③ Kyle Parsons and his team upcycle waste tires in order to solve a serious environmental problem.
④ Old motorcycle tires cause a serious environmental problem while decomposing.
⑤ Not all sandal parts are made of old motorcycle tires.

13

다음 글의 필자가 주장하는 바를 〈보기〉의 말을 바르게 배열하여 영어로 완성하시오.

> 〈보기〉 different objects / is / be / changed / into / valuable / for daily life / it / feasible / are / for useless things / to / that

What do you think can be done with old truck tarps, car seat belts, and bicycle inner tubes? Individually, these things look like trash, but with a little imagination the Freitag brothers, Markus and Daniel, repurpose them for something totally new: very strong bags. These bags are perfect for bicyclists going to work every day in all kinds of weather. Similarly, a man named Kyle Parsons and his partners have been creatively reusing old motorcycle tires from Bali, Indonesia. A shocking number of tires get thrown away there every year, and they are a serious environmental problem since they cannot decompose or be recycled. To solve this problem, Parsons and his team are turning them into sandal bottoms. They then use canvas and natural materials to make the other sandal parts. What a great reuse of resources!

Through upcycling, _____

_____

_____

14

다음 글의 밑줄 친 ⓐ~ⓔ가 다음 글에서 의미하는 바로 적절하지 <u>않은</u> 것을 <u>모두</u> 고르시오.

Through upcycling, a seemingly useless object can be transformed into something completely different that is useful for everyday life. What do you think can be done with old truck tarps, car seat belts, and bicycle inner tubes? Individually, these things look like trash, but with a little imagination the Freitag brothers, Markus and Daniel, repurpose ⓐ <u>them</u> for something totally new: very strong bags. These bags are perfect for bicyclists going to work every day in all kinds of weather. Similarly, a man named Kyle Parsons and his partners have been creatively reusing old motorcycle tires from Bali, Indonesia. A shocking number of tires get thrown away there every year, and ⓑ <u>they</u> are a serious environmental problem since ⓒ <u>they</u> cannot decompose or be recycled. To solve this problem, Parsons and his team are turning ⓓ <u>them</u> into sandal bottoms. Then canvas and natural materials are used to make the other sandal parts by ⓔ <u>them</u>. What a great reuse of resources!

① ⓐ: old truck tarps, car seat belts, and bike inner tubes
② ⓑ: old motorcycle tires from Bali
③ ⓒ: Kyle Parsons and his partners
④ ⓓ: old motorcycle tires from Bali
⑤ ⓔ: sandal bottoms

1회 등장 포인트

● 어휘 different

> Through upcycling, a seemingly useless object can be transformed into something completely different that is useful for everyday life.

● 어휘 imagination, strong

> Individually, these things look like trash, but with a little imagination the Freitag brothers, Markus and Daniel, repurpose them for something totally new: very strong bags.

● 어휘 serious

> A shocking number of tires get thrown away there every year, and they are a serious environmental problem since they cannot decompose or be recycled.

● 어휘 natural

> They then use canvas and natural materials to make the other sandal parts.

● 어휘 resources

> What a great reuse of resources!

01

다음 밑줄 친 부분 중, 문맥상 낱말의 쓰임이 어색한 것은?

Through upcycling, a seemingly useless object can be transformed into something completely ① different that is useful for everyday life. What do you think can be done with old truck tarps, car seat belts, and bicycle inner tubes? Individually, these things look like trash, but with a little ② imagination the Freitag brothers, Markus and Daniel, repurpose them for something totally new: very strong bags. These bags are perfect for bicyclists going to work every day in all kinds of weather. Similarly, a man named Kyle Parsons and his partners have been creatively reusing old motorcycle tires from Bali, Indonesia. A shocking number of tires get thrown away there every year, and they are a ③ minor environmental problem since they cannot decompose or be recycled. To solve this problem, Parsons and his team are turning them into sandal bottoms. They then use canvas and ④ natural materials to make the other sandal parts. What a great reuse of ⑤ resources!

● 빈칸 is useful for everyday life

> Through upcycling, a seemingly useless object can be transformed into something completely different that is useful for everyday life.

● 빈칸 repurpose them for something totally new

> Individually, these things look like trash, but with a little imagination the Freitag brothers, Markus and Daniel, repurpose them for something totally new: very strong bags.

● 빈칸 a serious environmental problem

> A shocking number of tires get thrown away there every year, and they are a serious environmental problem since they cannot decompose or be recycled.

02

다음 빈칸 ⓐ~ⓔ에 들어갈 말로 적절하지 <u>않은</u> 것은?

Through upcycling, a seemingly useless object can be transformed into something completely different that ⓐ_____. What do you think can be done with old truck tarps, car seat belts, and bicycle inner tubes? Individually, ⓑ_____ but with a little imagination the Freitag brothers, Markus and Daniel, ⓒ_____ _____: very strong bags. These bags are perfect for bicyclists going to work every day in all kinds of weather. Similarly, a man named Kyle Parsons and his partners have been creatively reusing old motorcycle tires from Bali, Indonesia. A shocking number of tires get thrown away there every year, and they are ⓓ_____ since they cannot decompose or be recycled. ⓔ_____, Parsons and his team are turning them into sandal bottoms. They then use canvas and natural materials to make the other sandal parts. What a great reuse of resources!

① ⓐ: is helpful for everyday life
② ⓑ: these things look useless
③ ⓒ: repurpose them for something totally valueless.
④ ⓓ: a serious environmental threat
⑤ ⓔ: In order to solve it

● 심경 추론

본문2의 앞, 뒤에 심경을 추론할 수 있을 만한 문장을 추가하고 글쓴이의 심경 변화를 묻는 문제가 종종 출제된다. 해당 유형의 문제가 나오면, 주어진 본문의 앞, 뒤 문장에 어떤 문장이 추가되었고, 그 문장이 어떤 심경을 나타내는지 꼭 체크하도록 하자.

03

다음 글에 드러난 글쓴이의 심경 변화로 가장 적절한 것은?

I was so worried about the global environmental destruction. However, a man named Kyle Parsons and his partners have been creatively reusing old motorcycle tires from Bali, Indonesia. A shocking number of tires get thrown away there every year, and they are a serious environmental problem since they cannot decompose or be recycled. To solve this problem, Parsons and his team are turning them into sandal bottoms. Like Parsons and his team, through upcycling, we can transform a seemingly useless object into something completely different that is useful for everyday life, and therefore we can protect our environment. Thank God there is something we can do to protect our environment!

① worried → discouraged
② surprised → embarrassed
③ excited → frustrated
④ delighted → depressed
⑤ concerned → relieved

● 문장 변형

> A shocking number of tires get thrown away there every year, and they are a serious environmental problem since they cannot decompose or be recycled.

'접속사(and)+대명사(they)'가 계속적 용법의 관계대명사 which로 변형되어 출제될 수 있다. 이때, 관계대명사절 속 be동사는 선행사가 되는 복수명사 A shocking number of tires에 수 일치하여 are이어야 한다는 점을 꼭 유의하자.

> To solve this problem, Parsons and his team are turning them into sandal bottoms.

To solve this problem이 앞 문장과 연결하는 연결어 Therefore로 변형되거나, 전체 문장이 〈so that+주어+can〉을 사용한 Parsons and his team are turning them into sandal bottoms so that they can solve this problem.으로 변형되어 출제될 수 있다. 또한, 대명사 them이 tires that are thrown away로 변형되어 출제될 수 있다. 이 변형 포인트들을 꼭 기억해두도록 하자.

> These bags are perfect for bicyclists going to work every day in all kinds of weather.

These와 bags 사이에 단어 long-lasting(오래 지속되는), strong, tough(튼튼한) 등의 단어가 포함되고, 해당 단어가 문맥상 적절한지 묻는 문제가 출제될 수 있다.

04

다음 글의 밑줄 친 부분 중 어법과 문맥상 <u>어색한</u> 것을 <u>모두</u> 고르시오.

Through upcycling, a seemingly useless object can be transformed into something completely different that is useful for everyday life. What do you think can be done with old truck tarps, car seat belts, and bicycle inner tubes? Individually, these things look like trash, but with a little imagination the Freitag brothers, Markus and Daniel, repurpose them for something totally new: very strong bags. These ① long-lasting bags are perfect for bicyclists ② who is going to work every day in all kinds of weather. Similarly, a man named Kyle Parsons and his partners have been creatively reusing old motorcycle tires from Bali, Indonesia. A shocking number of tires get thrown away there every year, ③ that are a serious environmental problem since they cannot decompose or be recycled. Parsons and his team are turning tires that ④ are thrown away into sandal bottoms ⑤ so that they can solve this problem. They then use canvas and natural materials to make the other sandal parts. What a great reuse of resources!

● 함축된 의미

These bags are perfect for bicyclists going to work every day in all kinds of weather.

'Freitag 형제가 쓰레기로 만든 가방은 튼튼해서 어떤 날씨에도 일하러 가는 자전거 이용자들에게 완벽하다'는 내용의 문장으로, 'Freitag 형제가 만든 그 가방은 튼튼해서 어떤 날씨에든 사람들이 자전거를 타고 일하러 갈 때 매우 도움이 된다'는 것을 의미한다.

출제 포인트 42.9% 정복!

리딩
본문[3]

22.2% 확률로 본문[3]에서 출제

Along with small everyday items, much bigger things can also be upcycled—even old buildings that cannot be used for their original purpose anymore. The German government showed us an excellent example of this with a former steel plant that closed in 1985. Rather than destroy the plant's buildings or abandon the entire facility, they decided to give it new meaning as a series of useful public structures. Many of the buildings kept their original shapes, but received extra equipment and new designs in their surrounding areas. For instance, old gas tanks became pools for divers. Concrete walls of iron storage towers were turned into ideal training fields for rock climbers. Can you believe a building for melting metal is now a viewing platform with a gorgeous 360-degree view? The final result is the Landscape Park Duisburg Nord. It has almost 570 acres of land filled with gardens, cycling paths, and pretty lights at night, in addition to its creatively repurposed buildings. This park proves that it's possible to preserve the heritage of a place as well as the environment.

내용 일치 〈출제 1위 유형〉

내용 일치 유형 문제에서는 글의 세부적인 내용에 유의해야 한다. 해당 단락에서 독일 정부는 오래된 공장의 가스탱크를 수영장으로, 콘크리트 벽을 암벽 전문가들을 위한 훈련장으로, 금속을 녹이는 데 쓰였던 건물을 전망대로 바꿈으로써 공장의 원래 형태는 유지하지만 새로운 의미를 부여했다는 것을 기억해두자.

일관성 〈출제 2위 유형〉

오래된 철강 공장이 독일의 뒤스부르크 환경 공원으로 업사이클된 사례를 서술하고 있다. 글의 순서, 문장 삽입, 무관한 문장 고르기 등 다양한 일관성 문제가 출제 되는데, 대명사 it, 연결사 For instance 등이 힌트가 될 수 있음을 알아두자.

대의 파악 〈출제 3위 유형〉

주제나 제목을 묻는 유형은 본문의 중심 내용을 잘 드러내고 있는지를 파악해야 한다. 본문의 일부만 나타내거나, 본문에는 언급되지 않는 상식적인 내용을 피하고, 본문 전체를 아우르는 보기를 골라야 함을 명심하자.

출제 1위 문장 ★★★

This park proves that it's possible to preserve the heritage of a place as well as the environment.

[가주어 it] 출제 1위 (문장편-문장10 → p.101)
[빈칸 it's possible ~ environment] 출제 2위 (문장편-문장10 → p.101)
[B as well as A] 출제 3위 (문장편-문장10 → p.102)

출제 2위 문장 ★★

Rather than destroy the plant's buildings or abandon the entire facility, they decided to give it new meaning as a series of useful public structures.

[Rather than] 출제 1위 (문장편-문장3 → p.92)

출제 3위 문장 ★

It has almost 570 acres of land filled with gardens, cycling paths, and pretty lights at night, in addition to its creatively repurposed buildings.

[과거분사 형용사 역할 — 명사 수식] 출제 1위 (문장편-문장9 → p.99)
[in addition to] 출제 2위 (문장편-문장9 → p.100)

문장1

> 비교급 강조
> Along with small everyday items, <u>much</u> bigger things can also
> be <u>upcycled</u>—even old buildings <u>that</u> cannot <u>be used</u> for their
> 수동태   주격관계대명사 that   수동태
> original purpose anymore.

┤ 출제 포인트 ├

1위	2위	3위
주격관계대명사 that	**비교급 강조**	**수동태**
문장 내 출제 확률 33.3%	문장 내 출제 확률 23.8%	문장 내 출제 확률 19.1%
본문[3] 문장편 내 출제 확률 4.3%	본문[3] 문장편 내 출제 확률 3.1%	본문[3] 문장편 내 출제 확률 2.4%

● 주격관계대명사 that

문장1에서 출제될 가능성은 2.7%이다. 이 문장에서 출제가 된다면 33.3%의 확률로 선행사 old buildings를 수식하는 주격관계대명사 that을 묻는다. 주격관계대명사 that 뒤에는 불완전한 문장이 온다는 사실을 명심하고, 뒤에 완전한 절이 이어지는 접속사 that과 구분할 필요가 있다. 선행사가 사물(old buildings)이기 때문에 which로 바꿔 쓸 수 있다. 또한, 이 문장은 서술형으로도 자주 출제되기 때문에 관계대명사 that을 활용해서 영작 연습도 해보자.

정답 which, that

뒤에 주어가 없는 불완전한 절이 오기 때문에, 선행사 old buildings를 수식하는 주격관계대명사가 쓰여야 함을 알 수 있다. 따라서, which와 that이 어법상 올바르다. 선행사가 사물이기 때문에 who는 적절하지 않고, 관계부사 where 뒤에는 완전한 절이 와야 하므로 어법상 적절하지 않다.

> **Q. 다음 괄호 안에서 어법상 옳은 것을 <u>모두</u> 고르시오.**
>
> Along with small everyday items, much bigger things can also be upcycled—even old buildings (which / who / that / where) cannot be used for their original purpose anymore.

● 비교급 강조

이 문장에서 23.8%의 확률을 차지하여 두 번째로 출제 확률이 높은 것은 비교급을 강조하는 much이다. much는 뒤에 오는 비교급(bigger)을 수식하기 위해 쓰였으며, '훨씬'이라는 의미이다. even, far, a lot, still로 바꿔 쓸 수 있으며, 원급을 강조하는 very와 구분하는 문제가 자주 출제된다.

정답

(A) much (B) that

(A) 뒤에 오는 비교급 bigger을 수식하기 위해서는 much를 쓰는 것이 적절하다.
(B) 뒤에 주어가 없는 불완전한 절이 왔기 때문에 선행사 a former steel plant를 수식하는 주격관계대명사가 쓰여야 함을 알 수 있다. 앞에 선행사가 있기 때문에, 선행사를 포함하는 관계대명사인 what은 쓸 수 없다.

> **Q. 다음 글의 (A), (B)의 각 네모 안에서 어법에 맞는 표현으로 적절한 것을 고르시오.**
>
> Along with small everyday items, (A) much / very bigger things can also be upcycled—even old buildings that cannot be used for their original purpose anymore. The German government showed us an excellent example of this with a former steel plant (B) that / what closed in 1985. Rather than destroy the plant's buildings or abandon the entire facility, they decided to give it new meaning as a series of useful public structures. Many of the buildings kept their original shapes, but received extra equipment and new designs in their surrounding areas.

● 수동태

이 문장에서는 수동태도 많이 묻는데, 출제 확률 19.1%를 차지한다. 주절의 주어 much bigger things는 업사이클되는 동작의 대상이므로 수동태로 쓴다. 또한, 관계대명사가 수식하는 선행사 old buildings도 사용되는 동작의 대상이므로 수동태를 쓴다. 두 경우 모두 조동사 can 뒤에 〈be p.p.〉의 형태로, be upcycled, be used가 되는 것에 유의하자.

> Q. 다음 글의 (A), (B)의 각 네모 안에서 어법에 맞는 표현을 고르시오.
>
> Along with small everyday items, much bigger things can also (A) | upcycle / be upcycled | —even old buildings that cannot (B) | use / be used | for their original purpose anymore. The German government showed us an excellent example of this with a former steel plant that closed in 1985.

정답
(A) be upcycled
(B) be used

(A) 주어 much bigger things가 동작의 대상이므로 수동태를 써야 한다. 수동태는 〈be p.p.〉인데 조동사 뒤에 동사원형이 와야 해서 be동사의 원형인 be 뒤에 upcycle의 과거분사 upcycled를 써야 한다.
(B) 선행사 old buildings는 사용되는 동작의 대상이므로, 관계사절 내의 조동사 cannot 뒤에 be p.p.의 수동태를 써야 한다.

● 빈칸 that cannot be used for their original purpose anymore

이 문장에서 출제가 된다면, 9.5%의 확률로 빈칸 유형이 출제될 수 있다. 타이어와 같은 일상생활 속의 용품과 마찬가지로, 더 이상 원래 용도로 쓰이지 않는 건물들도 업사이클될 수 있다는 것을 확인하는 문제가 자주 나오니 명심하자.

> Q. 다음 질문에 답하기 위해 빈칸에 들어갈 말을 본문에서 찾아 쓰시오.
>
> Along with small everyday items, much bigger things can also be upcycled—even old buildings that cannot be used for their original purpose anymore. The German government showed us an excellent example of this with a former steel plant that closed in 1985. Rather than destroy the plant's buildings or abandon the entire facility, they decided to give it new meaning as a series of useful public structures. Many of the buildings kept their original shapes, but received extra equipment and new designs in their surrounding areas. For instance, old gas tanks became pools for divers. Concrete walls of iron storage towers were turned into ideal training fields for rock climbers. Can you believe a building for melting metal is now a viewing platform with a gorgeous 360-degree view? The final result is the Landscape Park Duisburg Nord. It has almost 570 acres of land filled with gardens, cycling paths, and pretty lights at night, in addition to its creatively repurposed buildings. This park proves that it's possible to preserve the heritage of a place as well as the environment.
>
> 질문: Why did the German government decide to upcycle a former steel plant?
>
> 답: Because the plant lost its _____. (2 words)

정답 original purpose
[질문] 독일 정부는 왜 이전의 철강 공장을 업사이클하기로 결정했는가?
[답] 그 공장이 본래의 목적을 잃었기 때문이다.

● not ~ anymore

마찬가지로 9.5%의 확률로 not ~ anymore을 물을 수 있다. not ~ anymore은 '더 이상 ~가 아닌'이라는 의미이며, not ~ any longer로 바꿔 쓸 수 있다. 본문에서는 조동사 can의 부정형인 cannot과 함께 썼다.

정답 cannot

'더 이상 ~가 아니다'라는 의미를 전달하기 위해서 조동사 can을 부정형으로 써야 한다.

> **Q. 다음 괄호 안에서 적절한 말을 고르시오.**
>
> Along with small everyday items, much bigger things can also be upcycled—even old buildings that (can / cannot) be used for their original purpose anymore.

출제 포인트 44.8% 정복!

문장2

문장 출제 확률: 1.7%

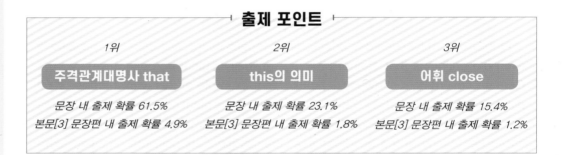

The German government showed us an excellent example of this with a former steel plant that closed in 1985.
this의 의미: 앞 문장 전체 　　　 주격관계대명사 that　　close: 닫다, 폐업하다

┤ 출제 포인트 ├

1위	2위	3위
주격관계대명사 that	**this의 의미**	**어휘 close**
문장 내 출제 확률 61.5% 본문[3] 문장편 내 출제 확률 4.9%	문장 내 출제 확률 23.1% 본문[3] 문장편 내 출제 확률 1.8%	문장 내 출제 확률 15.4% 본문[3] 문장편 내 출제 확률 1.2%

● 주격관계대명사 that

문장2에서 출제될 가능성은 1.7%이다. 이 문장에서 61.5% 확률로 가장 많이 출제되는 것은 주격관계대명사 that을 물어보는 어법 문제이다. 선행사 a former steel plant를 수식하는 주격관계대명사 that 뒤에는 주어가 없는 불완전한 절이 이어진다. 선행사가 사물이기 때문에 which로 바꿔 쓸 수 있다. 뒤에 완전한 절이 이어지는 접속사 that과 구별하는 문제, 영작 문제 등 다양한 형태로 출제되기 때문에 많이 연습해보자.

정답

that closed in 1985

선행사가 a former steel plant이고 관계사절에서 주어 역할을 하므로 주격관계대명사를 써야 한다. 선행사가 있기 때문에 선행사를 포함하는 관계대명사 what은 쓸 수 없다. 연도 앞에는 전치사 in을 쓴다.

> **Q. 다음 글의 밑줄 친 우리말과 같은 뜻이 되도록 〈보기〉에서 필요한 단어를 골라 어형 변화 없이 배열하여 쓰시오.**
>
> > 〈보기〉 in / 1985 / closed / that / what / on
>
> Along with small everyday items, much bigger things can also be upcycled—even old buildings that cannot be used for their original purpose anymore. The German government showed us an excellent example of this with a former steel plant <u>1985년에 문을 닫은</u>. Rather than destroy the plant's buildings or abandon the entire facility, they decided to give it new meaning as a series of useful public structures.
>
> _____

● this의 의미

이 문장에서 this가 지칭하는 바를 아는지 묻는 문제가 23.1% 확률로 자주 출제된다. 여기서 this는 앞 문장 전체를 지칭해서, 타이어와 같은 일상생활 속의 용품과 마찬가지로 더 이상 원래 용도로 쓰이지 않는 건물들도 업사이클될 수 있다는 사실을 가리킨다. 대명사가 지칭하는 내용을 본문에서 찾아 쓰거나, 일관성 문제로 출제될 수 있으니 꼭 기억하자.

Q. 다음 글의 밑줄 친 this가 의미하는 바를 다음과 같이 설명할 때, 빈칸에 들어갈 말을 본문에서 찾아 11단어로 쓰시오.

Along with small everyday items, much bigger things can also be upcycled— even old buildings that cannot be used for their original purpose anymore. The German government showed us an excellent example of <u>this</u> with a former steel plant that closed in 1985. Rather than destroy the plant's buildings or abandon the entire facility, they decided to give it new meaning as a series of useful public structures.

→ Much bigger things such as _____ can also be upcycled.

정답
old buildings that cannot be used for their original purpose anymore

this가 가리키는 것은 일상의 용품들뿐만 아니라 원래의 용도로 쓸 수 없게 된 건물들처럼 훨씬 큰 것들도 업사이클될 수 있다는 사실이다.

● 어휘 close

문장2에서는 close의 의미를 묻는 문제도 15.4% 확률로 출제된다. 여기서 close는 '문을 닫다, 폐업하다'라는 의미의 동사로 쓰였으며, 반의어는 open이다. close가 형용사, 부사로 쓰일 때와 혼동하지 않도록 하자.

Q. 다음 글에서 아래 영영풀이에 해당하는 단어를 찾아 기본형으로 쓰시오.

to stop the services or activities

The German government showed us an excellent example of this with a former steel plant that closed in 1985. Rather than destroy the plant's buildings or abandon the entire facility, they decided to give it new meaning as a series of useful public structures. Many of the buildings kept their original shapes, but received extra equipment and new designs in their surrounding areas.

_____

정답 close

[영영풀이] 서비스나 활동을 중단하는 것: 문을 닫다, 폐업하다

출제 포인트 46% 정복!

> rather than: ~라기 보다는   파괴하다 | 버리다
> **Rather than destroy** the plant's buildings or **abandon** the entire facility, they decided to give it new meaning as a series of useful public structures.

┤ 출제 포인트 ├

1위

> **Rather than**

문장 내 출제 확률 42.9%
본문[3] 문장편 내 출제 확률 7.3%

● Rather than

문장3에서 출제될 가능성은 3.6%이다. 이 문장에서 42.9% 확률로 가장 많이 출제된 것은 Rather than이다. rather than은 '~라기 보다는'이라는 의미이며, 동사원형 destroy와 abandon이 등위접속사 or에 의해 병렬 연결되어 있다. Rather than을 Instead of, Without과 같은 전치사로 원문을 바꿔 출제하는 경우가 많으므로, 뒤따라오는 동사의 형태에 주의를 기울여야 한다.

> **Q. 다음 괄호 안에서 어법상 옳은 것을 <u>모두</u> 고르시오.**
>
> The German government showed us an excellent example of this with a former steel plant that closed in 1985. (Rather than / Instead / Instead of / Without) destroying the plant's buildings or abandoning the entire facility, they decided to give it new meaning as a series of useful public structures.

정답
Rather than, Instead of, Without

뒤에 동명사 destroying이 쓰였기 때문에 Rather than, Instead of, Without을 쓰는 것이 올바르다. Instead는 부사이다.

[원문 변형]
destroy the plant's buildings or abandon ~ → destroying the plant's buildings or abandoning ~

● 빈칸 they decided to give it new meaning as a series of useful public structures

본문[3]의 주제를 빈칸으로 묻는 문제가 문장3에서 10.7% 확률로 빈번하게 출제되었다. 독일 정부는 1985년도에 문 닫은 철강 공장을 부수거나 전체 시설을 버리지 않고 새로운 의미를 부여해서 업사이클링의 예시를 보여주었다. 그 내용이 문장3의 they decided to give it new meaning as a series of useful public structures에 해당한다. 주어 they가 지칭하는 것은 the German government에 해당한다. 해당 문장이 다른 표현으로 변형되어 출제되는 경우도 많기 때문에 낯선 표현이 나와도 당황하지 않도록 하자.

> **Q. 다음 글의 밑줄 친 우리말 뜻과 일치하도록 〈조건〉에 맞게 영작하시오.**
>
> > 〈조건〉 1. 다음의 단어들을 반드시 포함시키되, 필요시 어형을 바꿀 것: decide, new meaning
> >   2. 총 7단어로 영작할 것
>
> Along with small everyday items, much bigger things can also be upcycled— even old buildings that cannot be used for their original purpose anymore. The

정답
they decided to give it new meaning

주어는 '그들'이기 때문에 대명사 they를 쓴다. 동사는 주어진 decide를 과거형으로 바꿔쓴다. decide는 to 부정사 형태의 목적어를 취하기 때문에 to give가 쓰인다. give는 수여 동사로 뒤에 간접목적어와 직접목적어를 써야 하므로 간접목적어 it을 쓰고, 직접목적어는 new meaning을 쓴다.

German government showed us an excellent example of this with a former steel plant that closed in 1985. Rather than destroy the plant's buildings or abandon the entire facility, <u>그들은 그것에게 새로운 의미를 주기로 결정했다</u> as a series of useful public structures.

___

● to부정사의 명사적 용법 – 목적어

이 문장에서 어법 문제가 출제되면 역시 10.7% 확률로 to give의 형태를 묻는 문제가 나올 수 있다. decide는 to부정사를 목적어로 취하는 동사로, decided 뒤에 to give가 왔다. give 또는 giving이 오답으로 많이 제시된다.

Q. 다음 글의 밑줄 친 (A), (B)를 어법에 맞게 고쳐 쓰시오.

Along with small everyday items, much bigger things can also be upcycled— even old buildings that cannot (A) <u>use</u> for their original purpose anymore. The German government showed us an excellent example of this with a former steel plant that closed in 1985. Rather than destroy the plant's buildings or abandon the entire facility, they decided (B) <u>give</u> it new meaning as a series of useful public structures.

(A) _____   (B) _____

___

● 어휘 destroy

이 문장에서 단어 destroy의 의미를 묻는 문제 역시 10.7% 확률로 많이 출제된다. destroy는 destruct로 바꿔 쓸 수 있고, 영영풀이인 to damage something so badly that it cannot be used도 알아두면 도움이 된다. 양자택일 문제에서는 반의어 construct, build가 오답으로 빈번하게 출제된다.

Q. 다음의 영영풀이에 해당하는 단어를 본문에서 찾아 쓰시오.

to damage something so badly that it cannot be used

The German government showed us an excellent example of this with a former steel plant that closed in 1985. Rather than destroy the plant's buildings or abandon the entire facility, they decided to give it new meaning as a series of useful public structures.

_____

● 어휘 abandon

destroy와 병렬 구조로 연결된 abandon 역시 10.7% 확률로 자주 출제되는 어휘이다. '버리다, 포기하다'라는 의미로 leave로 바꿔 쓸 수 있다. 오답으로는 build, preserve, install 등이 출제되었다. 영영풀이는 to leave or never return to some place이다.

> **Q. 다음의 영영풀이에 해당하는 단어를 본문에서 찾아 쓰시오.**
>
> | to leave or never return to some place |
> | --- |
>
> The German government showed us an excellent example of this with a former steel plant that closed in 1985. Rather than destroy the plant's buildings or abandon the entire facility, they decided to give it new meaning as a series of useful public structures.
>
> _____

● 어휘 facility

facility의 영영풀이를 확인하는 문제도 10.7% 확률로 빈번하게 출제되었다. '시설, 설비'라는 의미로, 영영풀이는 a place that is designed or built for a particular purpose이다.

> **Q. 다음의 영영풀이에 해당하는 단어를 본문에서 찾아 쓰시오.**
>
> | a place designed or built for a particular purpose |
> | --- |
>
> The German government showed us an excellent example of this with a former steel plant that closed in 1985. Rather than destroy the plant's buildings or abandon the entire facility, they decided to give it new meaning as a series of useful public structures.
>
> _____

출제 포인트 48.5% 정복!

문장4

문장 출제 확률: 1.8%

동사1: 과거 시제. keep: 유지하다   동사2: 과거 시제

Many of the buildings kept their original shapes, but received extra equipment and new designs in their surrounding areas.

현재분사 형용사 역할 – 명사 수식

● 시제 일치

문장4에서 출제될 가능성은 1.8%이다. 문장4에서는 42.9% 확률로, 동사의 형태를 묻는 문제가 가장 자주 출제되었다. 주어 Many of the buildings 뒤에 동사 2개가 등위접속사 but으로 병렬 연결되어 있다. 첫 번째 동사가 과거형 kept이므로, 두 번째 동사 역시 과거형 received로 쓰인 것을 확인하자.

> Q. 다음 문장에서 어법상 <u>어색한</u> 것을 찾아 바르게 고치시오.
>
> Many of the buildings kept their original shapes, but receiving extra equipment and new designs in their surrounding areas.
>
> _____ → _____

정답

receiving → received

주어 Many of the buildings 뒤에 동사 2개가 등위접속사 but으로 병렬 연결되어 있다. 첫 번째 동사가 과거형 이므로, 두 번째 동사도 과 거형으로 쓴다.

● 현재분사 형용사 역할 – 명사 수식

문장4에서는 28.6% 확률로, 분사의 형태를 묻는 문제가 두 번째로 많이 출제되었다. surround는 '둘러싸다'를 의미하고, 분사의 수식을 받는 areas는 건물의 주변을 둘러싸는 주체이므로, 능동 관계이다. 따라서, 능동을 나타내는 현재분사 surrounding이 areas를 수식한다. 오답으로 과거분사 surrounded가 자주 출제된다.

> Q. 다음 글의 (A), (B)의 각 네모 안에서 어법에 맞는 표현을 고르시오.
>
> Many of the buildings kept their original shapes, but received extra equipment and new designs in their (A) surrounding / surrounded areas. For instance, old gas tanks became pools for divers. Concrete walls of iron storage towers were turned into ideal training fields for rock climbers. Can you believe a building for melting metal is now a viewing platform with a gorgeous 360-degree view? The final result is the Landscape Park Duisburg Nord. It has almost 570 acres of land (B) filling / filled with gardens, cycling paths, and pretty lights at night, in addition to its creatively repurposed buildings. This park proves that it's possible to preserve the heritage of a place as well as the environment.

정답

(A) surrounding
(B) filled

(A) 분사의 수식을 받는 areas는 건물의 주변을 둘러 싸는 주체이므로, 능동 관계이다. 따라서, 능동을 나타내는 현재분사 surrounding이 맞다.

(B) 분사의 수식을 받는 land는 정원, 자전거 길, 조명 등으로 채워지는 동작의 대상이므로 수동 관계이다. 따라서, 수동을 나타내는 과거분사 filled가 맞다.

이 문장에서 단어 keep의 의미를 묻는 문제도 14.3% 확률로 많이 출제된다. 본문에서 '유지하다'라는 의미로 쓰였고, retained, maintained로 바꿔 쓸 수 있다. 문맥상 어색한 어휘를 고르는 문제나 양자택일 문제로 자주 출제된다.

> **Q. 다음 글의 밑줄 친 부분 중, 문맥상 낱말의 쓰임이 적절하지 않은 것은?**
>
> Along with small everyday items, much bigger things can also be upcycled—even old buildings that cannot be used for their original purpose anymore. The German government showed us an excellent example of this with a ① former steel plant that closed in 1985. Rather than destroy the plant's buildings or abandon the entire facility, they decided to give it ② new meaning as a series of useful public structures. Many of the buildings ③ lost their original shapes, but received extra equipment and new designs in their surrounding areas. For instance, old gas tanks became pools for divers. ④ Concrete walls of iron storage towers were turned into ideal training fields for rock climbers. Can you believe a building for melting metal is now a viewing platform with a gorgeous 360-degree view? The final result is the Landscape Park Duisburg Nord. It has almost 570 acres of land filled with gardens, cycling paths, and pretty lights at night, in addition to its creatively repurposed buildings. This park ⑤ proves that it's possible to preserve the heritage of a place as well as the environment.

정답 ③

건물을 파괴하거나 전체 시설을 버리지 않고 새로운 의미를 부여했다는 내용이 앞서 언급되었으므로, 건물의 많은 부분이 원래의 모양을 '유지했다'는 것이 흐름상 적절하다. '잃어버렸다'는 의미인 lost를 kept, retained, maintained 등으로 고쳐야 한다.

출제 포인트 49.7% 정복!

문장5

구체적인 사례를 제시하기 위한 연결어
For instance, old gas tanks became pools for divers.

┤ **출제 포인트** ├

1위

연결어 For instance

문장 내 출제 확률 100.0%
본문[3] 문장편 내 출제 확률 1.8%

● 연결어 For instance

문장5에서 출제될 가능성은 0.4%이다. 이 문장에서 출제되는 경우 100.0%의 확률로 연결어 For instance가 출제되었다. 앞서 제시된 내용을 뒷받침하는 예를 제시할 때 쓰는 연결어로, '예를 들면'의 의미이다. 같은 의미를 가진 연결어 For example로 출제되기도 한다.

> **Q. 다음 글의 (A), (B)의 각 네모 안에서 문맥상 적절한 표현을 고르시오.**
>
> Along with small everyday items, much bigger things can also be upcycled—even old buildings that cannot be used for their original purpose anymore. The

정답
(A) Rather than
(B) For example

(A) 건물을 파괴하거나 전체 시설을 버린다는 내용과 그것(건물)에 새로운 의미를 부여한다는 주절의 내용은 서로 상반되기 때문에 '~라기 보다는'을 뜻하는 Rather than이 적절하다.

German government showed us an excellent example of this with a former steel plant that closed in 1985. (A) In order to / Rather than destroy the plant's buildings or abandon the entire facility, they decided to give it new meaning as a series of useful public structures. Many of the buildings kept their original shapes, but received extra equipment and new designs in their surrounding areas. (B) For example / What's more , old gas tanks became pools for divers. Concrete walls of iron storage towers were turned into ideal training fields for rock climbers. Can you believe a building for melting metal is now a viewing platform with a gorgeous 360-degree view? The final result is the Landscape Park Duisburg Nord.

(B) 앞에서는 건물의 원래 형태를 유지하면서 추가 설비가 설치되고 새로운 디자인이 입혀지는 건물 업사이클링 방식을 설명하고, 뒤에서는 가스탱크를 다이빙풀로 바꾸고 콘크리트 벽을 암벽 훈련장으로 바꾼 구체적인 사례를 제시했으므로, 예시를 나타내는 For example 이 적절하다.

[원문 변형] For instance → For example

출제 포인트 49.9% 정복!

문장6

문장 출제 확률: 2.7%

주어: 복수명사

turn A into B: A를 B로 바꾸다
수동태 be p.p.

Concrete walls of iron storage towers **were turned into** ideal training fields for rock climbers.

─┤ 출제 포인트 ├─

1위

수 일치와 수동태

문장 내 출제 확률 90.5%
본문[3] 문장편 내 출제 확률 11.6%

● 수 일치와 수동태

문장6에서 출제될 가능성은 2.7%이다. 문장6에서는 동사의 형태를 묻는 문제가 90.5% 확률로, 압도적으로 많이 출제됐다. 〈turn A into B〉는 'A를 B로 바꾸다'라는 의미이고, 주어 Concrete walls가 이상적인 훈련장으로 바뀐 동작의 대상이므로, 수동태 were turned로 써야 한다. turn을 유의어인 convert 또는 change로 바꿔서 출제되기도 하니, 다른 단어가 나와도 당황하지 말자.

Q. 다음 글의 (A), (B)의 각 네모 안에서 어법상 적절한 것을 고르시오.

Many of the buildings kept their original shapes, but (A) receive / received extra equipment and new designs in their surrounding areas. For instance, old gas tanks became pools for divers. Concrete walls of iron storage towers (B) turned / were turned into ideal training fields for rock climbers.

정답
(A) received
(B) were turned

(A) 동사 2개가 등위접속사 but으로 병렬 연결된다. 첫 번째 동사가 과거형 kept으로 쓰였기 때문에 두 번째 동사인 receive 역시 과거형으로 써야 한다.
(B) 주어 Concrete walls가 이상적인 훈련장으로 바뀐 동작의 대상이므로, 수동태로 써야 한다.

출제 포인트 51.7% 정복!

> 동명사+명사
>
> Can you believe a building for melting metal is now a **viewing platform** with a **gorgeous** 360-degree view?
>
> 아주 멋진

출제 포인트

1위	2위
어휘 gorgeous	동명사 + 명사
문장 내 출제 확률 37.5%	문장 내 출제 확률 25%
본문[3] 문장편 내 출제 확률 1.8%	본문[3] 문장편 내 출제 확률 1.2%

● 어휘 gorgeous

문장7에서 출제될 가능성은 1.0%이다. 이 문장에서 단어 gorgeous의 의미를 묻는 문제가 37.5%로 가장 많이 출제되었다. '아주 멋진'이라는 뜻이며, 영영풀이는 very beautiful or attractive이다. 본문에서는 업사이클링의 결과로 탄생한 전망대의 멋진 경관을 설명하기 위해 쓰였으니 문맥을 잘 기억하도록 하자.

> **Q. 다음의 영영풀이에 해당하는 단어를 본문에서 찾아 쓰시오.**
>
> | very beautiful or attractive |
> |---|
>
> Many of the buildings kept their original shapes, but received extra equipment and new designs in their surrounding areas. For instance, old gas tanks became pools for divers. Concrete walls of iron storage towers were turned into ideal training fields for rock climbers. Can you believe a building for melting metal is now a viewing platform with a gorgeous 360-degree view? The final result is the Landscape Park Duisburg Nord.
>
> _____

정답 gorgeous

[영영풀이] 매우 아름답고 매력적인: 아주 멋진

● 동명사 + 명사

문장7에서는 viewing의 형태를 묻는 문제가 25% 확률로 많이 출제되었다. viewing platform은 전망대를 의미한다. 〈동명사+명사〉는 '~를 하기 위한 명사'의 의미로 사물의 용도를 나타낸다. viewing platform은 '보기 위한 단(壇)'으로 '전망대'라고 해석할 수 있다. 오답으로 viewed가 자주 출제된다는 점에 유의하자.

정답

(A) surrounding
(B) viewing (C) filled

(A) 분사의 수식을 받는 areas는 건물의 주변을 둘러싸는 주체이므로, 능동의 관계이다. 따라서 능동을 나타내는 현재분사 surrounding으로 써야 한다.

> **Q. 다음 글의 밑줄 친 동사원형 (A)~(C)를 어법에 맞게 바꿔 쓰시오.**
>
> Many of the buildings kept their original shapes, but received extra equipment and new designs in their (A) surround areas. For instance, old gas tanks became pools for divers. Concrete walls of iron storage towers were turned into ideal

training fields for rock climbers. Can you believe a building for melting metal is now a (B) <u>view</u> platform with a gorgeous 360-degree view? The final result is the Landscape Park Duisburg Nord. It has almost 570 acres of land (C) <u>fill</u> with gardens, cycling paths, and pretty lights at night, in addition to its creatively repurposed buildings. This park proves that it's possible to preserve the heritage of a place as well as the environment.

(A) _____ (B) _____ (C) _____

(B) 전망대는 '보기 위한 단'이므로 〈동명사+명사〉 형태로 쓴다. view를 동명사로 바꾸면 viewing이다.
(C) 분사의 수식을 받는 land는 정원, 자전거 길, 조명 등으로 채워지는 동작의 대상이므로 수동의 관계이다. 따라서 수동을 나타내는 과거분사 filled를 쓴다.

출제 포인트 52.2% 정복!

문장8

문장 출제 확률: 0.0%

The final result is the Landscape Park Duisburg Nord.

AI 분석 결과, 문장8에서 출제될 가능성은 없다. (0.0%)

문장9

문장 출제 확률: 3.1%

과거분사 형용사 역할 – 명사 수식

It has almost 570 acres of land <u>filled</u> with gardens, cycling paths, and pretty lights at night, <u>in addition to</u> its creatively <u>repurposed</u> buildings.
~ 외에도

과거분사 형용사 역할 – 명사 수식

┤ 출제 포인트 ├

1위	2위
과거분사 형용사 역할 – 명사 수식	**in addition to**
문장 내 출제 확률 83.3%	문장 내 출제 확률 8.3%
본문[3] 문장편 내 출제 확률 12.2%	본문[3] 문장편 내 출제 확률 1.2%

● 과거분사 형용사 역할 – 명사 수식

문장9에서 출제될 가능성은 3.1%이다. 문장9에서 출제되는 경우 대부분(83.3%) 문장에 두 번 출현하는 분사의 형태를 묻는 문제가 출제되었다. 첫 번째 fill은 '채우다'를 의미하고, 수식 받는 명사 land가 정원, 자전거 길, 조명으로 채워지는 수동의 대상이기 때문에 과거분사 filled를 쓰는 것이 적절하다. 전치사 with가 함께 쓰여서 filled with는 '~로 가득 찬'이라는 의미이다. 또한, 분사의 수식을 받는 buildings는 사람들에 의해서 다른 용도로 목적이 바뀐 동작의 대상이므로 수동 관계이다. 따라서, 수동을 나타내는 repurposed로 buildings를 수식한다. 서술형 문제로도 자주 출제되는 문장이다.

Q. 다음 글의 밑줄 친 우리말 뜻과 일치하게 〈보기〉의 단어를 모두 활용해서 영작하시오. (필요 시, 어형을 바꿀 것)

〈보기〉 repurpose, in, to, its, creative, addition, buildings

The final result is the Landscape Park Duisburg Nord. It has almost 570 acres of land filled with gardens, cycling paths, and pretty lights at night, <u>그것의 창의적으로 개조된 건물들 이외에도</u>.

_____

● **in addition to**

문장9에서 in addition to는 8.3%의 2순위로 출제된다. in addition to는 '~ 외에도, ~에 더하여'라는 의미이며, 뒤에 명사(구)가 온다. 의미는 같지만 연결어로 쓰이는 in addition과 혼동하지 않도록 하자.

Q. 다음 글의 빈칸 (A), (B)에 들어갈 말을 쓰시오.

For instance, old gas tanks became pools for divers. Concrete walls of iron storage towers were turned (A)_____ ideal training fields for rock climbers. Can you believe a building for melting metal is now a viewing platform with a gorgeous 360-degree view? The final result is the Landscape Park Duisburg Nord. It has almost 570 acres of land filled with gardens, cycling paths, and pretty lights at night, in addition (B)_____ its creatively repurposed buildings. This park proves that it's possible to preserve the heritage of a place as well as the environment.

출제 포인트 54.3% 정복!

문장10 문장 출제 확률: 4.2% (771개의 출제 포인트 중 32회 출현, 46개 문장 중 8위)

가주어 it
This park proves that <u>it</u>'s possible <u>to preserve</u> the heritage of a place <u>as well as</u> the environment. 진주어
B as well as A: A뿐만 아니라 B도

┤ **출제 포인트** ├

1위	2위	3위
가주어 it	**빈칸 it's possible ~ environment**	**B as well as A**
문장 내 출제 확률 34.4%	문장 내 출제 확률 18.8%	문장 내 출제 확률 15.6%
본문[3] 문장편 내 출제 확률 7.4%	본문[3] 문장편 내 출제 확률 3.7%	본문[3] 문장편 내 출제 확률 3.1%

● 가주어 it

문장10에서 출제될 가능성은 4.2%이다. 본문[3]의 마지막 문장에서는 가주어 it을 가지고 문제를 많이 낸다(34.4%). 접속사 that절의 주어 it은 가주어이고, 진주어는 to preserve the heritage of a place as well as the environment이다. 이때의 it은 해석하지 않으며, to부정사는 문장에서 주어 역할을 하는 명사적 용법임에 유의한다. 아래 문제를 통해 가주어-진주어 구문에 익숙해져보자.

> **Q. 다음 글의 밑줄 친 it이 가리키는 것을 본문에서 찾아 쓰시오.**
>
> The final result is the Landscape Park Duisburg Nord. It has almost 570 acres of land filled with gardens, cycling paths, and pretty lights at night, in addition to its creatively repurposed buildings. This park proves that it's possible to preserve the heritage of a place as well as the environment.
>
> _____

정답

to preserve the heritage of a place as well as the environment

it은 가주어이고, 진주어는 to preserve 이하이다.

● 빈칸 it's possible to preserve the heritage of a place as well as the environment

이 문장에서는 18.8%의 확률로, it's possible ~ the environment 부분을 빈칸 문제로 묻는다. 이 부분은, 문 닫은 철강 공장을 뒤스부르크 환경 공원으로 바꾼 것은 업사이클링을 통해서 환경과 한 장소의 유산을 모두 보존할 수 있다는 것을 보여준 사례라는 의의를 밝힌다. that절 이하가 빈칸으로 출제되거나 영작 문제로 출제되는 경우가 흔하고, 상관접속사 as well as를 다른 상관접속사로 바꿔서 나오기도 한다. preserve, heritage, environment와 같은 핵심 단어 역시 다른 유의어로 바꿔서 출제되기 때문에 다양한 표현을 익히는 것이 중요하다.

> **Q. 다음 빈칸에 들어갈 말로 적절하지 않은 것은?**
>
> Along with small everyday items, much bigger things can also be upcycled—even old buildings that cannot be used for their original purpose anymore. The German government showed us an excellent example of this with a former steel plant that closed in 1985. Rather than destroy the plant's buildings or abandon the entire facility, they decided to give it new meaning as a series of useful public structures. Many of the buildings kept their original shapes, but received extra equipment and new designs in their surrounding areas. For instance, old gas tanks became pools for divers. Concrete walls of iron storage towers were turned into ideal training fields for rock climbers. Can you believe a building for melting metal is now a viewing platform with a gorgeous 360-degree view? The final result is the Landscape Park Duisburg Nord. It has almost 570 acres of land filled with gardens, cycling paths, and pretty lights at night, in addition to its creatively repurposed buildings. This park proves that _____.
>
> ① both the heritage of a place and the environment can be protected
> ② it is important to break the artistic tradition and make a new attempt
> ③ upcycling allows heritage of a place and the environment to coexist in harmony
> ④ it is possible to preserve our surroundings together with the heritage of a place
> ⑤ it is possible to create a cultural value and protect the environment all at once

정답 ②

문 닫은 철강 공장을 뒤스부르크 환경 공원으로 바꾼 것은 업사이클링을 통해서 환경과 한 장소의 유산을 모두 보존할 수 있다는 것을 보여준 사례이다. '예술적 전통을 깨고 새로운 시도를 하는 것이 중요하다'는 ②는 빈칸에 들어갈 수 없다.
① 한 장소의 유산과 환경 둘 다 보호될 수 있다
③ 업사이클링은 한 장소의 유산과 환경이 조화롭게 공존할 수 있도록 해준다
④ 한 장소의 유산과 함께 우리의 주변을 보호하는 것이 가능하다
⑤ 문화적 가치를 창출하며 동시에 환경을 보호하는 것이 가능하다

● B as well as A

문장10에서는 〈B as well as A〉 표현 관련해서도 15.6% 확률로 문제가 나온다. 'A뿐만 아니라 B도'라는 의미이며, 〈not only A but also B〉로 바꿔 쓸 수 있다. 이 문장 전환을 서술형 문제로 자주 다루고 있다.

> **Q. 다음 빈칸에 들어갈 말로 가장 적절한 것은?**
>
> The final result is the Landscape Park Duisburg Nord. It has almost 570 acres of land filled with gardens, cycling paths, and pretty lights at night, in addition to its creatively repurposed buildings. This park proves that it's possible to preserve the heritage of a place _____ the environment.
>
> ① as far as   ② as well as   ③ as long as
> ④ as soon as   ⑤ as much as

● 명사절 접속사 that

문장10의 접속사 that도 9.4% 확률로 자주 출제되는 문법 포인트이다. 접속사 that, 관계대명사 that, which를 비교하는 어법 문제가 나올 수 있다. 해당 문장에서는 동사 proves 뒤에 목적어 역할을 하는 완전한 절을 이끌고 있다.

> **Q. 다음 빈칸에 들어갈 말을 쓰시오.**
>
> This park proves _____ it's possible to preserve the heritage of a place as well as the environment.

● 어휘 preserve

이 문장에서는 다양한 어휘 문제가 출제되었는데, 그 중에서도 preserve의 문맥상 쓰임을 묻는 문제가 9.4%로 가장 많이 출제되었다. preserve는 '보존하다'라는 의미이며, conserve, protect 등으로 바꿔 쓸 수 있다. 영영풀이 maintain or keep something in original or current state도 기억해두자.

> **Q. 다음의 영영풀이에 해당하는 단어를 본문에서 찾아 쓰시오.**
>
> | maintain or keep something in original or current state |
> |---|
>
> The final result is the Landscape Park Duisburg Nord. It has almost 570 acres of land filled with gardens, cycling paths, and pretty lights at night, in addition to its creatively repurposed buildings. This park proves that it's possible to preserve the heritage of a place as well as the environment.
>
> _____

● 어휘 heritage

이 문장에서 heritage 역시 6.3% 확률로 출제되었는데, 주로 영영풀이를 묻는 문제가 출제되었다. 영영풀이는 the cultural and historical qualities, traditions, or features that is passed down from previous generations이다.

> **Q. 다음의 영영풀이에 해당하는 단어를 본문에서 찾아 쓰시오.**
>
> | the cultural and historical qualities, traditions, or features that is passed down from previous generations |
> | --- |
>
> The final result is the Landscape Park Duisburg Nord. It has almost 570 acres of land filled with gardens, cycling paths, and pretty lights at night, in addition to its creatively repurposed buildings. This park proves that it's possible to preserve the heritage of a place as well as the environment.
>
> _____

정답 heritage

[영영풀이] 이전 세대로부터 전해 내려오는 문화적, 역사적 특성, 전통 또는 특징: 유산

● 어휘 prove

본문[3]의 마지막 출제 포인트로 다룰 문제는 역시 6.3% 확률로 출제되는 prove이다. prove는 '증명하다'라는 의미이며, 영영풀이는 to demonstrate the truth of something이다. 철자가 비슷한 improve가 오답으로 자주 출제된다.

> **Q. 다음의 영영풀이에 해당하는 단어를 본문에서 찾아 기본형으로 쓰시오.**
>
> | to demonstrate the truth of something |
> | --- |
>
> The final result is the Landscape Park Duisburg Nord. It has almost 570 acres of land filled with gardens, cycling paths, and pretty lights at night, in addition to its creatively repurposed buildings. This park proves that it's possible to preserve the heritage of a place as well as the environment.
>
> _____

정답 prove

[영영풀이] 어떤 것의 진실성을 입증하다: 증명하다

출제 포인트 57.3% 정복!

01

다음 빈칸 (A), (B)에 들어갈 말로 가장 적절한 것은?

Along with small everyday items, much bigger things can also be upcycled—even old buildings that cannot be used for their original purpose anymore. The German government showed us an excellent example of this with a former steel plant that closed in 1985. Rather than destroy the plant's buildings or abandon the entire facility, they decided to give it new meaning as a series of useful public structures. Many of the buildings kept their original shapes, but received extra equipment and new designs in their surrounding areas. For instance, old gas tanks became pools for divers. Concrete walls of iron storage towers were turned into ideal training fields for rock climbers. Can you believe a building for melting metal is now a viewing platform with a gorgeous 360-degree view? The final result is the Landscape Park Duisburg Nord. It has almost 570 acres of land filled with gardens, cycling paths, and pretty lights at night, in addition to its creatively repurposed buildings. This park proves that it's possible to preserve the _____(A)_____ of a place as well as the _____(B)_____.

	(A)		(B)
①	reputation	–	peace
②	heritage	–	civil rights
③	heritage	–	environment
④	reputation	–	environment
⑤	environment	–	civil rights

02

다음 중, 밑줄 친 that이 (A) that과 쓰임이 같은 것은?

Along with small everyday items, much bigger things can also be upcycled—even old buildings (A) that cannot be used for their original purpose anymore.

① She said that the story was not true.
② Where is the letter that came last week?
③ The fact that he is American is not important.
④ I heard the news that she finally became a singer.
⑤ There are so many things that I have to do before leaving.

03

밑줄 친 (A)를 다음과 같이 바꿔 쓸 때 빈칸에 알맞은 말을 쓰시오. (한 칸에 한 단어)

For instance, old gas tanks became pools for divers. (A) They turned concrete walls of iron storage towers into ideal training fields for rock climbers.

→ Concrete walls of iron storage towers _____ _____ _____ ideal training fields for rock climbers.

04

밑줄 친 단어의 영영풀이가 적절하지 않은 것은?

Along with small everyday items, much bigger things can also be upcycled—even old buildings that cannot be used for their original purpose anymore. The German government showed us an excellent example of this with a former steel ⓐ plant that closed in 1985. Rather than destroy the plant's buildings or abandon the entire ⓑ facility, they decided to give it new meaning as a series of useful public structures. Many of the buildings kept their original shapes, but received extra equipment and new designs in their surrounding areas. For instance, old gas tanks became pools for divers. Concrete walls of iron ⓒ storage towers were turned into ideal training fields for rock climbers. Can you believe a building for melting metal is now a viewing platform with a gorgeous 360-degree view? The final result is the Landscape Park Duisburg Nord. It has almost 570 acres of land filled with gardens, cycling paths, and pretty lights at night, in addition to its ⓓ creatively repurposed buildings. This park proves that it's possible to preserve the ⓔ heritage of a place as well as the environment.

① ⓐ: a living thing that usually has a stem, leaves, and roots, and produces seeds
② ⓑ: something that is built for a specific purpose
③ ⓒ: the state of being kept in a place when not being used
④ ⓓ: in a way that produces or uses original and unusual ideas
⑤ ⓔ: a feature that has continued over many years

05

다음 글의 밑줄 친 (A)~(C) 중, 생략 가능한 것은?

Along with small everyday items, much bigger things can also be upcycled—even old buildings (A) that cannot be used for their original purpose anymore. The German government showed us an excellent example of this with a former steel plant (B) that closed in 1985. Rather than destroy the plant's buildings or abandon the entire facility, they decided to give it new meaning as a series of useful public structures. Many of the buildings kept their original shapes, but received extra equipment and new designs in their surrounding areas. For instance, old gas tanks became pools for divers. Concrete walls of iron storage towers were turned into ideal training fields for rock climbers. Can you believe a building for melting metal is now a viewing platform with a gorgeous 360-degree view? The final result is the Landscape Park Duisburg Nord. It has almost 570 acres of land filled with gardens, cycling paths, and pretty lights at night, in addition to its creatively repurposed buildings. This park proves (C) that it's possible to preserve the heritage of a place as well as the environment.

06

다음 글의 밑줄 친 부분 중, 문맥상 낱말의 쓰임이 적절하지 않은 것은?

Along with small everyday items, much bigger things can also be upcycled—even ① old buildings that cannot be used for their original purpose anymore. The German government showed us an ② excellent example of this with a former steel plant that closed in 1985. Rather than destroy the plant's buildings or abandon the entire facility, they decided to give it ③ new meaning as a series of useful public structures. Many of the buildings kept their original shapes, but received extra equipment

and new designs in their surrounding areas. For instance, old gas tanks became pools for divers. Concrete walls of iron storage towers were turned into ideal training fields for rock climbers. Can you believe a building for melting metal is now a viewing platform with a gorgeous 360-degree view? The final ④ result is the Landscape Park Duisburg Nord. It has almost 570 acres of land filled with gardens, cycling paths, and pretty lights at night, in addition to its creatively repurposed buildings. This park ⑤ improves that it's possible to preserve the heritage of a place as well as the environment.

07

다음 글의 밑줄 친 부분 중, 어법상 틀린 것은?

Along with small everyday items, much bigger things can also be upcycled—even old buildings ① that cannot be used for their original purpose anymore. The German government showed us an excellent example of this with a former steel plant that ② closed in 1985. Rather than destroy the plant's buildings or abandon the entire facility, they decided to ③ giving it new meaning as a series of useful public structures. Many of the buildings kept their original shapes, but received extra equipment and new designs in their ④ surrounding areas. For instance, old gas tanks became pools for divers. Concrete walls of iron storage towers were ⑤ turned into ideal training fields for rock climbers.

08

다음 글의 밑줄 친 부분 중, 문맥상 낱말의 쓰임이 적절하지 않은 것은?

Along with small everyday items, much bigger things can also be upcycled—even old buildings that cannot be used for their original purpose anymore. The German government showed us an excellent example of this with a former steel plant that closed in 1985. Rather than destroy the plant's buildings or ① utilize the entire facility, they decided to give it new meaning as a series of useful public structures. Many of the buildings ② kept their original shapes, but received extra equipment and new designs in their surrounding areas. For instance, old gas tanks became pools for divers. Concrete walls of iron storage towers were ③ turned into ideal training fields for rock climbers. Can you believe a building for melting metal is now a viewing platform with a gorgeous 360-degree view? The final ④ result is the Landscape Park Duisburg Nord. It has almost 570 acres of land filled with gardens, cycling paths, and pretty lights at night, in addition to its creatively repurposed buildings. This park ⑤ proves that it's possible to preserve the heritage of a place as well as the environment.

09

우리말과 같은 뜻이 되도록 영작할 때, 빈칸에 들어갈 말을 차례로 쓰시오.

이 공원은 환경뿐만 아니라 어떤 장소의 유산도 보호할 수 있다는 것을 증명한다.

→ This park proves that it's possible to preserve the heritage of a place _____ _____ _____ the environment.

10

다음 빈칸 (A), (B)에 들어갈 말로 가장 적절한 것은?

Many of the buildings kept their original shapes, but received extra equipment and new designs in their surrounding areas. _____(A)_____, old gas tanks became pools for divers. Concrete walls of iron storage towers were turned into ideal training fields for rock climbers. Can you believe a building for melting metal is now a viewing platform with a gorgeous 360-degree view? The final result is the Landscape Park Duisburg Nord. It has almost 570 acres of land filled with gardens, cycling paths, and pretty lights at night, _____(B)_____ its creatively repurposed buildings. This park proves that it's possible to preserve the heritage of a place as well as the environment.

	(A)	(B)
①	Therefore	– due to
②	In addition	– due to
③	However	– in addition
④	For instance	– in addition to
⑤	In other words	– in addition to

11

다음 (A), (B), (C)의 각 네모 안에서 어법에 맞는 표현으로 가장 적절한 것은?

Can you believe a building for melting metal is now a viewing platform with a gorgeous (A) 360-degree / 360-degrees view? The final result is the Landscape Park Duisburg Nord. It has almost 570 acres of land (B) fill / filled with gardens, cycling paths, and pretty lights at night, in addition to its creatively repurposed buildings. This park proves that it's possible (C) preserve / to preserve the heritage of a place as well as the environment.

	(A)	(B)	(C)
①	360-degree	– fill	– preserve
②	360-degree	– filled	– preserve
③	360-degrees	– fill	– to preserve
④	360-degree	– filled	– to preserve
⑤	360-degrees	– filled	– to preserve

12

다음 글의 밑줄 친 동사원형을 어법에 맞게 바꿀 때, 그 형태가 나머지와 다른 하나는?

Can you believe a building for melting metal is now a ① view platform with a gorgeous 360-degree view? The final result is the Landscape Park Duisburg Nord. It has almost 570 acres of land ② fill with gardens, cycling paths, and pretty lights at night, in addition to its creatively ③ repurpose buildings. This park proves that it's possible to preserve the heritage of a place as well as the environment.

When artists add their own creative touches, things that most people consider junk are reborn as beautiful works of art. The giant pictures ④ make from trash by environmental artist Tom Deininger are one of a kind. Up close, these brightly ⑤ color creations look like a mixed-up mess of broken plastic, unwanted toys, and bent wire—all things that cannot be recycled.

13

다음 글의 밑줄 친 부분 중, 문맥상 낱말의 쓰임이 적절하지 않은 것은?

Along with small everyday items, much bigger things can also be upcycled—even old buildings that cannot be used for their ① original purpose anymore. The German government showed us an excellent example of this with a former steel plant that ② closed in 1985. Rather than destroy the plant's buildings or abandon the entire facility, they decided to give it ③ old meaning as a series of useful public structures. Many of the buildings kept their original shapes, but received extra equipment and new designs in their surrounding areas. … (중략) … The final result is the Landscape Park Duisburg Nord. It has almost 570 acres of land filled with gardens, cycling paths, and pretty lights at night, in addition to its creatively ④ repurposed buildings. This park ⑤ proves that it's possible to preserve the heritage of a place as well as the environment.

14

다음 문장의 밑줄 친 우리말 뜻과 일치하도록 〈조건〉에 맞게 영작하시오.

This park proves that 환경뿐만 아니라 어떤 장소의 유산도 보호할 수 있다.

〈조건〉	1. 가주어 it을 포함할 것
	2. be, possible, the heritage of a place, well, preserve, the environment를 반드시 사용하되, 필요시 어형을 바꿀 것
	3. 총 15단어로 영작할 것

_____

_____

15

다음 글의 밑줄 친 부분 중, 어법상 틀린 것은?

The German government showed us an excellent example of this with a former steel plant that closed in 1985. Rather than destroy the plant's buildings or abandon the entire facility, they decided ① to give it new meaning as a series of useful public structures. Many of the buildings kept their original shapes, but received extra equipment and new designs in their ② surrounded areas. For instance, old gas tanks became pools for divers. Concrete walls of iron storage towers ③ were turned into ideal training fields for rock climbers. Can you believe a building for melting metal is now a ④ viewing platform with a gorgeous 360-degree view? The final result is the Landscape Park Duisburg Nord. It has almost 570 acres of land filled with gardens, cycling paths, and pretty lights at night, in addition to its ⑤ creatively repurposed buildings.

16

다음 글의 밑줄 친 ⓐ~ⓔ의 동사원형을 어법에 맞게 바꿀 때, 적절하지 **않은** 것은?

Along with small everyday items, much bigger things can also be upcycled—even old buildings that cannot ⓐ <u>use</u> for their original purpose anymore. The German government showed us an excellent example of this with a former steel plant that closed in 1985. Rather than ⓑ <u>destroy</u> the plant's buildings or abandon the entire facility, they decided to give it new meaning as a series of useful public structures. Many of the buildings kept their original shapes, but ⓒ <u>receive</u> extra equipment and new designs in their surrounding areas. For instance, old gas tanks ⓓ <u>become</u> pools for divers. Concrete walls of iron storage towers ⓔ <u>turn</u> into ideal training fields for rock climbers.

① ⓐ: be used
② ⓑ: destroy
③ ⓒ: receive
④ ⓓ: became
⑤ ⓔ: were turned

17

다음 글의 밑줄 친 **this**의 내용으로 가장 적절한 것은?

Along with small everyday items, much bigger things can also be upcycled—even old buildings that cannot be used for their original purpose anymore. The German government showed us an excellent example of <u>this</u> with a former steel plant that closed in 1985. Rather than destroy the plant's buildings or abandon the entire facility, they decided to give it new meaning as a series of useful public structures.

① It is common to convert the old buildings to a park.
② Many factories had to close themselves down in 1900s.
③ The German government has been investing in new plant.
④ Old buildings that lost their original purpose can be upcycled.
⑤ Upcycling is a great way to reduce waste and has been gaining more attention.

18

다음 글의 (A), (B), (C)의 각 네모 안에서 문맥에 맞는 낱말로 가장 적절한 것은?

Along with small everyday items, much bigger things can also be upcycled—even old buildings that cannot be used for their original purpose anymore. The German government showed us an excellent example of this with a (A) formal / former steel plant that closed in 1985. Rather than destroy the plant's buildings or abandon the entire facility, they decided to give it new meaning as a series of useful public structures. Many of the buildings (B) altered / kept their original shapes, but received extra equipment and new designs in their surrounding areas. For instance, old gas tanks became pools for divers. Concrete walls of iron storage towers were turned into ideal training fields for rock climbers. Can you believe a building for melting metal is now a viewing platform with a gorgeous 360-degree view? The final result is the Landscape Park Duisburg Nord. It has almost 570 acres of land filled with gardens, cycling paths, and pretty lights at night, in addition to its creatively repurposed buildings. This park proves that it's possible to (C) observe / preserve the heritage of a place as well as the environment.

(A)	(B)	(C)
① former	kept	observe
② formal	kept	preserve
③ former	kept	preserve
④ formal	altered	observe
⑤ former	altered	preserve

19

다음 글의 밑줄 친 부분 중, 문맥상 낱말의 쓰임이 적절하지 않은 것은?

Many of the buildings kept their original shapes, but received ① extra equipment and new designs in their surrounding areas. For instance, old gas tanks became pools for divers. Concrete walls of iron storage towers were turned into ② ideal training fields for rock climbers. Can you believe a building for melting metal is now a viewing platform with a ③ gorgeous 360-degree view? The final result is the Landscape Park Duisburg Nord. It has almost 570 acres of land filled with gardens, cycling paths, and pretty lights at night, in addition to its creatively ④ repurposed buildings. This park proves that it's possible to ⑤ destroy the heritage of a place as well as the environment.

20

다음 글의 밑줄 친 부분 중, 어법상 틀린 것은?

Along with small everyday items, much bigger things can also be upcycled—even old buildings ① that cannot be used for their original purpose anymore. The German government ② showed us an excellent example of this with a former steel plant that closed in 1985. Rather than destroy the plant's buildings or abandon the entire facility, they decided to give it new meaning as a series of useful public structures. Many of the buildings kept their original shapes, but received extra equipment and new designs in their ③ surrounding areas. For instance, old gas tanks became pools for divers. Concrete walls of iron storage towers were turned into ideal training fields for rock climbers. Can you believe a building for melting metal is now a ④ viewed platform with a gorgeous 360-degree view? The final result is the Landscape Park Duisburg Nord. It has almost 570 acres of land filled with gardens, cycling paths, and pretty lights at night, in addition to its creatively repurposed buildings. This park proves that ⑤ it's possible to preserve the heritage of a place as well as the environment.

21

다음 중, 밑줄 친 부분의 쓰임이 (A) that과 다른 것은?

Along with small everyday items, much bigger things can also be upcycled—even old buildings that cannot be used for their original purpose anymore. The German government showed us an excellent example of this with a former steel plant (A) that closed in 1985. Rather than destroy the plant's buildings or abandon the entire facility, they decided to give it new meaning as a series of useful public structures.

① I know that I'm in trouble.
② We have a dog that is very small.
③ I know a girl that can speak Korean.
④ We like singing a song that is exciting.
⑤ He wants to buy a new smartphone that is made by Samsung.

22

다음 글의 밑줄 친 부분 중, 문맥상 낱말의 쓰임이 적절하지 않은 것은?

Along with small everyday items, much ① bigger things can also be upcycled—even old buildings that cannot be used for their original purpose anymore. The German government showed us an excellent example of this with a former steel plant that ② closed in 1985. Rather than destroy the plant's buildings or abandon the entire facility, they decided to give it new meaning as a series of useful public structures. Many of the buildings ③ lost their original shapes, but received extra equipment and new designs in their surrounding areas. For instance, old gas tanks became pools for divers. Concrete walls of iron storage towers were turned into ideal training fields for rock climbers. Can you believe a building for melting metal is now a viewing platform with a gorgeous 360-degree view? The final result is the Landscape Park Duisburg Nord. It has almost 570 acres of land filled with gardens, cycling paths, and pretty lights at night, in addition to its creatively ④ repurposed buildings. This park proves that it's ⑤ possible to preserve the heritage of a place as well as the environment.

23

다음 빈칸에 들어갈 말로 가장 적절한 것은?

The German government showed us an excellent example of this with a former steel plant that closed in 1985. _____ destroying the plant's buildings or abandoning the entire facility, they decided to give it new meaning as a series of useful public structures. Many of the buildings kept their original shapes, but received extra equipment and new designs in their surrounding areas. For instance, old gas tanks became pools for divers. Concrete walls of iron storage towers were turned into ideal training fields for rock climbers. Can you believe a building for melting metal is now a viewing platform with a gorgeous 360-degree view? The final result is the Landscape Park Duisburg Nord. It has almost 570 acres of land filled with gardens, cycling paths, and pretty lights at night, in addition to its creatively repurposed buildings. This park proves that it's possible to preserve the heritage of a place as well as the environment.

① Despite   ② Instead of   ③ Because of
④ In order to   ⑤ In addition to

24

다음 밑줄 친 to부정사 중, (A) to preserve와 쓰임이 같은 것은?

The final result is the Landscape Park Duisburg Nord. It has almost 570 acres of land filled with gardens, cycling paths, and pretty lights at night, in addition to its creatively repurposed buildings. This park proves that it's possible (A) to preserve the heritage of a place as well as the environment.

① I want to be a doctor.
② He grew up to be an actor.
③ Bring me a pencil to write with.
④ It is not easy to study English.
⑤ To solve the problem, we held a meeting.

25

다음 빈칸에 들어갈 말로 가장 적절한 것은?

Along with small everyday items, much bigger things can also be upcycled—even old buildings that cannot be used for their original purpose anymore. The German government showed us an excellent example of this with a former steel plant that closed in 1985. Rather than destroy the plant's buildings or abandon the entire facility, they decided to give it new meaning as a series of useful public structures. Many of the buildings kept their original shapes, but received extra equipment and new designs in their surrounding areas. _____, old gas tanks became pools for divers. Concrete walls of iron storage towers were turned into ideal training fields for rock climbers. Can you believe a building for melting metal is now a viewing platform with a gorgeous 360-degree view? The final result is the Landscape Park Duisburg Nord. It has almost 570 acres of land filled with gardens, cycling paths, and pretty lights at night, in addition to its creatively repurposed buildings. This park proves that it's possible to preserve the heritage of a place as well as the environment.

① However   ② In addition   ③ Nonetheless
④ For instance   ⑤ On the contrary

본문[3]

출제 포인트

1위	2위	3위
내용 일치	일관성	대의 파악
본문[3] 문단편 내 출제 확률 52.7%	본문[3] 문단편 내 출제 확률 32.4%	본문[3] 문단편 내 출제 확률 8.1%

● 내용 일치

이 문단에서는 내용 일치 유형이 52.7%로 가장 많이 출제되었다. 오래된 철강 공장이 뒤스부르크 환경 공원으로 업사이클되는 과정을 사실적으로 서술하고 있는 문단으로, '건물의 많은 부분들이 원래 형태를 유지했다'라는 부분과, 다이버들과 암벽등반가들을 위한 업사이클링 사례를 헷갈리지 않도록 주의하자.

문장1	Along with small everyday items, much bigger things can also be upcycled—even old buildings that cannot be used for their original purpose anymore.	13.1%
문장2	The German government showed us an excellent example of this with a former steel plant that closed in 1985.	12.3%
문장3	Rather than destroy the plant's buildings or abandon the entire facility, they decided to give it new meaning as a series of useful public structures.	11.5%
문장4	Many of the buildings kept their original shapes, but received extra equipment and new designs in their surrounding areas.	10.0%
문장5	For instance, old gas tanks became pools for divers.	9.2%
문장6	Concrete walls of iron storage towers were turned into ideal training fields for rock climbers.	12.3%
문장7	Can you believe a building for melting metal is now a viewing platform with a gorgeous 360-degree view?	12.3%
문장8	The final result is the Landscape Park Duisburg Nord.	0.0%
문장9	It has almost 570 acres of land filled with gardens, cycling paths, and pretty lights at night, in addition to its creatively repurposed buildings.	5.4%
문장10	This park proves that it's possible to preserve the heritage of a place as well as the environment.	13.9%

Q. 글의 내용과 일치하면 T, 일치하지 않으면 F에 표시하시오.

(1) 뒤스부르크 환경 공원은 한 장소의 유산도 보호할 수 있음을 증명한다. (T / F)
(2) 독일 정부는 철강 공장을 유용한 공공 구조물로 업사이클하기로 결정했다. (T / F)
(3) 뒤스부르크 환경 공원은 자전거 길과 아름다운 야간 조명을 갖추고 있다. (T / F)
(4) 철을 저장하는 콘크리트 벽은 360도의 경치를 즐길 수 있는 전망대가 되었다. (T / F)
(5) 작은 일상적인 물건뿐만 아니라 오래된 건물도 업사이클될 수 있다. (T / F)
(6) 건물들은 기존 건물 구조를 잃고 완전히 다른 모습으로 탈바꿈되었다. (T / F)
(7) 독일 정부는 1985년에 문을 닫은 철강 공장으로 업사이클링의 훌륭한 예시를 보여줬다. (T / F)
(8) 금속을 녹이기 위한 건물은 이제 다이버들을 위한 수영장이 되었다. (T / F)
(9) 오래된 가스 탱크는 암벽 등반가들을 위한 훈련장으로 바뀌었다. (T / F)

정답

1	T	2	T	3	T
4	F	5	T	6	F
7	T	8	F	9	F
10	T	11	F	12	T
13	F	14	F	15	F
16	F	17	T	18	T

(10) 그 공원은 환경 보호뿐만 아니라 유산 보존 측면에서도 가치가 있다.
(11) 철강 공장은 완전히 철거된 뒤에 공공 구조물로 재건되었다.
(12) 뒤스부르크 환경 공원은 전망대뿐만 아니라 자전거 길을 갖추고 있다.
(13) 철을 저장하는 타워의 콘크리트 벽은 암벽 등반가들을 위해 철거되었다.

(14) 작은 일상적인 것들과 달리, 오래된 건물과 같은 큰 것들은 업사이클될 가능성이 낮다.

(15) 건물의 원래 모습을 유지하기 위해 추가 설비를 설치하지 않았다.

(16) 독일 정부는 금속 제품을 여전히 생산했던 오래된 철강 공장을 업사이클하기로 결정했다.

(17) 건물은 아름다운 경관을 제공하는 전망대를 갖춘 장소로 탈바꿈되었다.

(18) 오래된 가스 탱크는 다이버들을 위한 수영장으로 업사이클링 되었다.

(10) The Park is valuable in terms of not only environmental protection but also heritage conservation. (T / F)

(11) The steel factory was entirely demolished and then rebuilt into public structures. (T / F)

(12) The Landscape Park Duisburg Nord has cycle tracks as well as a viewing platform. (T / F)

(13) The concrete walls of the iron storage tower were demolished for rock climbers. (T / F)

(14) Unlike small daily things, large things such as old buildings are unlikely to be upcycled. (T / F)

(15) No additional facilities were installed to maintain the original appearance of the building. (T / F)

(16) The German government decided to upcycle an old steel plant that still produced metal goods. (T / F)

(17) The building was transformed into a place with a viewing platform that offers wonderful scenery. (T / F)

(18) Old gas tanks were upcycled into pools for divers. (T / F)

● 일관성

일관성 문제도 32.4% 확률로 많이 출제된다. 오래된 철강 공장이 독일의 뒤스부르크 환경 공원으로 업사이클된 사례를 시간 순서대로 설명하는 가운데, 앞뒤 내용을 긴밀하게 연결하는 대명사 it, 연결사 For instance(예를 들면)와 같은 포인트에 주목하자.

Q. 다음 글에서 전체 흐름과 관계 없는 문장은?

Along with small everyday items, much bigger things can also be upcycled—even old buildings that cannot be used for their original purpose anymore. The German government showed us an excellent example of this with a former steel plant that closed in 1985. Rather than destroy the plant's buildings or abandon the entire facility, they decided to give it new meaning as a series of useful public structures. ① Many of the buildings kept their original shapes, but received extra equipment and new designs in their surrounding areas. ② For instance, old gas tanks became pools for divers. ③ Nevertheless, the tanks turned out to have their own potential in terms of energy efficiency. ④ Concrete walls of iron storage towers were turned into ideal training fields for rock climbers. ⑤ Can you believe a building for melting metal is now a viewing platform with a gorgeous 360-degree view? The final result is the Landscape Park Duisburg Nord. It has almost 570 acres of land filled with gardens, cycling paths, and pretty lights at night, in addition to its creatively repurposed buildings. This park proves that it's possible to preserve the heritage of a place as well as the environment.

정답 ③

오래된 철강 공장에 추가 설비를 설치하고 새로운 디자인을 하는 등 공장을 업사이클하는 구체적인 예시를 설명하고 있다. ③은 '그럼에도 불구하고, 그 탱크들은 에너지 효율 측면에서 그들만의 잠재력을 가지고 있는 것으로 밝혀졌다'라는 의미로, 전체적인 흐름에서 벗어나 있다.

● 대의 파악

대의 파악 문제는 8.1%의 확률로 출제되었다. 이 단락은 오래된 철강 공장이 뒤스부르크 환경 공원으로 업사이클된 과정을 설명하면서, 그것의 의의가 환경 보호뿐만 아니라 유산 보존이라는 내용으로 마무리하고 있다. 주제, 제목, 요지 등과 같은 문제 유형에 대비해두자.

Q. 다음 글의 요지로 가장 적절한 것은?

Along with small everyday items, much bigger things can also be upcycled—even old buildings that cannot be used for their original purpose anymore. The

German government showed us an excellent example of this with a former steel plant that closed in 1985. Rather than destroy the plant's buildings or abandon the entire facility, they decided to give it new meaning as a series of useful public structures. Many of the buildings kept their original shapes, but received extra equipment and new designs in their surrounding areas. For instance, old gas tanks became pools for divers. Concrete walls of iron storage towers were turned into ideal training fields for rock climbers. Can you believe a building for melting metal is now a viewing platform with a gorgeous 360-degree view? The final result is the Landscape Park Duisburg Nord. It has almost 570 acres of land filled with gardens, cycling paths, and pretty lights at night, in addition to its creatively repurposed buildings. This park proves that it's possible to preserve the heritage of a place as well as the environment.

① Only huge buildings with a valuable cultural heritage can be upcycled.
② The benefits of upcycling small everyday items outweigh the costs.
③ It is absurd to rebuild old buildings in Germany by adding new designs.
④ German public parks are suitable for those who enjoy extreme sports.
⑤ Upcycling larger structures as well as small everyday items is worthwhile.

정답 ⑤

뒤스부르크 환경 공원의 사례를 통해 작은 일상 물품들뿐만 아니라 더 큰 건물도 업사이클하는 것이 가능하다는 것을 보여주는 글이다. 따라서 글의 요지로 가장 적절한 것은 ⑤ '작은 일상적인 것뿐만 아니라 더 큰 구조물을 업사이클링하는 것은 가치가 있다.'이다.
① 귀중한 문화유산이 있는 거대한 건물만이 업사이클될 수 있다.
② 사소한 일상 물품을 업사이클하는 것의 이득은 비용 이상이다.
③ 독일에서 새 디자인을 추가하여 오래된 건물을 재건하는 것은 터무니없다.
④ 독일 대중 공원은 익스트림 스포츠를 즐기는 사람들에게 적합하다.

● 요약

요약 문제는 4.1% 확률로 출제되었다. 이 단락을 한 문장으로 요약하면 '오래된 철강 공장을 뒤스부르크 공원으로 업사이클함으로써 환경을 보호할 뿐만 아니라, 장소의 유산을 보존할 수 있다'로 마지막 문장에 해당한다. 또한, 철강 공장의 업사이클링 과정을 사실적으로 전달하고 있는 부분으로, 한 문단으로 요약하는 유형도 출제될 수 있다.

Q. 다음 글의 내용을 한 문단으로 요약하고자 한다. 주어진 철자로 시작하는 빈칸 (A)~(C)에 들어갈 말을 쓰시오.

Along with small everyday items, much bigger things can also be upcycled—even old buildings that cannot be used for their original purpose anymore. The German government showed us an excellent example of this with a former steel plant that closed in 1985. Rather than destroy the plant's buildings or abandon the entire facility, they decided to give it new meaning as a series of useful public structures. Many of the buildings kept their original shapes, but received extra equipment and new designs in their surrounding areas. For instance, old gas tanks became pools for divers. Concrete walls of iron storage towers were turned into ideal training fields for rock climbers. Can you believe a building for melting metal is now a viewing platform with a gorgeous 360-degree view? The final result is the Landscape Park Duisburg Nord. It has almost 570 acres of land filled with gardens, cycling paths, and pretty lights at night, in addition to its creatively repurposed buildings. This park proves that it's possible to preserve the heritage of a place as well as the environment.

> The German government made the Landscape Park Duisburg Nord by (A) u_____ an old steel plant. They turned it into a helpful public building that had pools for divers, (B) t_____ f_____ for rock climbers, a viewing platform, etc. Therefore, it is proved that we can not only protect the nature but also preserve the (C) h_____ of a place.

정답
(A) upcycling
(B) training fields
(C) heritage

[요약문] 독일 정부가 오래된 철강 공장을 (A) 업사이클함으로써 뒤스부르크 환경 공원을 만들었다. 그들은 그것을 다이버들을 위한 풀과, 암벽등반가들을 위한 이상적인 (B) 훈련장, 전망대 등을 갖춘 유용한 공공건물로 바꾸었다. 따라서 우리가 자연을 보호할 수 있을 뿐만 아니라 장소의 (C) 유산도 보존할 수 있다는 것이 증명되었다.

01

뒤스부르크 환경 공원에 관한 다음 글의 내용과 일치하지 <u>않</u>는 것은?

For instance, old gas tanks became pools for divers. Concrete walls of iron storage towers were turned into ideal training fields for rock climbers. Can you believe a building for melting metal is now a viewing platform with a gorgeous 360-degree view? The final result is the Landscape Park Duisburg Nord. It has almost 570 acres of land filled with gardens, cycling paths, and pretty lights at night, in addition to its creatively repurposed buildings.

① 가스탱크였던 곳에서는 다이빙을 할 수 있다.
② 전망대는 원래 금속을 녹이기 위한 용도로 쓰이는 건물이었다.
③ 전망대는 공원 앞쪽만을 볼 수 있도록 설계되었다.
④ 공원에서는 자전거를 탈 수 있다.
⑤ 밤에는 조명이 켜진다.

02

주어진 글 다음에 이어질 내용의 순서로 가장 적절한 것은?

Along with small everyday items, much bigger things can also be upcycled—even old buildings that cannot be used for their original purpose anymore. The German government showed us an excellent example of this with a former steel plant that closed in 1985.

(A) The final result is the Landscape Park Duisburg Nord. It has almost 570 acres of land filled with gardens, cycling paths, and pretty lights at night, in addition to its creatively repurposed buildings. This park proves that it's possible to preserve the heritage of a place as well as the environment.

(B) For instance, old gas tanks became pools for divers. Concrete walls of iron storage towers were turned into ideal training fields for rock climbers. Can you believe a building for melting metal is now a viewing platform with a gorgeous 360-degree view?

(C) Rather than destroy the plant's buildings or abandon the entire facility, they decided to give it new meaning as a series of useful public structures. Many of the buildings kept their original shapes, but received extra equipment and new designs in their surrounding areas.

① (A) – (C) – (B)
② (B) – (A) – (C)
③ (B) – (C) – (A)
④ (C) – (A) – (B)
⑤ (C) – (B) – (A)

03

다음 글의 내용과 일치하는 것을 <u>모두</u> 고르시오.

Along with small everyday items, much bigger things can also be upcycled—even old buildings that cannot be used for their original purpose anymore. The German government showed us an excellent example of this with a former steel plant that closed in 1985. Rather than destroy the plant's buildings or abandon the entire facility, they decided to give it new meaning as a series of useful public structures. Many of the buildings kept their original shapes, but received extra equipment and new designs in their surrounding areas. For instance, old gas tanks became pools for divers. Concrete walls of iron storage towers were turned into ideal training fields for rock climbers. Can you believe a building for melting metal is now a viewing platform with a gorgeous 360-degree view? The final result is the Landscape Park Duisburg Nord. It has almost 570 acres of land filled with gardens, cycling paths, and pretty lights at night, in addition to its creatively repurposed buildings. This park proves that it's possible to preserve the heritage of a place as well as the environment.

① Not only small things but also large things such as buildings can be upcycled.
② The old steel factory was transformed entirely using new designs and materials.
③ The Landscape Park Duisburg Nord offers a training field for rock climbers and a viewing platform.
④ Landscape Park Duisburg Nord demonstrates it is possible to not only protect the nature but also preserve the legacy.
⑤ Millions of people visit the Landscape Park Duisburg Nord every year.

04

다음 글의 내용을 한 문장으로 요약하고자 한다. 빈칸 (A), (B)에 들어갈 말로 가장 적절한 것은?

Along with small everyday items, much bigger things can also be upcycled—even old buildings that cannot be used for their original purpose anymore. The German government showed us an excellent example of this with a former steel plant that closed in 1985. Rather than destroy the plant's buildings or abandon the entire facility, they decided to give it new meaning as a series of useful public structures. Many of the buildings kept their original shapes, but received extra equipment and new designs in their surrounding areas. For instance, old gas tanks became pools for divers. Concrete walls of iron storage towers were turned into ideal training fields for rock climbers. Can you believe a building for melting metal is now a viewing platform with a gorgeous 360-degree view? The final result is the Landscape Park Duisburg Nord. It has almost 570 acres of land filled with gardens, cycling paths, and pretty lights at night, in addition to its creatively repurposed buildings. This park proves that it's possible to preserve the heritage of a place as well as the environment.

> It _____(A)_____ that we can preserve the _____(B)_____ of a place as well as protect the environment by upcycling an old steel plant as a public park.

	(A)		(B)
①	turns out	–	legacy
②	is rejected	–	peace
③	is admitted	–	reputation
④	is denied	–	order
⑤	is proved	–	dignity

05

다음 글의 내용과 일치하지 <u>않는</u> 것은?

Along with small everyday items, much bigger things can also be upcycled—even old buildings that cannot be used for their original purpose anymore. The German government showed us an excellent example of this with a former steel plant that closed in 1985. Rather than destroy the plant's buildings or abandon the entire facility, they decided to give it new meaning as a series of useful public structures. Many of the buildings kept their original shapes, but received extra equipment and new designs in their surrounding areas. For instance, old gas tanks became pools for divers. Concrete walls of iron storage towers were turned into ideal training fields for rock climbers. Can you believe a building for melting metal is now a viewing platform with a gorgeous 360-degree view? The final result is the Landscape Park Duisburg Nord. It has almost 570 acres of land filled with gardens, cycling paths, and pretty lights at night, in addition to its creatively repurposed buildings. This park proves that it's possible to preserve the heritage of a place as well as the environment.

① Repurposing the abandoned steel plant for a eco-friendly park is a great example of upcycling.
② The German government tranformed the factory that closed in 1985 into a helpful public building.
③ The steel factory was reformed partially by building additional facilities with its original shapes maintained.
④ The Landscape Park Duisburg Nord offers a pool for divers, cycle tracks, beautiful lights, etc.
⑤ The meaning of Landscape Park Duisburg Nord is legacy preservation and regional economic revival.

06

다음 글의 흐름으로 보아, 주어진 문장이 들어가기에 가장 적절한 곳은?

> Rather than destroy the plant's buildings or abandon the entire facility, they decided to give it new meaning as a series of useful public structures.

Along with small everyday items, much bigger things can also be upcycled—even old buildings that cannot be used for their original purpose anymore. (①) The German government showed us an excellent example of this with a former steel plant that closed in 1985. (②) Many of the buildings kept their original shapes, but received extra equipment and new designs in their surrounding areas. (③) For instance, old gas tanks became pools for divers. (④) Concrete walls of iron storage towers were turned into ideal training fields for rock climbers. (⑤) Can you believe a building for melting metal is now a viewing platform with a gorgeous 360-degree view? The final result is the Landscape Park Duisburg Nord. It has almost 570 acres of land filled with gardens, cycling paths, and pretty lights at night, in addition to its creatively repurposed buildings. This park proves that it's possible to preserve the heritage of a place as well as the environment.

07

다음 글의 제목으로 가장 적절한 것은?

Along with small everyday items, much bigger things can also be upcycled—even old buildings that cannot be used for their original purpose anymore. The German government showed us an excellent example of this with a former steel plant that closed in 1985. Rather than destroy the plant's buildings or abandon the entire facility, they decided to give it new meaning as a series of useful public structures. Many of the buildings kept their original shapes, but received extra equipment and new designs in their surrounding areas. For instance, old gas tanks became pools for divers. Concrete walls of iron storage towers were turned into ideal training fields for rock climbers. Can you believe a building for melting metal is now a viewing platform with a gorgeous 360-degree view? The final result is the Landscape Park Duisburg Nord. It has almost 570 acres of land filled with gardens, cycling paths, and pretty lights at night, in addition to its creatively repurposed buildings. This park proves that it's possible to preserve the heritage of a place as well as the environment.

① Positive Influence on German Public Parks
② An Old Park That Creates Steel and Concrete
③ From Steel Factory to Eco-friendly Public Park
④ Creative Transformation of Old Gas Tanks
⑤ Why Germany Decided to Demolish the Plant

08

다음 글에서 전체 흐름과 관계 없는 문장은?

Along with small everyday items, much bigger things can also be upcycled—even old buildings that cannot be used for their original purpose anymore. ① The German government showed us an excellent example of this with a former steel plant that closed in 1985. ② Rather than destroy the plant's buildings or abandon the entire facility, they decided to give it new meaning as a series of useful public structures. ③ Many of the buildings kept their original shapes, but received extra equipment and new designs in their surrounding areas. ④ Thus, many old buildings must not be demolished in consideration of the enormous cost and effort that will be put into them. ⑤ For instance, old gas tanks became pools for divers. Concrete walls of iron storage towers were turned into ideal training fields for rock climbers. Can you believe a building for melting metal is now a viewing platform with a gorgeous 360-degree view? The final result is the Landscape Park Duisburg Nord. It has almost 570 acres of land filled with gardens, cycling paths, and pretty lights at night, in addition to its creatively repurposed buildings. This park proves that it's possible to preserve the heritage of a place as well as the environment.

09

다음 글의 주제로 가장 적절한 것은?

Along with small everyday items, much bigger things can also be upcycled—even old buildings that cannot be used for their original purpose anymore. The German government showed us an excellent example of this with a former steel plant that closed in 1985. Rather than destroy the plant's buildings or abandon the entire facility, they decided to give it new meaning as a series of useful public structures. Many of the buildings kept their original shapes, but received extra equipment and new designs in their surrounding areas. For instance, old gas tanks became pools for divers. Concrete walls of iron storage towers were turned into ideal training fields for rock climbers. Can you believe a building for melting metal is now a viewing platform with a gorgeous 360-degree view? The final result is the Landscape Park Duisburg Nord. It has almost 570 acres of land filled with gardens, cycling paths, and pretty lights at night, in addition to its creatively repurposed buildings. This park proves that it's possible to preserve the heritage of a place as well as the environment.

① the difference between the Landscape Park Duisburg Nord and other German parks
② the importance of ingenious and groundbreaking designs in rebuilding public structures
③ the effects of upcycling old buildings on a decrease in the human labor force in large cities
④ the process of establishing the Landscape Park Duisburg Nord and its significance
⑤ the necessity of preserving cultural heritages in terms of national competitiveness

10

다음 글의 흐름으로 보아, 주어진 문장이 들어가기에 가장 적절한 곳은?

> For instance, old gas tanks became pools for divers.

Along with small everyday items, much bigger things can also be upcycled—even old buildings that cannot be used for their original purpose anymore. (①) The German government showed us an excellent example of this with a former steel plant that closed in 1985. (②) Rather than destroy the plant's buildings or abandon the entire facility, they decided to give it new meaning as a series of useful public structures. (③) Many of the buildings kept their original shapes, but received extra equipment and new designs in their surrounding areas. (④) Concrete walls of iron storage towers were turned into ideal training fields for rock climbers. (⑤) Can you believe a building for melting metal is now a viewing platform with a gorgeous 360-degree view? The final result is the Landscape Park Duisburg Nord. It has almost 570 acres of land filled with gardens, cycling paths, and pretty lights at night, in addition to its creatively repurposed buildings. This park proves that it's possible to preserve the heritage of a place as well as the environment.

기타 연습 문제

1회 등장 포인트

● 전치사 along with

> Along with small everyday items, much bigger things can also be upcycled—even old buildings that cannot be used for their original purpose anymore.

● 어휘 public

> Rather than destroy the plant's buildings or abandon the entire facility, they decided to give it new meaning as a series of useful public structures.

01

다음 글의 밑줄 친 부분 중, 제시된 표현으로 바꿔 쓸 수 없는 것은?

ⓐ Along with small everyday items, much bigger things can also be upcycled—even old buildings that cannot be used for their original purpose anymore. The German government showed us an excellent example of this with a former steel plant that closed in 1985. Rather than destroy the plant's buildings or abandon the entire facility, they decided to give it new meaning as a series of useful ⓑ public structures. Many of the buildings kept their original shapes, but ⓒ received extra equipment and new designs in their surrounding areas. For instance, old gas tanks became pools for divers. Concrete walls of iron storage towers were ⓓ turned into ideal training fields for rock climbers. Can you believe a building for melting metal is now a viewing platform with a gorgeous 360-degree view? The final result is the Landscape Park Duisburg Nord. It has almost 570 acres of land filled with gardens, cycling paths, and pretty lights at night, in addition to its creatively repurposed buildings. This park proves that it's possible to ⓔ preserve the heritage of a place as well as the environment.

① ⓐ: In addition to
② ⓑ: private
③ ⓒ: supplemented
④ ⓓ: converted
⑤ ⓔ: protect

● 어휘 receive, extra

> Many of the buildings kept their original shapes, but received extra equipment and new designs in their surrounding areas.

02

다음 글의 밑줄 친 부분 중, 낱말의 쓰임이 적절하지 않은 것은?

The German government showed us an excellent example of upcycling a building with a former steel plant that closed in 1985. Rather than destroy the plant's buildings or ① abandon the entire facility, they decided to give it new meaning as a series of useful public structures. Many of the buildings kept their original shapes, but ② received extra equipment and new designs in their surrounding areas. For instance, old gas tanks became pools for divers. Concrete walls of iron storage towers were turned into ③ unsuitable training fields for rock climbers. Can you believe a building for melting metal is now a viewing platform with a gorgeous 360-degree view? The final result is the Landscape Park Duisburg Nord. It has almost 570 acres of land filled with gardens, cycling paths, and pretty lights at night, in addition to its creatively ④ repurposed buildings. This park proves that it's possible to ⑤ preserve the heritage of a place as well as the environment.

● 어휘 storage, ideal

> Concrete walls of iron storage towers were turned into ideal training fields for rock climbers.

● 전치사＋동명사

Can you believe a building for melting metal is now a viewing platform with a gorgeous 360-degree view?

03

다음 글의 밑줄 친 부분 중, 어법상 틀린 것은?

Along with small everyday items, much bigger things can also be upcycled—even old buildings ① what cannot be used for their original purpose anymore. The German government showed us an excellent example of this with a former steel plant that closed in 1985. Rather than destroy the plant's buildings or abandon the entire facility, they decided ② to give it new meaning as a series of useful public structures. Many of the buildings kept their original shapes, but received extra equipment and new designs in their surrounding areas. For instance, old gas tanks became pools for divers. Concrete walls of iron storage towers ③ were turned into ideal training fields for rock climbers. Can you believe a building for ④ melting metal is now a viewing platform with a gorgeous 360-degree view? The final result is the Landscape Park Duisburg Nord. It has almost 570 acres of land ⑤ filled with gardens, cycling paths, and pretty lights at night, in addition to its creatively repurposed buildings.

● 수 일치, 어휘 degree

Can you believe a building for melting metal is now a viewing platform with a gorgeous 360-degree view?

04

다음 글의 밑줄 친 부분 중, 어법상 틀린 것은?

Along with small everyday items, ① much bigger things can also be upcycled—even old buildings that cannot be used for their original purpose anymore. The German government showed us an excellent example of this with a former steel plant that closed in 1985. Rather than destroy the plant's buildings or abandon the entire facility, they decided ② to give it

new meaning as a series of useful public structures. Many of the buildings kept their original shapes, but received extra equipment and new designs in their surrounding areas. For instance, old gas tanks became pools for divers. Concrete walls of iron storage towers ③ were turned into ideal training fields for rock climbers. Can you believe a building for melting metal ④ are now a viewing platform with a gorgeous 360-degree view? The final result is the Landscape Park Duisburg Nord. It has almost 570 acres of land filled with gardens, cycling paths, and pretty lights at night, in addition to its creatively repurposed buildings. This park proves that it's possible ⑤ to preserve the heritage of a place as well as the environment.

05

밑줄 친 우리말 (A)와 같은 뜻이 되도록 〈조건〉에 맞추어 영작하시오.

Can you believe that (A) 금속을 녹이기 위한 건물이 360도의 멋진 경치를 보여주는 전망대이다?

〈조건〉   1. 다음 표현들을 반드시 포함할 것
with, a gorgeous 360-degree view,
a viewing platform, a building
2. 필요한 단어를 추가해서 총 14단어로 영작할 것

_____

_____

● 어휘 creatively

It has almost 570 acres of land filled with gardens, cycling paths, and pretty lights at night, in addition to its creatively repurposed buildings.

06

글의 밑줄 친 부분 중, 낱말의 쓰임이 적절하지 <u>않은</u> 것은?

The German government showed us an excellent example of this with a former steel plant that closed in 1985. ① <u>Rather than</u> destroy the plant's buildings or abandon the entire facility, they decided to give it new meaning as a series of ② <u>useful</u> public structures. Many of the buildings kept their original shapes, but received extra equipment and new designs in their ③ <u>surrounding</u> areas. For instance, old gas tanks became pools for divers. Concrete walls of iron storage towers were turned into ideal training fields for rock climbers. Can you believe a building for melting metal is now a viewing platform with a gorgeous ④ <u>360-degree</u> view? The final result is the Landscape Park Duisburg Nord. It has almost 570 acres of land filled with gardens, cycling paths, and pretty lights at night, in addition to its ⑤ <u>unsuitably</u> repurposed buildings.

● 목적

07

다음 글의 목적으로 가장 적절한 것은?

Along with small everyday items, much bigger things can also be upcycled—even old buildings that cannot be used for their original purpose anymore. The German government showed us an excellent example of this with a former steel plant that closed in 1985. Rather than destroy the plant's buildings or abandon the entire facility, they decided to give it new meaning as a series of useful public structures. Many of the buildings kept their original shapes, but received extra equipment and new designs in their surrounding areas. For instance, old gas tanks became pools for divers. Concrete walls of iron storage towers were turned into ideal training fields for rock climbers. Can you believe a building for melting metal is now a viewing platform with a gorgeous 360-degree view? The final result is the Landscape Park Duisburg Nord. It has almost 570 acres of land filled with gardens, cycling paths, and pretty lights at night, in addition to its creatively repurposed buildings. This park proves that it's possible to preserve the heritage of a place as well as the environment.

① to tell people about the German government's frustrating attempts
② to motivate German people to help upcycle a huge public structure
③ to warn of the risks and costs of demolishing old public offices
④ to inform people of a great example of upcycling a large building
⑤ to promote an eco-friendly park with attractive tourist destinations

● 지칭 추론

08

다음 글의 밑줄 친 (A), (B)가 각각 가리키는 것을 본문에서 찾아 그대로 쓰시오.

Along with small everyday items, much bigger things can also be upcycled—even old buildings that cannot be used for their original purpose anymore. The German government showed us an excellent example of this with a former steel plant that closed in 1985. Rather than destroy the plant's buildings or abandon the entire facility, they decided to give (A) <u>it</u> new meaning as a series of useful public structures. Many of the buildings kept their original shapes, but received extra equipment and new designs in their surrounding areas. For instance, old gas tanks became pools for divers. Concrete walls of iron storage towers were turned into ideal training fields for rock climbers. Can you believe a building for melting metal is now a viewing platform with a gorgeous 360-degree view? The final result is the Landscape Park Duisburg Nord. (B) <u>It</u> has almost 570 acres of land filled with gardens, cycling paths, and pretty lights at night, in addition to its creatively repurposed buildings. This park proves that it's possible to preserve the heritage of a place as well as the environment.

(A) _____

(B) _____

09

다음 글의 요지로 가장 적절한 것은?

Along with small everyday items, much bigger things can also be upcycled—even old buildings that cannot be used for their original purpose anymore. The German government showed us an excellent example of this with a former steel plant that closed in 1985. Rather than destroy the plant's buildings or abandon the entire facility, they decided to give it new meaning as a series of useful public structures. Many of the buildings kept their original shapes, but received extra equipment and new designs in their surrounding areas. For instance, old gas tanks became pools for divers. Concrete walls of iron storage towers were turned into ideal training fields for rock climbers. Can you believe a building for melting metal is now a viewing platform with a gorgeous 360-degree view? The final result is the Landscape Park Duisburg Nord. It has almost 570 acres of land filled with gardens, cycling paths, and pretty lights at night, in addition to its creatively repurposed buildings. This park proves that it's possible to preserve the heritage of a place as well as the environment.

① When building a new factory, various purposes of use should be considered.

② Metal-making factories need an observatory to properly check all processes.

③ The German government invested in various factories to strengthen the key industry.

④ The German government imposed regulations on factories that emit a lot of environmental pollutants.

⑤ The German government transformed an abandoned plant into a public park by creatively repurposing the building.

출제 포인트 65.2% 정복!

리딩
본문[4]

24.8% 확률로 본문[4]에서 출제

★★
When artists add their own creative touches, things that most people consider junk are reborn as beautiful works of art. The giant pictures ★ made from trash by environmental artist Tom Deininger are one of a kind. Up close, these brightly colored creations look like a mixed-up mess of broken plastic, unwanted toys, and bent wire—all things that cannot be recycled. From farther away, however, they appear to blend together into marvelous landscapes or other paintings. There is also an artist who shows that even disposable cups can be reused as artistic material. For years, Gwyneth Leech has turned used coffee cups into brilliant art exhibits. After a cup is used by someone, she paints a unique design on it and hangs it with many other painted cups in front of a window or pretty background. ★★★ These works from Leech and Deininger are not only pleasing to the eye, but they also naturally provoke an interest in environmental conservation in people.

일관성 〈출제 1위 유형〉

예술가들이 쓰레기를 예술작품으로 다시 탄생시킨다는 내용의 글로, Tom Deininger과 Gwyneth Leech의 작품을 예로 들며 글이 전개된다. 특히, Deininger의 작품 설명에서 작품을 가까이서 봤을 때의 모습과 멀리서 봤을 때의 모습을 역접 관계를 나타내는 연결어 however를 사용하여 상반되도록 설명하고 있다는 점을 기억하자. 부사 also를 사용하여 Deininger처럼 쓰레기로 예술작품을 만드는 Leech의 작품 소개가 이어진다는 점도 기억하자.

대의 파악 〈출제 2위 유형〉

사람들이 쓰레기라고 여기는 물건에 Tom Deininger과 Gwyneth Leech와 같은 예술가들의 창의적 솜씨가 더해지면 예술작품으로 다시 태어나고, 이런 업사이클을 통해 사람들에게 즐거움뿐만 아니라 환경 보존에 대한 관심을 유발한다는 내용의 글이다. 글의 키워드를 활용하여 선택지가 출제되므로, 키워드 creative의 유의어인 inventive, imaginative, original과 같은 어휘를 알아두자.

내용 일치 〈출제 3위 유형〉

키워드를 변형하여 내용 일치 여부를 묻는 선택지가 출제되므로 핵심 내용을 확실히 이해하자. 예술가들은 쓰레기를 원래의 용도로 재사용하지 않고 예술작품으로 업사이클했다는 점, 재활용할 수 없는 물건으로 만든 Deininger의 그림은 가까이서 볼 때와 멀리서 볼 때 다른 인상을 준다는 점, Leech는 사용된 커피컵에 디자인을 그려서 다른 컵들과 함께 매달아 놓았다는 점, Deininger와 Leech의 전시품은 자연스럽게 환경에 대한 관심을 유발한다는 점을 명확히 파악하자.

출제 1위 문장 ★★★

These works from Leech and Deininger are not only pleasing to the eye, but they also naturally provoke an interest in environmental conservation in people.

[감정동사의 현재분사] 출제 1위 (문장편-문장8 → p.140)

[빈칸 provoke an interest in environmental conservation] 출제 2위 (문장편-문장8 → p.140)

출제 2위 문장 ★★

When artists add their own creative touches, things that most people consider junk are reborn as beautiful works of art.

[목적격관계대명사 that] 출제 1위 (문장편-문장1 → p.124)

[수 일치] 출제 2위 (문장편-문장1 → p.124)

[어휘 junk] 출제 3위 (문장편-문장1 → p.125)

출제 3위 문장 ★

The giant pictures made from trash by environmental artist Tom Deininger are one of a kind.

[수 일치] 출제 1위 (문장편-문장2 → p.126)

[과거분사 형용사 역할 — 명사 수식] 출제 2위 (문장편-문장2 → p.126)

[어휘 trash] 출제 3위 (문장편-문장2 → p.127)

문장1 문장 출제 확률: 4.3% (총 771개의 출제 포인트 중 33회 출현, 46개 문장 중 6위)

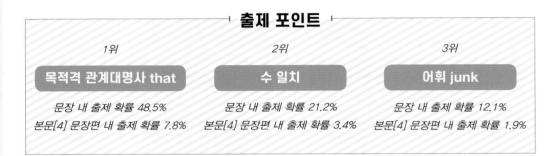

목적격 관계대명사 that

When artists add their own creative touches, things <u>that</u> most people consider <u>junk</u> <u>are</u> reborn as beautiful works of art.

쓰레기 수 일치

┤ **출제 포인트** ├

1위	2위	3위
목적격 관계대명사 that	**수 일치**	**어휘 junk**
문장 내 출제 확률 48.5%	문장 내 출제 확률 21.2%	문장 내 출제 확률 12.1%
본문[4] 문장편 내 출제 확률 7.8%	본문[4] 문장편 내 출제 확률 3.4%	본문[4] 문장편 내 출제 확률 1.9%

● 목적격관계대명사 that

문장1은 4.3% 확률로 출제된다. 이 문장에서 48.5%의 확률로 목적격관계대명사 that을 묻는다. 관계사절 내에서 동사 consider의 목적어 역할을 하는 목적격관계대명사이며, 선행사 things가 사물이므로 which와 바꿔 쓸 수 있지만, who와 바꿔 쓸 수 없다는 것을 유의하자. 앞에 선행사가 있으므로, 관계대명사 what과 바꿔 쓸 수 없지만, things that을 관계대명사 what으로 바꿔 쓸 수 있으므로 what most people consider junk로 쓸 수 있다는 점을 알아두자.

> **Q. 다음 두 문장을 한 문장으로 바르게 바꿔 쓴 것은?**
>
> | Most people consider things junk. Things are reborn as beautiful works of art. |
>
> ① Things are reborn as beautiful works of art that most people consider junk.
> ② Things are reborn as beautiful works of art and most people consider junk.
> ③ What most people consider them junk are reborn as beautiful works of art.
> ④ Things that most people consider junk are reborn as beautiful works of art.
> ⑤ Things and most people consider junk are reborn as beautiful works of art.

● 수 일치

21.2%의 확률로 수 일치 문제를 물어볼 수 있다. 주절의 동사 바로 앞에 나온 명사 junk는 관계사절(that most people consider junk) 내에서 목적격 보어 역할을 하는 명사이므로, 주어로 혼동하지 않도록 하자. 주어는 things이고, 이에 수 일치하여 복수동사 are이 쓰인 점을 유의하자.

> **Q. 다음 문장의 괄호 안에서 어법에 맞는 것을 고르시오.**
>
> When artists add their own creative touches, things that most people consider junk (is / are) reborn as beautiful works of art.

● 어휘 junk

12.1% 확률로 어휘 junk에 대해 묻는 경우가 많다. 이 글의 핵심 소재 중 하나로, 더 이상 가치가 없거나 쓸모없는 물건을 의미하는 junk의 유의어 trash, garbage, rubbish, litter, waste까지 함께 숙지하여 대비하자. junk의 뜻을 묻거나, 빈칸에 들어갈 어휘를 나타내는 영영풀이를 묻는 유형이 출제되기도 하므로, 영영풀이 things that are considered to be useless, low-quality, or unwanted(쓸모가 없거나, 질이 낮거나, 원치 않는다고 여겨지는 것들)도 익혀두자.

Q. 다음 글의 밑줄 친 부분 중, 문맥상 낱말의 쓰임이 적절하지 <u>않은</u> 것은?

When artists add their own creative touches, things that most people consider ① <u>gems</u> are reborn as beautiful works of art. The giant pictures made from trash by environmental artist Tom Deininger are one of a kind. Up ② <u>close</u>, these brightly colored creations look like a mixed-up mess of broken plastic, ③ <u>unwanted</u> toys, and bent wire—all things that cannot be recycled. From farther away, however, they appear to blend together into marvelous landscapes or other paintings. There is also an artist who shows that even disposable cups can be ④ <u>reused</u> as artistic material. For years, Gwyneth Leech has turned used coffee cups into brilliant art exhibits. After a cup is used by someone, she paints a unique design on it and hangs it with many other painted cups in front of a window or pretty background. These works from Leech and Deininger are not only ⑤ <u>pleasing</u> to the eye, but they also naturally provoke an interest in environmental conservation in people.

정답 ①

쓰레기와 사용된 컵으로 만든 예술 작품 설명이 뒤에 이어지며, 예술가들이 사람들이 쓸모없다고 여기는 물건들에 창의적인 솜씨를 더한다는 것이 문맥상 적절하므로, gems(보석)가 아닌 junk(쓰레기)와 같은 낱말이 문맥상 적절하다.

● reborn의 형태

9.1%의 확률로 reborn의 형태를 묻는 문제가 나오기도 한다. reborn은 과거분사 형태로만 쓰인다. 이 문장에서도 수동태 are reborn으로 쓰인 것을 잘 기억해두도록 하자.

Q. 다음 중, 괄호 안의 단어를 알맞게 변형하지 <u>않은</u> 것은?

When artists add their own creative touches, things that most people consider junk ⓐ (reborn) as beautiful works of art. The giant pictures made from trash by environmental artist Tom Deininger are one of a kind. Up close, these brightly ⓑ (color) creations look like a mixed-up mess of broken plastic, unwanted toys, and bent wire—all things that cannot ⓒ (recycle). From farther away, however, they appear ⓓ (blend) together into marvelous landscapes or other paintings. There is also an artist who shows that even disposable cups can be reused as artistic material. For years, Gwyneth Leech ⓔ (turn) used coffee cups into brilliant art exhibits. After a cup is used by someone, she paints a unique design on it and hangs it with many other painted cups in front of a window or pretty background. These works from Leech and Deininger are not only pleasing to the eye, but they also naturally provoke an interest in environmental conservation in people.

① ⓐ → reborns
② ⓑ → colored
③ ⓒ → be recycled
④ ⓓ → to blend
⑤ ⓔ → has turned

정답 ①

ⓐ 앞에 나온 관계대명사 that부터 명사 junk까지 관계사절이므로 관계대명사의 선행사이면서 문장의 주어인 복수 명사 things와 수 일치를 해야 하는데, 이 때 주어 things가 문맥상 재탄생되는 대상이므로 수동태 are reborn으로 어형을 바꿔야 한다.

출제 포인트 68% 정복!

문장2

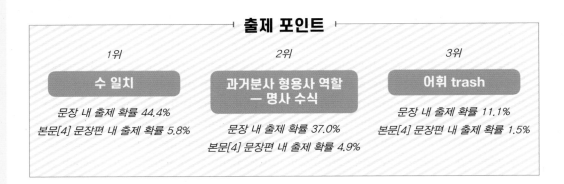

The giant pictures <u>made</u> from <u>trash</u> by environmental artist Tom Deininger <u>are</u> one of a kind.

과거분사 (명사 수식)　　쓰레기　　수 일치

출제 포인트

1위	*2위*	*3위*
수 일치	**과거분사 형용사 역할 – 명사 수식**	**어휘 trash**
문장 내 출제 확률 44.4%	문장 내 출제 확률 37.0%	문장 내 출제 확률 11.1%
본문[4] 문장편 내 출제 확률 5.8%	본문[4] 문장편 내 출제 확률 4.9%	본문[4] 문장편 내 출제 확률 1.5%

● 수 일치

문장2에서 출제될 가능성은 3.5%이다. 이 문장에서는 44.4%의 확률로 수 일치를 물을 수 있다. 이 문장의 주어는 The giant pictures이고 are이 동사이다. 주어 The giant pictures와 수 일치하여 복수동사 are이 와야 한다는 것을 알아두자. 주어를 수식하는 과거분사 made를 본동사로 착각하지 않도록 하자.

> **Q. 다음 문장의 괄호 안에서 어법에 맞는 것을 고르시오.**
>
> The giant pictures made from trash by environmental artist Tom Deininger (is / are) one of a kind.

정답 are

주어 The giant pictures와 수 일치하여 복수동사 are이 적절하다.

● 과거분사 형용사 역할 – 명사 수식

37.0%의 확률로 과거분사 형용사 역할을 묻는다. 동사 make의 과거형과 과거분사형이 동일한 형태이기 때문에, 본동사인지 준동사인지 구별하는 문제가 출제될 가능성이 높다. made를 본동사로 혼동할 수 있지만, 주어 The giant pictures가 만드는(made) 동작의 대상이므로 본동사라면 are made가 되어야 한다. 또한, 본동사 are이 있으므로 준동사가 적절하다는 점을 이해하고, 현재분사와 과거분사를 구별하는 문제에서는 수식을 받는 명사 The giant pictures가 '만들어진' 것이므로 수동 의미를 나타내는 과거분사를 써야 한다는 것도 유의하자.

> **Q. 다음 문장의 괄호 안에서 어법에 맞는 것을 고르시오.**
>
> The giant pictures (are made / made) from trash by environmental artist Tom Deininger are one of a kind.

정답 made

이 문장의 본동사는 are이기 때문에 괄호에는 준동사가 들어가야 한다. 따라서 주어 The giant pictures를 수식하는 과거분사가 어법상 적절하다.

● 어휘 trash

11.1%의 확률로 어휘 trash를 묻는 문제가 출제될 수 있다. 예술가가 사람들이 쓸모없는 물건이라고 여기는 것들에 창의적인 솜씨를 더해 만든 예술작품의 예시에 해당하는 내용으로, 예술작품(the giant pictures)을 만든 재료는 trash(쓰레기)와 같은 어휘로 표현될 수 있다. 해당 어휘가 다른 말로 바뀌어 출제될 수 있으니, 유의어 junk, garbage, rubbish, litter, waste도 함께 알아두자. 영영풀이인 things that are no longer useful or wanted and that have been thrown away(더 이상 쓸모가 없거나 필요하지 않으며 버려진 것들)에서 useful (↔ useless), wanted(↔ unwanted) 등의 핵심 표현도 숙지해 두자.

Q. 다음 빈칸에 들어갈 말로 가장 적절한 것은?

   When artists add their own creative touches, things that most people consider junk are reborn as beautiful works of art. The giant pictures made from _____ by environmental artist Tom Deininger are one of a kind. Up close, these brightly colored creations look like a mixed-up mess of broken plastic, unwanted toys, and bent wire—all things that cannot be recycled. From farther away, however, they appear to blend together into marvelous landscapes or other paintings. There is also an artist who shows that even disposable cups can be reused as artistic material. For years, Gwyneth Leech has turned used coffee cups into brilliant art exhibits. After a cup is used by someone, she paints a unique design on it and hangs it with many other painted cups in front of a window or pretty background. These works from Leech and Deininger are not only pleasing to the eye, but they also naturally provoke an interest in environmental conservation in people.

① glass   ② trash   ③ metal   ④ coffee   ⑤ cash

정답 ②

쓸모가 없는 물건이 예술가의 손길을 통해 아름다운 예술작품으로 재탄생된다고 앞에서 언급했으므로, 더 이상 가치가 없거나 쓸모없는 물건으로 만들어진 그림을 소개하는 것이 문맥상 적절하다. 따라서 빈칸에 들어가기에 가장 적절한 것은 ② 'trash(쓰레기)'이다.
① 유리 ③ 금속
④ 커피 ⑤ 현금

● 어휘 one of a kind

7.4%의 확률로 one of a kind의 뜻을 물어볼 수 있다. 이 표현은 '독특한 것[사람]'이라는 의미이다. 쓰레기로 예술작품을 만들었다는 내용으로, 이렇게 만든 예술작품은 세상에서 단 하나뿐인 독특한 것이라는 의미를 one of a kind를 써서 나타냈다. 해당 표현의 영영풀이 a person or thing that is unlike anything or anyone else(다른 어떤 것이나 사람과는 다른 사람 또는 사물)을 활용하여, 어휘에 대한 설명을 묻거나 영영풀이에 해당하는 어휘를 본문에서 찾는 유형이 출제되었으므로 영영풀이도 기억해두자.

Q. 다음 중, 밑줄 친 단어의 영영풀이로 가장 적절한 것은?

   When artists add their own creative touches, things that most people consider junk are reborn as beautiful works of art. The giant pictures made from trash by environmental artist Tom Deininger are <u>one of a kind</u>.

① old things that are viewed as having no use or value
② a thing that is unlike anything else
③ not straight
④ designed to be thrown away after use
⑤ good in a way that gives pleasure or satisfaction

정답 ②

one of a kind는 '독특한 것'이라는 뜻이므로, 영영풀이로 가장 적절한 것은 ② '다른 어떤 것과도 다른 사물'이다.
① 쓸모도 가치도 없는 것으로 간주되는 낡은 것들
③ 곧지 않은
④ 사용 후에 버려지도록 디자인된
⑤ 즐거움이나 만족감을 주는 방식으로 좋은

출제 포인트 70.5% 정복!

문장3

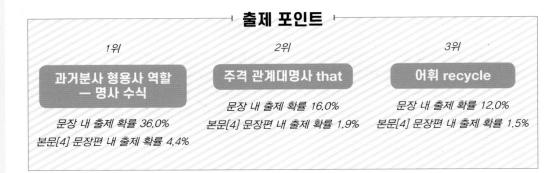

과거분사 (명사 수식)

Up close, these brightly <u>colored</u> creations look like a mixed-

과거분사 (명사 수식)

up mess of <u>broken</u> plastic, unwanted toys, and <u>bent</u> wire—all

과거분사 (명사 수식)

things <u>that</u> cannot be <u>recycled</u>.

주격 관계대명사 that   recycle: 재활용하다

┤ 출제 포인트 ├

1위	2위	3위
과거분사 형용사 역할 — 명사 수식	**주격 관계대명사 that**	**어휘 recycle**
	문장 내 출제 확률 16.0%	문장 내 출제 확률 12.0%
문장 내 출제 확률 36.0%	본문[4] 문장편 내 출제 확률 1.9%	본문[4] 문장편 내 출제 확률 1.5%
본문[4] 문장편 내 출제 확률 4.4%		

● 과거분사 형용사 역할 – 명사 수식

문장3에서 출제될 확률은 3.2%이다. 이 문장에서는 36.0% 확률로, 과거분사 형용사 역할을 가장 많이 묻는다. 수식을 받는 명사 creations, plastic, wire 모두 각 동작(color(색칠하다), break(부수다), bend(구부리다))의 대상이기 때문에, 수동 의미를 나타내는 과거분사를 사용한다는 점을 기억하자.

> **Q. 다음 글의 밑줄 친 (A), (B), (C)의 단어를 각각 알맞은 형태로 고치시오.**
>
> When artists add their own creative touches, things that most people consider junk are reborn as beautiful works of art. The giant pictures made from trash by environmental artist Tom Deininger are one of a kind. Up close, these brightly (A) <u>color</u> creation look like a mixed-up mess of (B) <u>break</u> plastic, unwanted toys, and (C) <u>bend</u> wire—all things that cannot be recycled.
>
> (A) _____
>
> (B) _____
>
> (C) _____

● 주격관계대명사 that

주격관계대명사 that 역시 16.0% 확률로 많이 나오는 포인트이다. 관계사절 내에서의 역할, 접속사 that과의 쓰임을 구별할 수 있는지를 확인하는 문제가 주로 출제된다. 이 문장에서 that은 뒤에 주어가 없는 불완전한 문장이 이어지므로 접속사가 될 수 없기 때문에, 주어 역할을 하는 관계대명사임을 알 수 있다. 이때, 형용사 all이 선행사 things를 수식하므로 관계대명사 that을 썼다. 선행사가 사물이므로 who로 바꿔 쓸 수 없고, 선행사가 있기 때문에 관계대명사 what을 쓸 수 없다는 것을 유의하자.

> **Q. 다음 문장의 밑줄 친 that과 쓰임이 다른 것은?**
>
> Up close, these brightly colored creations look like a mixed-up mess of broken plastic, unwanted toys, and bent wire—all things <u>that</u> cannot be recycled.
>
> ① His father scolded Jason <u>that</u> came home late.
> ② The school curriculum <u>that</u> stresses cultural diversity makes students open-minded.
> ③ It was Professor William <u>that</u> wrote a letter of recommendation for me.
> ④ A detective is someone <u>that</u> investigates crimes to catch criminals.
> ⑤ Hatred is an emotion <u>that</u> cannot be explained clearly.

정답 ③

주어진 문장에서, 앞에 선행사 all things가 있고, 뒤에 주어가 없는 불완전한 문장이 이어지므로, 밑줄 친 that은 주격관계대명사이다.

오답

①, ②, ④, ⑤도 각각 Jason, The school curriculum, someone, an emotion을 선행사로 하는 주격 관계대명사이다. 반면, ③의 that은 It was와 that 사이에 주어 Professor William을 두어서 주어를 강조하는 강조구문의 that이다.
① Jason의 아버지는 집에 늦게 들어온 그를 꾸짖었다.
② 문화적 다양성을 강조하는 학교 교육과정은 학생들을 편견이 없게 만든다.
③ 나를 위해 추천서를 쓴 사람은 William 교수님이었다.
④ 탐정은 범죄자들을 잡기 위해 범죄를 조사하는 사람이다.
⑤ 증오는 분명하게 설명될 수 없는 감정이다.

● 어휘 recycle

12.0% 확률로 어휘 recycle을 묻는다. 앞에 나열된 깨진 플라스틱, 버려진 장난감, 휘어진 선에 대한 부가 설명으로, 이것들을 '재활용'될 수 없는 물건들이라고 재언급하는 부분이다. 이때, 본문[1]을 바탕으로 재활용과 업사이클링을 구분할 수 있어야 한다. 또한, 해당 어휘의 영영풀이 to turn things that have already been used into new products(이미 사용된 것들을 새로운 제품으로 바꾸다)를 학습하여 영영풀이 활용 문제에 대비하자.

> **Q. 다음 빈칸에 들어갈 말로 가장 적절한 것을 고르시오.**
>
> The giant pictures made from trash by environmental artist Tom Deininger are one of a kind. Up close, these brightly colored creations look like a mixed-up mess of broken plastic, unwanted toys, and bent wire—all things that cannot be _____.
>
> ① discarded   ② delivered   ③ melted
> ④ assembled   ⑤ recycled

정답 ⑤

쓰레기로 예술작품을 만들었다는 내용이며, 쓰레기의 구체적인 예시로 깨진 플라스틱, 버려진 장난감, 휘어진 선들이 나열됨에 따라, 이 모든 것들은 '재활용될' 수 없는 물건들이라는 내용이 자연스럽다.
① 버려진 ② 전달된
③ 녹은 ④ 모인

● 어휘 mess

정답 ③

빈칸이 있는 문장 다음에 역접 관계를 나타내는 연결어 however가 있으므로, 빈칸이 있는 문장에는 뒷 내용과 반대되는 내용이 나와야 한다. 이어지는 내용에서, 그림을 멀리서 보는 경우에는 물건들이 보기 좋게 조합된다고 했으므로, 반대로 조합을 이루지 않고 엉망인 상태를 뜻하는 어휘가 빈칸에 들어가야 적절하다. 따라서 영영풀이로 적절한 것은 ③ '매우 지저분하거나 정돈되지 않은 상태 또는 환경'이다.
① 무언가를 개선하기 위해 그것에 추가된 작은 세부사항
② 가열되면 다른 모양으로 만들어지는 가볍고 튼튼한 재료
④ 대중에게 공개된 것들의 모음집
⑤ 얇고 유연한 금속사

8%의 확률로 mess의 뜻을 묻는다. 뒤에 역접 관계를 연결하는 연결어 however와 함께 물건들이 보기 좋게 조합된다는 내용이 이어지고, 이 문장에서는 이와 반대로 '부정적인 인상'을 준다는 내용이 나오는 흐름이다. 이를 mess(엉망인 상태)로 나타냈다. 영영풀이 a very dirty or disordered state or condition(매우 어수선하거나 정돈되지 않은 상태 또는 환경)도 함께 알아두자.

> **Q. 다음 빈칸에 들어갈 단어의 영영풀이로 가장 적절한 것은?**
>
> The giant pictures made from trash by environmental artist Tom Deininger are one of a kind. Up close, these brightly colored creations look like a mixed-up _____ of broken plastic, unwanted toys, and bent wire—all things that cannot be recycled. From farther away, however, they appear to blend together into marvelous landscapes or other paintings.
>
> ① a small detail added to something in order to improve it
> ② a light strong material made into different shapes when heated
> ③ a very dirty or untidy state or condition
> ④ a collection of things that are shown to the public
> ⑤ a thin, flexible thread of metal

● 어휘 creation

역시 8%의 확률로 creation의 뜻을 묻는다. 앞에 언급된 쓰레기로 만든 거대한 그림을 나타내므로, 창작물을 나타내는 명사 creation이 적절하며, 동사 create에서 파생된 다른 명사 creativity(창의력), creature(생물)와 혼동하지 않도록 유의하자. 해당 어휘의 영영풀이를 숙지하여 대비하자.

creation: a noble thing that somebody has made to show one's ability or imagination
　　　　(누군가가 자신의 능력이나 상상력을 보여주기 위해 만든 참신한 것)

정답

(A) trash　(B) creations

(A) 앞 문장에서 '대부분의 사람들이 쓰레기로 여기던 사물들이 아름다운 예술작품으로 다시 태어난다'는 내용이 있으므로, (A)에는 '쓰레기'로 만들어진 그림이라는 내용이 되어야 한다.
treasure: 보물
(B) 앞에서 예술가들의 작품에 대해 이야기하고 있으므로, (B)에는 '작품들'이 들어가는 것이 적절하다.
creature: 생물

> **Q. 다음 글의 (A), (B)의 각 네모 안에서 문맥상 적절한 낱말을 고르시오.**
>
> When artists add their own creative touches, things that most people consider junk are reborn as beautiful works of art. The giant pictures made from (A) treasure / trash by environmental artist Tom Deininger are one of a kind. Up close, these brightly colored (B) creations / creatures look like a mixed-up mess of broken plastic, unwanted toys, and bent wire—all things that cannot be recycled.

출제 포인트 72.4% 정복!

130

> ~인 것 같다   빈칸 appear to ~ paintings
> **From farther away**, **however**, **they** appear to blend together into marvelous landscapes or other paintings.

출제 포인트

공동 1위	공동 1위	3위
빈칸 appear to ~ paintings	**빈칸 From farther away**	**어휘 appear**
문장 내 출제 확률 28.6%	문장 내 출제 확률 28.6%	문장 내 출제 확률 23.8%
본문[4] 문장편 내 출제 확률 2.9%	본문[4] 문장편 내 출제 확률 2.9%	본문[4] 문장편 내 출제 확률 2.4%

● **빈칸 appear to blend together into marvelous landscapes or other paintings**

문장4는 2.7% 확률로 출제될 수 있다. 이 문장에서는 appear to ~ paintings를 빈칸으로 묻는 문제가 28.6%로 출제될 수 있다. '물건들이 엉망인 상태로 섞여 있는 것 같다'는 앞 내용이 연결어 however로 연결되면서, 앞 내용과 반대되는 내용, 즉 긍정적인 묘사가 포함된 부분이다. 빈칸 부분이 본문에서 변형되어 출제되는 경우가 있으니 이에 대비할 수 있어야 한다. blend, put together, mix, mingle, match와 같은 어휘를 사용해서 '물건들이 보기 좋게 조화된다'는 내용을 고르도록 하자.

> **Q. 다음 빈칸에 들어갈 말로 가장 적절한 것은?**
>
> When artists add their own creative touches, things that most people consider junk are reborn as beautiful works of art. The giant pictures made from trash by environmental artist Tom Deininger are one of a kind. Up close, these brightly colored creations look like a mixed-up mess of broken plastic, unwanted toys, and bent wire—all things that cannot be recycled. From farther away, however, they _____. There is also an artist who shows that even disposable cups can be reused as artistic material. For years, Gwyneth Leech has turned used coffee cups into brilliant art exhibits. After a cup is used by someone, she paints a unique design on it and hangs it with many other painted cups in front of a window or pretty background. These works from Leech and Deininger are not only pleasing to the eye, but they also naturally provoke an interest in environmental conservation in people.
>
> ① seem like a playground for living creatures
> ② prove to be an imitation of a famous masterpiece
> ③ are found to be the source of the unpleasant odor
> ④ obstruct magnificent views of the surrounding countryside
> ⑤ appear to blend together into marvelous landscapes or other paintings

정답 ⑤

⑤ 역접 관계를 나타내는 연결어 however가 그림을 가까이서 보는 경우와 반대되는 내용을 연결하는 흐름으로, ⑤ '보기 좋게 조합되어, 멋진 풍경이나 다른 그림들처럼 보인다'가 적절하다.
① 생명체들의 놀이터처럼 보인다
② 유명한 걸작의 모조품인 것으로 판명된다
③ 불쾌한 냄새의 원인으로 밝혀진다
④ 주변 전원의 웅장한 경치를 가로막는다

● 빈칸 From farther away

이 문장을 시작하는 표현인 From farther away를 묻는 문제 역시 28.6% 확률로 출제될 수 있다. 앞서 '그림을 가까이서 보는 경우'가 언급되었고 연결어 however와 함께 뒤에는 반대되는 내용인 '멀리서 보는 경우'가 이어지는 흐름이다. '더 먼' 거리에서 보는 경우를 나타내기 위해 far의 비교급 farther와 further 중에서 farther가 쓰였다. '한 층 더 깊은' 정도를 나타내는 further와 혼동하지 않도록 유의하자.

정답 farther

연결어 however로 보아, 가까이서 보는 경우를 나타내는 앞 내용과 반대되는 내용이 이어져야 하므로, '거리상으로 더 먼' 경우를 나타내는 farther가 적절하다.

> **Q. 다음 글의 괄호 안에서 어법에 맞는 것을 고르시오.**
>
> The giant pictures made from trash by environmental artist Tom Deininger are one of a kind. Up close, these brightly colored creations look like a mixed-up mess of broken plastic, unwanted toys, and bent wire—all things that cannot be recycled. From (farther / further) away, however, they appear to blend together into marvelous landscapes or other paintings.

● 어휘 appear

어휘 appear의 의미를 묻는 문제도 23.8% 확률로 자주 출제된다. appear는 여러 의미가 있으므로, 본문에서 어떤 의미로 쓰였는지 잘 파악해야 한다. '나타나다', '생기다', '출연하다'라는 의미 외에도, 〈appear to-v〉의 형태로 쓰여 '~인 것 같다'라는 의미를 갖는다.

정답 ①

주어진 문장과 ①의 appear는 각각 뒤에 to부정사와 that절과 함께 쓰여 '~인 것 같다'라는 의미를 갖는다.
① 양측 모두 할 말이 많은 것 같다.
② 난데없이 길 잃은 개가 나타났다.
③ 그는 공룡이 언제 지구에 나타났는지 알지도 모른다.
④ 그녀가 금메달을 딴 사진이 신문에 실려 있다.
⑤ 이 나무들은 한국의 천연기념물 목록에 올라 있다.

> **Q. 다음 문장의 밑줄 친 appear와 같은 의미로 쓰인 것은?**
>
> From farther away, however, they appear to blend together into marvelous landscapes or other paintings.
>
> ① It appears that both sides have much to say.
> ② A stray dog appeared out of nowhere.
> ③ He might know when dinosaurs appeared on the earth.
> ④ A picture of her winning a gold medal appears in the paper.
> ⑤ These trees appear on a list of Korea's natural monuments.

● 연결어 however

연결어 however를 묻는 문제는 9.5% 확률로 출제된다. 앞 문장에서 그림을 가까이서 보는 경우를 다루고, 이 문장에서는 그림을 멀리서 보는 경우를 다루기 때문에, 역접 관계를 나타내는 연결어 however가 쓰였다. 이와 비슷한 의미를 가진 though도 함께 알아두자.

정답 ②

(A) 앞에서 그림을 가까이서 보는 경우를 서술했으며, 이어지는 내용에서는 그림을 멀리서 보는 경우를 서술하고 있으므로, 역접 관계를 나타내는 연결어 however나 in contrast가 적절하다.
(B) 앞 문장에서는 쓰레기들을 활용한 예술작품으로 거대한 그림을 제시했으며, 이어지는 문장에서는 또 다른 예시를 제시하고 있으므로, 첨가를 나타내는 연결어 Furthermore나 Moreover가 적절하다.
[원문 변형] There is also an artist → Furthermore, there is an artist

> **Q. 글의 빈칸 (A), (B)에 들어갈 말로 가장 적절한 것은?**
>
> When artists add their own creative touches, things that most people consider junk are reborn as beautiful works of art. The giant pictures made from trash by environmental artist Tom Deininger are one of a kind. Up close, these brightly colored creations look like a mixed-up mess of broken plastic, unwanted toys, and bent wire—all things that cannot be recycled. From farther away, _____(A)_____, they appear to blend together into marvelous landscapes or other paintings. _____(B)_____, there is an artist who shows that even disposable cups can be reused as artistic material. For years, Gwyneth Leech has turned used coffee cups into brilliant art exhibits.

	(A)	(B)
①	likewise	– In short
②	however	– Furthermore
③	for instance	– Instead
④	in contrast	– Otherwise
⑤	moreover	– In fact

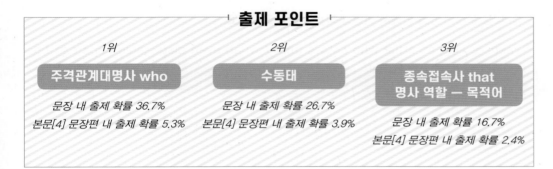

① 마찬가지로 – 요약하면
③ 예를 들어 – 대신에
④ 대조적으로 – 그렇지 않으면
⑤ 게다가 – 사실

출제 포인트 74.2% 정복!

문장5

문장 출제 확률: 3.9% (총 771개의 출제 포인트 중, 30회 출현, 46개 문장 중 3위)

주격관계대명사 who   종속접속사 that 명사 역할 – 목적어

There is also an artist <u>who</u> shows <u>that</u> even disposable cups can be reused as artistic material.

수동태

출제 포인트

1위	*2위*	*3위*
주격관계대명사 who	**수동태**	**종속접속사 that 명사 역할 — 목적어**
문장 내 출제 확률 36.7%	*문장 내 출제 확률 26.7%*	*문장 내 출제 확률 16.7%*
본문[4] 문장편 내 출제 확률 5.3%	*본문[4] 문장편 내 출제 확률 3.9%*	*본문[4] 문장편 내 출제 확률 2.4%*

● **주격관계대명사 who**

문장5에서 문제가 출제될 확률은 3.9%이다. 이 문장에서는 36.7% 확률로 주격관계대명사 who에 관한 문제가 출제될 수 있다. 주격관계대명사 who는 사람이 선행사이고, 관계사가 관계사절 안에서 주어 역할을 할 때 사용한다. 여기서는 which와 who, what과 who, 또는 관계부사와 관계대명사를 구별하는 문제로 출제될 수 있으니, 주격관계대명사 who의 문법적 특징에 대한 이해를 점검할 수 있도록 관련 문제를 풀어보며 대비하자. 또한, 〈주격관계대명사 + 동사〉 대신 분사로 바꿔 쓴 형태로, who shows가 showing으로 변형되어 출제될 수 있다는 점도 기억하자.

> **Q. 다음 문장의 괄호 안에서 어법상 적절한 것을 고르시오.**
>
> There is also an artist (who / what) shows that even disposable cups can be reused as artistic material.

정답 who

괄호 뒤에 주어가 없는 불완전한 절이 이어지므로, 주어 역할을 하며 두 문장을 연결하는 주격관계대명사가 와야 한다. 선행사가 an artist이기 때문에, 사람이 선행사일 때 사용하는 주격관계대명사 who가 적절하다.

● 수동태

that절에서 쓰인 수동태에 관련된 문제가 26.7% 확률로 출제될 수 있다. that절의 주어 disposable cups가 재사용될 수 있는 것이므로 주어와 동사는 수동관계이다. 동사의 수동태 형태는 〈be동사＋과거분사〉의 형태로 사용되는데, 조동사 can이 있으므로 〈조동사＋be＋과거분사〉로 써야 한다. 주로 동사의 태를 구별하는 문제가 출제되기 때문에, 주어와 동사의 관계를 한 번 더 확인하자.

> **Q. 다음 문장에서 주어진 동사를 빈칸에 알맞은 형태로 고치시오.**
>
> There is also an artist who shows that even disposable cups can _____ (reuse) as artistic material.
>
> _____

● 종속접속사 that 명사 역할 – 목적어

명사절을 이끄는 종속접속사 that에 관한 문제가 16.7% 확률로 출제될 수 있다. 접속사 that은 뒤에 주어와 동사가 포함된 완전한 절을 이끌며, that이 이끄는 절은 문장에서 명사 역할을 할 수 있다. which 또는 what과 같이 관계대명사와 구별하는 문제가 주로 출제된다. 관계대명사 뒤에는 불완전한 절이 온다는 차이점을 확실히 알고 있어야 한다.

> **Q. 다음 문장의 괄호 안에서 어법상 적절한 것을 고르시오.**
>
> There is also an artist who shows (that / what) even disposable cups can be reused as artistic material.

● 어휘 reuse, disposable

6.7% 확률로 문장5의 reuse와 disposable이 문제로 나올 수 있다. reuse는 환경에 긍정적인 영향을 미치는 뜻의 어휘이며, '재사용하다'라는 의미를 가지고 있다. repurpose, recycle, upcycle 등의 낱말도 환경에 도움이 되는 유사한 기능을 나타낸다고 볼 수 있다. 반면, abandon, desert, dump 등은 '버리다'라는 의미로, 환경에 부정적인 영향을 미치는 뜻의 어휘이다. 한편, disposable은 '일회용의'라는 뜻으로, 영영풀이는 designed to be thrown away after use(사용 후 버려지도록 디자인된)이다. single-use, non-reusable, throwaway와 같은 어휘로 바꿔 쓸 수 있다. recyclable, reusable과 같은 반대 의미의 단어도 함께 익혀두도록 하자.

> **Q. 다음 빈칸에 들어갈 알맞은 단어를 주어진 영영풀이에 맞게 쓰시오.**
>
> | designed to be thrown away after use |
> |---|
>
> There is also an artist who shows that even _____ cups can be reused as artistic material. For years, Gwyneth Leech has turned used coffee cups into brilliant art exhibits. After a cup is used by someone, she paints a unique design on it and hangs it with many other painted cups in front of a window or pretty background.
>
> _____

● 부사 Also

이 문장에서 6.7% 확률로, 연결어 역할을 하는 부사 also에 관해 물을 수 있다. Tom Deininger처럼 사람들이 쓰레기라고 여기는 것들을 활용하는 또 다른 예술가 Gwyneth Leech를 추가로 소개하기 위해 '또한'이라는 뜻의 부사가 쓰였다. 비슷한 의미를 가진 Besides, In addition으로 바꿔 쓰는 표현이 문제로 출제될 수 있다. also를 단서로 하여 순서나 문장 삽입 유형 문제도 자주 출제되므로, 이 문장의 위치도 눈여겨보자.

> **Q. 다음 빈칸에 들어갈 수 있는 것을 <u>모두</u> 고르시오.**
>
> When artists add their own creative touches, things that most people consider junk are reborn as beautiful works of art. The giant pictures made from trash by environmental artist Tom Deininger are one of a kind. Up close, these brightly colored creations look like a mixed-up mess of broken plastic, unwanted toys, and bent wire—all things that cannot be recycled. From farther away, however, they appear to blend together into marvelous landscapes or other paintings. _____, there is an artist who shows that even disposable cups can be reused as artistic material. For years, Gwyneth Leech has turned used coffee cups into brilliant art exhibits. After a cup is used by someone, she paints a unique design on it and hangs it with many other painted cups in front of a window or pretty background.
>
> ① Also ② Besides ③ Nevertheless ④ However ⑤ Otherwise

정답 ①, ②

빈칸 이후에 오는 문장은 앞서 설명된 Tom Deininger와 더불어 쓰레기로 예술작품을 만드는 예술가를 추가로 제시하고 있다. 따라서 빈칸에 들어갈 연결어는 추가 정보를 제시하는 Also(또한)와 Besides(게다가)이다.
[원문 변형]
There is also an artist ~ →
Also, there is an artist ~
③ 그럼에도 불구하고
④ 그러나
⑤ 그렇지 않으면

● 빈칸 can be reused as artistic material

마찬가지로 6.7% 확률로, can be reused as artistic material 부분을 빈칸으로 하는 문제가 출제된다. 예술가 Tom Deininger처럼 쓰레기로 예술작품을 재탄생시키는 예술가 Gwyneth Leech를 소개하는 내용으로, '일회용품이 예술적 소재가 된다'는 핵심이 빈칸으로 출제된다.

> **Q. 다음 빈칸에 들어갈 말로 가장 적절한 것은?**
>
> When artists add their own creative touches, things that most people consider junk are reborn as beautiful works of art. The giant pictures made from trash by environmental artist Tom Deininger are one of a kind. Up close, these brightly colored creations look like a mixed-up mess of broken plastic, unwanted toys, and bent wire—all things that cannot be recycled. From farther away, however, they appear to blend together into marvelous landscapes or other paintings. There is also an artist who shows that even disposable cups can be reused as _____. For years, Gwyneth Leech has turned used coffee cups into brilliant art exhibits. After a cup is used by someone, she paints a unique design on it and hangs it with many other painted cups in front of a window or pretty background. These works from Leech and Deininger are not only pleasing to the eye, but they also naturally provoke an interest in environmental conservation in people.
>
> ① renewable energy resources ② toys for children ③ artistic material
> ④ eco-friendly flowerpots ⑤ shelters for birds

정답 ③

본문에 제시된 예술가들은 모두 쓰레기나 다시 쓸 수 없을 것이라고 생각되는 것들을 가지고서 아름다운 작품으로 만드는 일을 한다. 따라서 빈칸에는 ③ 'artistic material(예술적 재료)'이 적절하다.
① 재생 에너지 자원
② 아이들을 위한 장난감
④ 친환경 화분
⑤ 새들을 위한 피난처

출제 포인트 77% 정복!

현재완료 – 계속

For years, Gwyneth Leech **has turned** used coffee cups into brilliant art **exhibits**.

능동태

exhibit: 전시품

출제 포인트

1위	2위	3위
현재완료 – 계속	능동태	어휘 exhibit
문장 내 출제 확률 27.8%	문장 내 출제 확률 22.2%	문장 내 출제 확률 16.7%
본문[4] 문장편 내 출제 확률 2.4%	본문[4] 문장편 내 출제 확률 1.9%	전체 지문 내 출제 확률 1.5%

● 현재완료 – 계속

문장6에서 출제될 확률은 2.3%이다. 이 문장에서는 현재완료 시제가 출제될 확률이 27.8%이다. 과거부터 지금까지 계속되는 일을 나타낼 때 현재완료 시제를 쓴다. 예술가 Gwyneth Leech가 과거부터 지금까지 수년 동안 사용된 커피컵을 미술 전시품으로 '바꿔 왔다'는 내용을 현재완료 시제로 나타냈다는 점을 기억하자. 옳지 않게 쓰인 과거완료 시제를 파악해 내는 문제가 출제되었으니, 이 점도 잘 기억해두자.

> **Q. 다음 글의 밑줄 친 (A)와 (B)의 형태를 알맞게 고치시오.**
>
> There is also an artist who shows that even disposable cups can (A) reuse as artistic material. For years, Gwyneth Leech (B) turned used coffee cups into brilliant art exhibits. After a cup is used by someone, she paints a unique design on it and hangs it with many other painted cups in front of a window or pretty background.
>
> (A) _____ (B) _____

● 능동태

22.2%의 확률로 동사의 태를 묻는 문제가 출제될 수 있다. 주어 Gwyneth Leech가 사용된 커피컵을 멋진 예술작품으로 '바꾸는' 주체이므로 주어와 동사 turn은 능동 관계이다. 동사의 태를 묻는 문제에 대비하여 주어와 동사의 관계를 파악해두자.

> **Q. 다음 글에서 어법상 어색한 부분을 찾아 올바르게 고치시오.**
>
> There is also an artist who shows that even disposable cups can be reused as artistic material. For years, Gwyneth Leech has been turned used coffee cups into brilliant art exhibits. After a cup is used by someone, she paints a unique design on it and hangs it with many other painted cups in front of a window or pretty background.
>
> _____ → _____

정답

(A) be reused
(B) has turned

(A) 일회용 컵이 스스로 무언가를 '재사용하는' 것이 아니라 예술적 재료로 '재사용되는' 것이므로, 수동태 be reused를 쓰는 것이 적절하다.
(B) 앞뒤 문장이 모두 현재 시제로 기술하고 있고, 해당 문장에 기간을 나타내는 For과 함께 '수년 동안 바꿔 왔다'는 의미로 현재완료 시제가 적절하다.

정답

has been turned
→ (has) turned

주어 Gwyneth Leech가 바꾸는(turn) 행위의 주체이므로 능동태를 써야 한다.

● 어휘 exhibit

어휘 exhibit의 의미를 묻는 문제가 16.7% 확률로 출제될 수 있다. 이 문장에서 exhibit은 동사가 아닌 명사로 '전시품'이라는 의미를 나타낸다. 유의어로 item, piece, work 등이 있으며, 영영풀이 an object or collection of objects presented or displayed for others to view in a gallery or museum(미술관 또는 박물관에서 다른 사람들이 볼 수 있도록 제시되거나 전시된 물건 또는 수집품)도 함께 알아두자.

> **Q. 다음 영영풀이에 해당하는 단어를 아래 글에서 찾아 쓰시오. (단, 기본형으로 쓸 것)**
>
> | an object or collection of objects presented or displayed for others to view in a gallery or museum |
> | --- |
>
> There is also an artist who shows that even disposable cups can be reused as artistic material. For years, Gwyneth Leech has turned used coffee cups into brilliant art exhibits. After a cup is used by someone, she paints a unique design on it and hangs it with many other painted cups in front of a window or pretty background.
>
> _____

정답 exhibit
영영풀이는 '미술관 또는 박물관에서 다른 사람들이 볼 수 있도록 제시되거나 전시된 물건 또는 수집품'이라고 설명하고 있다. 이는 '전시품'으로, 본문의 exhibit에 해당한다.

● 과거분사 used

이 문장에서 과거분사 used의 형태에 관해 문제가 출제될 확률은 11.1%이다. 동사 use는 과거형과 과거분사가 동일한 형태이므로 쓰임을 구분할 줄 아는 것이 중요하다. 이 문장에서 used는 명사 coffee cups를 수식하는 형용사 역할을 하는 준동사이다. 여기서 수식을 받는 대상이 사용되는 것이므로 수동 관계를 나타내는 과거분사가 적절하며, 현재분사와 과거분사 비교 문제로 많이 출제되기 때문에, 문제를 풀 때 분사와 수식을 받는 대상의 관계가 무엇인지 유의하자.

> **Q. 다음 글에서 어법상 어색한 부분을 찾아 바르게 고치시오.**
>
> For years, Gwyneth Leech has turned using coffee cups into brilliant art exhibits. After a cup is used by someone, she paints a unique design on it and hangs it with many other painted cups in front of a window or pretty background. These works from Leech and Deininger are not only pleasing to the eye, but they also naturally provoke an interest in environmental conservation in people.
>
> _____ → _____

정답 using → used
커피컵은 '사용된' 것이기 때문에 수동 의미를 나타내는 과거분사 used로 고쳐야 한다.

● 어휘 brilliant

어휘 brilliant에 관한 문제가 11.1% 확률로 출제될 수 있다. 예술가들이 쓰레기를 아름다운 예술 작품으로 다시 탄생시킨다는 내용의 글이므로, 예술가 Leech가 만든 예술작품에 대한 긍정적인 수식어가 오는 것이 문맥상 적절하다. 해당 문장에서는 '멋진, 근사한'이라는 의미의 brilliant를 사용했으며, 유의어로는 splendid, gorgeous, beautiful, awesome 등이 있다. 반면에, unpleasant, gross, offensive, awful과 같은 반의어를 활용한 선택지가 출제되기도 하므로 참고하도록 하자.

> **Q. 다음 빈칸에 들어갈 말로 적절하지 않은 것은?**
>
> When artists add their own creative touches, things that most people consider junk are reborn as beautiful works of art. The giant pictures made from trash by environmental artist Tom Deininger are one of a kind. Up close, these brightly

colored creations look like a mixed-up mess of broken plastic, unwanted toys, and bent wire—all things that cannot be recycled. From farther away, however, they appear to blend together into marvelous landscapes or other paintings. There is also an artist who shows that even disposable cups can be reused as artistic material. For years, Gwyneth Leech has turned used coffee cups into _____ art exhibits. After a cup is used by someone, she paints a unique design on it and hangs it with many other painted cups in front of a window or pretty background. These works from Leech and Deininger are not only pleasing to the eye, but they also naturally provoke an interest in environmental conservation in people.

① brilliant   ② splendid   ③ gorgeous   ④ awful   ⑤ outstanding

---

출제 포인트 78.5% 정복!

문장7

문장 출제 확률: 2.8%

> 수동태   병렬 구조
> **After a cup <u>is used</u> by someone, she <u>paints</u> a unique design on it <u>and hangs</u> it with many other <u>painted</u> cups in front of a window or pretty background.** 과거분사 형용사 역할 – 명사 수식

출제 포인트

1위	2위	3위
병렬 구조	**과거분사 형용사 역할 — 명사 수식**	**수동태**
문장 내 출제 확률 56.3%	문장 내 출제 확률 25.0%	문장 내 출제 확률 12.5%
본문[4] 문장편 내 출제 확률 4.4%	본문[4] 문장편 내 출제 확률 1.9%	본문[4] 문장편 내 출제 확률 1.0%

● 병렬 구조

이 문장에서 문제가 출제될 확률은 2.8%이다. 이 문장에서는 56.3%로 등위접속사 and로 연결된 병렬 구조를 묻는 문제가 나올 확률이 높다. 이와 같은 문제를 풀기 위해서는 우선 문맥을 파악하여 등위접속사로 연결되는 어구를 파악하는 것이 중요하다. 문법적 형태가 같은 paints와 hangs가 병렬 구조를 이루고 있다는 것을 숙지하자.

> Q. 다음 빈칸에 알맞도록 주어진 동사를 어법에 맞게 바꿔 쓰시오.
>
> After a cup is used by someone, she paints a unique design on it and _____ (hang) it with many other painted cups in front of a window or pretty background.
>
> _____

● 과거분사 형용사 역할 – 명사 수식

과거분사인 painted에 관해 묻는 문제가 25.0%의 확률로 출제될 수 있다. 과거분사는 '~된, ~(해)진'이라는 의미이다. 여기서 분사와 수식을 받는 대상(cups)은 수동 관계로, '그려진'의 의미인 과거분사 painted가 쓰였다. 알맞은 분사의 종류를 묻는 문제가 많이 출제되므로, 분사와 수식을 받는 대상과의 관계를 다시 한번 확인하도록 하자.

> Q. 다음 문장에서 어법상 어색한 부분을 찾아 바르게 고치시오.
>
> After a cup is used by someone, she paints a unique design on it and hangs it with many other painting cups in front of a window or pretty background.
>
> _____ → _____

정답
painting → painted
컵이 '(그림이) 그려진' 대상이므로 능동 의미를 나타내는 현재분사 painting을 수동 의미를 나타내는 과거분사 painted로 고쳐야 한다.

● 수동태

부사절에 쓰인 수동태에 관한 문제가 12.5% 확률로 출제될 수 있다. 접속사 After가 이끄는 부사절의 주어 a cup이 '사용되는' 것으로, 동작의 대상임을 나타내는 수동태가 쓰였다. 이 문장을 능동태를 사용하여 바꾸면 After someone uses a cup ~.이 된다. 주어에 따라 동사의 태를 전환하는 영작 유형 문제를 대비해야 하며, 이러한 문제를 풀 때는 먼저 주어를 파악하여 태를 결정하자.

> Q. 다음 문장에서 어법상 어색한 부분을 찾아 바르게 고치시오.
>
> After a cup uses by someone, she paints a unique design on it and hangs it with many other painted cups in front of a window or pretty background.
>
> _____ → _____

정답
uses → is used
문장에서 a cup은 (누군가에 의해) '사용된' 대상으로, 주어 a cup과 동사 use는 수동 관계이다. 따라서 능동태 형태인 uses를 수동태 is used로 고쳐야 한다.

출제 포인트 79.7% 정복!

문장8   문장 출제 확률: 4.7% (총 771개의 출제 포인트 중 36회 출현, 46개 문장 중 2위)

감정동사의 현재분사

These works from Leech and Deininger are not only <u>pleasing</u> **to the eye, but they also naturally** <u>provoke an interest in environmental conservation</u> **in people.**   빈칸 provoke ~ conservation

―― 출제 포인트 ――

1위	2위
감정동사의 현재분사	빈칸 provoke ~ conservation
문장 내 출제 확률 52.8%	문장 내 출제 확률 30.6%
본문[4] 문장편 내 출제 확률 9.2%	본문[4] 문장편 내 출제 확률 5.3%

● 감정동사의 현재분사

문장8에서 출제될 확률은 4.7%로, 2과 전체에서 두 번째로 많이 출제된 문장이다. 이 문장에서는 감정동사의 현재분사가 출제될 확률이 52.8%로 가장 높다. pleasing은 감정동사 please(기쁘게 하다)의 분사형으로, 주어 These works가 감정을 유발하기 때문에 현재분사 v-ing의 형태로 썼으며, '기쁨을 주는, 기쁘게 하는'의 의미이다. 현재분사와 과거분사를 비교하는 문제가 자주 출제되기 때문에, 주어가 감정을 유발하는지 또는 느끼는지를 파악해 두도록 하자. pleasing의 유의어 enjoyable, delightful과, 반의어인 unpleasant, nasty, disagreeable도 숙지해 두자.

정답

pleased → pleasing

주어 These works가 '기쁨을 느끼게 하는' 것이므로, 과거분사 pleased를 현재분사 pleasing으로 고쳐야 한다.

> **Q. 다음 문장에서 어법상 어색한 부분을 찾아 바르게 고치시오.**
>
> These works from Leech and Deininger are not only pleased to the eye, but they also naturally provoke an interest in environmental conservation in people.
>
> _____ → _____

● 빈칸 provoke an interest in environmental conservation

업사이클링을 거친 예술작품이 환경보호에 미치는 효과를 함축적으로 전달하는 내용이다. 이 글의 핵심 내용을 담은 부분으로, 유의어를 활용하여 주제나 제목을 묻는 문제가 나오거나, 빈칸 또는 요약 유형으로 출제될 가능성이 높다. provoke를 대신하여 stimulate, trigger, arouse, inspire, ignite, generate와 같은 어휘가, conservation 대신에 preservation, protection과 같은 어휘가 나올 수 있다는 점을 유의하자.

정답 ③

쓸모 없어진 물건들을 예술가들이 업사이클함으로써 사람들에게 즐거움을 줄 뿐만 아니라 ③ '환경 보존'에 대한 관심을 불러일으켰다는 것이 적절하다.
① 컵을 사용하는 새로운 방법
② 틀에 박히지 않은 예술 주제
④ 새로운 예술 장르
⑤ 오래된 유산의 보전

> **Q. 다음 글에서 빈칸에 들어갈 말로 적절한 것은?**
>
> When artists add their own creative touches, things that most people consider junk are reborn as beautiful works of art. The giant pictures made from trash by environmental artist Tom Deininger are one of a kind. Up close, these brightly colored creations look like a mixed-up mess of broken plastic, unwanted toys, and bent wire—all things that cannot be recycled. From farther away, however, they appear to blend together into marvelous landscapes or other paintings. There is also an artist who shows that even disposable cups can be reused as artistic material. For years, Gwyneth Leech has turned used coffee cups into brilliant art exhibits. After a cup is used by someone, she paints a unique design on it and hangs it with many other painted cups in front of a window or pretty background. These works from Leech and Deininger are not only pleasing to the eye, but they also naturally provoke an interest in _____ in people.
>
> ① new ways to use a cup　　　　② unconventional art themes
> ③ environmental conservation　　④ a new art genre
> ⑤ preservation of old heritages

01

다음 빈칸에 들어갈 말로 가장 적절한 것을 고르시오.

When artists add their own creative touches, things that most people consider junk are reborn as beautiful works of art. The giant pictures made from trash by environmental artist Tom Deininger are one of a kind. Up close, these brightly colored creations look like a mixed-up mess of broken plastic, unwanted toys, and bent wire—all things that cannot be recycled. From farther away, however, they appear to blend together into marvelous landscapes or other paintings. There is also an artist who shows that even disposable cups can be reused as artistic material. For years, Gwyneth Leech has turned used coffee cups into brilliant art exhibits. After a cup is used by someone, she paints a unique design on it and hangs it with many other painted cups in front of a window or pretty background. These works from Leech and Deininger are not only pleasing to the eye, but they also naturally _____ _____ in people.

① provoke an interest in environmental preservation
② inspire an interest in the conservation of cultural heritage
③ stimulate curiosity about the new artistic style
④ encourage an appreciation for nature's creation
⑤ provoke an interest in emerging artists of the new generation

02

다음 글의 밑줄 친 부분 중, 문맥상 적절하지 않은 것은?

When artists add their own creative ① touches, things that most people consider junk are ② reborn as beautiful works of art. The giant pictures made from trash by environmental artist Tom Deininger are one of a kind. Up close, these brightly colored ③ creations look like a mixed-up mess of broken plastic, unwanted toys, and bent wire—all things that cannot be recycled. From farther away, however, they appear to ④ blend together into marvelous landscapes or other paintings. There is also an artist who shows that even disposable cups can be reused as artistic material. For years, Gwyneth Leech has turned used coffee cups into brilliant art exhibits. After a cup is used by someone, she paints a unique design on it and hangs it with many other painted cups in front of a window or pretty background. These works from Leech and Deininger are not only pleasing to the eye, but they also naturally ⑤ discourage an interest in environmental conservation in people.

03

다음 글의 밑줄 친 부분 중, 우리말 해석이 적절하지 않은 것은?

There is also an artist who shows that even disposable cups can ① be reused as artistic material. For years, Gwyneth Leech has turned ② used coffee cups into brilliant art exhibits. After a cup ③ is used by someone, she paints a unique design on it and hangs it with many other painted cups in front of a window or pretty background. These works from Leech and Deininger ④ are not only pleasing to the eye, but they also naturally ⑤ provoke an interest in environmental conservation in people.

① 예술적 재료로 다시 사용되다
② 사용된 커피컵
③ 누군가에 의해 사용된다
④ 즐거움을 느낄 뿐만 아니라
⑤ 관심을 유발한다

04

다음 글의 밑줄 친 부분 중, 어법상 어색한 것을 찾아 번호를 쓰고 바르게 고쳐 쓰시오.

When artists add their own creative touches, things that most people consider junk are reborn as beautiful works of art. ① The giant pictures made from trash by environmental artist Tom Deininger are one of a kind. Up close, these brightly colored creations look like a mixed-up mess of broken plastic, unwanted toys, and bent wire—② all things that cannot be recycled. From farther away, however, ③ they appear to blend together into marvelous landscapes or other paintings. There is also an artist who shows that even disposable cups can be reused as artistic material. For years, Gwyneth Leech has turned used coffee cups into brilliant art exhibits. After a cup is used by someone, she paints a unique design on it and ④ hangs it with many other painted cups in front of a window or pretty background. ⑤ These works from Leech and Deininger are not only pleased to the eye, but they also naturally provoke an interest in environmental conservation in people.

(   ) _____ → _____

05

다음 글의 밑줄 친 부분 중, 어법상 어색한 부분을 알맞게 고치지 않은 것은?

When artists add their own creative touches, things that most people consider junk ① is reborn as beautiful works of art. The giant pictures ② making from trash by environmental artist Tom Deininger ③ is one of a kind. Up close, these brightly colored creations look like a mixed-up mess of broken plastic, unwanted toys, and bent wire—all things that cannot ④ recycle. From farther away, however, they appear to blend together into marvelous landscapes or other paintings. There is also an artist

⑤ which shows that even disposable cups can be reused as artistic material. For years, Gwyneth Leech has turned used coffee cups into brilliant art exhibits. After a cup is used by someone, she paints a unique design on it and hangs it with many other painted cups in front of a window or pretty background. These works from Leech and Deininger are not only pleasing to the eye, but they also naturally provoke an interest in environmental conservation in people.

① is → are   ② making → made
③ is → are   ④ recycle → be recycled
⑤ which → what

06

다음 빈칸에 들어갈 말로 가장 적절한 것은?

When artists add their own creative touches, things that most people consider junk are reborn as beautiful works of art. The giant pictures made from trash by environmental artist Tom Deininger are one of a kind. Up close, these brightly colored creations look like a mixed-up mess of broken plastic, unwanted toys, and bent wire—all things that cannot be recycled. From farther away, however, they appear to blend together into marvelous landscapes or other paintings. There is also an artist who shows that even _____ cups can be reused as artistic material. For years, Gwyneth Leech has turned used coffee cups into brilliant art exhibits. After a cup is used by someone, she paints a unique design on it and hangs it with many other painted cups in front of a window or pretty background. These works from Leech and Deininger are not only pleasing to the eye, but they also naturally provoke an interest in environmental conservation in people.

① indispensable   ② reusable   ③ glowing
④ disposable   ⑤ portable

07

다음 글의 밑줄 친 (A) that과 쓰임이 같은 것을 모두 고르시오.

When artists add their own creative touches, things that most people consider junk are reborn as beautiful works of art. The giant pictures made from trash by environmental artist Tom Deininger are one of a kind. Up close, these brightly colored creations look like a mixed-up mess of broken plastic, unwanted toys, and bent wire—all things that cannot be recycled. From farther away, however, they appear to blend together into marvelous landscapes or other paintings. There is also an artist who shows (A) that even disposable cups can be reused as artistic material. For years, Gwyneth Leech has turned used coffee cups into brilliant art exhibits. After a cup is used by someone, she paints a unique design on it and hangs it with many other painted cups in front of a window or pretty background. These works from Leech and Deininger are not only pleasing to the eye, but they also naturally provoke an interest in environmental conservation in people.

① The cookies that my mother made were sugar-free cookies.
② The book that I'm reading right now is very interesting.
③ He told me that he was running late for the meeting.
④ The restaurant that we went to last week had really good food.
⑤ She reminded me that we need to bring our passports to the airport.

08

다음 중, 괄호 안에 주어진 단어의 형태를 알맞게 변형하지 않은 것은?

When artists add their own creative touches, things that most people consider junk ①_____(be) reborn as beautiful works of art. The giant pictures ②_____(make) from trash by environmental artist Tom Deininger are one of a kind. Up close, these brightly colored creations look like a mixed-up mess of broken plastic, unwanted toys, and bent wire—all things that cannot ③_____ (recycle). From farther away, however, they appear ④_____(blend) together into marvelous landscapes or other paintings. There is also an artist who shows that even disposable cups can ⑤_____(reuse) as artistic material. For years, Gwyneth Leech has turned used coffee cups into brilliant art exhibits. After a cup is used by someone, she paints a unique design on it and hangs it with many other painted cups in front of a window or pretty background. These works from Leech and Deininger are not only pleasing to the eye, but they also naturally provoke an interest in environmental conservation in people.

① are　　　② made　　　③ be recycled
④ to blend　　　⑤ reuse

09

다음 중, 밑줄 친 우리말을 나타내기에 어법상 어색한 것은?

When artists add their own creative touches, 대부분의 사람들이 쓰레기로 여기는 사물들이 are reborn as beautiful works of art.

① things which most people consider junk
② what most people consider things junk
③ what most people consider junk
④ things that most people consider junk
⑤ things most people consider junk

10

다음 글의 밑줄 친 (A)와 같은 용법으로 사용된 것은?

There is also an artist who shows that even disposable cups can be reused as artistic material. For years, Gwyneth Leech (A) has turned used coffee cups into brilliant art exhibits. After a cup is used by someone, she paints a unique design on it and hangs it with many other painted cups in front of a window or pretty background. These works from Leech and Deininger are not only pleasing to the eye, but they also naturally provoke an interest in environmental conservation in people.

① I have lost my wallet on my way home.
② Have you ever been to Egypt?
③ I have already finished my homework.
④ She has just finished her dessert.
⑤ I haven't met him since I was a kid.

① an object or a collection of objects displayed in a public space
② a piece of land that possesses a particular quality or appearance
③ things that are unwanted or useless
④ the protection of the natural environment and resources
⑤ something new and original that is made, using one's imagination and skill

11

다음 빈칸에 들어갈 단어의 영영풀이로 가장 적절한 것은?

When artists add their own creative touches, things that most people consider _____ are reborn as beautiful works of art. The giant pictures made from trash by environmental artist Tom Deininger are one of a kind. Up close, these brightly colored creations look like a mixed-up mess of broken plastic, unwanted toys, and bent wire—all things that cannot be recycled. From farther away, however, they appear to blend together into marvelous landscapes or other paintings. There is also an artist who shows that even disposable cups can be reused as artistic material. For years, Gwyneth Leech has turned used coffee cups into brilliant art exhibits. After a cup is used by someone, she paints a unique design on it and hangs it with many other painted cups in front of a window or pretty background. These works from Leech and Deininger are not only pleasing to the eye, but they also naturally provoke an interest in environmental conservation in people.

12

다음 글의 밑줄 친 부분의 어법 설명으로 옳지 않은 것은?

When artists add their own creative touches, things (a) that most people consider junk are reborn as beautiful works of art. The giant pictures made from trash by environmental artist Tom Deininger (b) are one of a kind. Up close, these (c) brightly colored creations look like a mixed-up mess of broken plastic, unwanted toys, and (d) bent wire— all things that cannot be (e) recycled.

① (a): 뒤에 주어와 동사가 있는 완전한 형태의 명사절을 이끄는 접속사 역할을 한다.
② (b): 과거분사구 made from trash by environmental artist Tom Deininger의 수식을 받는 복수명사 The giant pictures가 주어이므로 수 일치를 하여 복수동사를 썼다.
③ (c): 과거분사 colored를 수식하는 부사로, '밝게'라고 해석한다.
④ (d): 수식을 받는 명사 wire가 휘어진 것이므로, 수동 관계를 나타내는 과거분사가 적절하다.
⑤ (e): 주어 all things가 재활용될 수 없는 대상임을 나타내는 수동태 표현의 일부이다.

13

다음 글의 (A), (B), (C)의 각 네모 안에서 어법상 알맞은 말로 바르게 연결된 것은?

When artists add their own creative touches, things that most people consider junk (A) is / are reborn as beautiful works of art. The giant pictures made from trash by environmental artist Tom Deininger (B) is / are one of a kind. Up close, these brightly colored creations look like a mixed-up mess of broken plastic, unwanted toys, and bent wire—all things that cannot be recycled. From farther away, however, they appear to (C) blend / blending together into marvelous landscapes or other paintings. There is also an artist who shows that even disposable cups can be reused as artistic material. For years, Gwyneth Leech has turned used coffee cups into brilliant art exhibits. After a cup is used by someone, she paints a unique design on it and hangs it with many other painted cups in front of a window or pretty background. These works from Leech and Deininger are not only pleasing to the eye, but they also naturally provoke an interest in environmental conservation in people.

```
     (A)      (B)       (C)
① is   −  is    −  blend
② is   −  are   −  blend
③ are  −  are   −  blend
④ are  −  are   −  blending
⑤ are  −  is    −  blending
```

14

다음 빈칸에 들어갈 단어의 영영풀이로 가장 적절한 것은?

When artists add their own creative touches, things that most people consider junk are reborn as beautiful works of art. The giant pictures made from trash by environmental artist Tom Deininger are one of a kind. Up close, these brightly colored creations look like a mixed-up mess of broken plastic, unwanted toys, and bent wire—all things that cannot be _____(e)d. From farther away, however, they appear to blend together into marvelous landscapes or other paintings. There is also an artist who shows that even disposable cups can be reused as artistic material. For years, Gwyneth Leech has turned used coffee cups into brilliant art exhibits. After a cup is used by someone, she paints a unique design on it and hangs it with many other painted cups in front of a window or pretty background. These works from Leech and Deininger are not only pleasing to the eye, but they also naturally provoke an interest in environmental conservation in people.

① to put things together thoroughly and usually with good results
② to suspend something, or to be suspended, at the top
③ to arouse a particular reaction or have a particular effect
④ to mix or mingle a thing with other things
⑤ to get used things processed in order to use them again

15

다음 글의 괄호 안에 주어진 단어의 형태를 바르게 변형하지 않은 것은?

When artists add their own creative touches, things that most people consider junk ⓐ (reborn) as beautiful works of art. The giant pictures ⓑ (make) from trash by environmental artist Tom Deininger are one of a kind. Up close, these brightly colored creations look like a mixed-up mess of broken plastic, unwanted toys, and ⓒ (bend) wire— all things that cannot be recycled. From ⓓ (far) away, however, they appear to blend together into marvelous landscapes or other paintings. There is also an artist who shows that even disposable cups can be reused as artistic material. For years, Gwyneth Leech has turned ⓔ (use) coffee cups into brilliant art exhibits. After a cup is used by someone, she paints a unique design on it and hangs it with many other painted cups in front of a window or pretty background. These works from Leech and Deininger are not only pleasing to the eye, but they also naturally provoke an interest in environmental conservation in people.

① ⓐ → are reborn   ② ⓑ → to make
③ ⓒ → bent   ④ ⓓ → farther
⑤ ⓔ → used

16

다음 글의 밑줄 친 부분 중, 문맥상 어색한 것은?

When artists add their own creative touches, things that most people consider junk are reborn as beautiful works of art. ① The giant pictures made from trash by environmental artist Tom Deininger are the usual things. Up close, these brightly colored creations look like a mixed-up mess of broken plastic, unwanted toys, and bent wire—all things that cannot be recycled. From farther away, however, ② they appear to blend together into marvelous landscapes or other paintings. There is also an artist who shows that even disposable cups can be reused as artistic material. For years, ③ Gwyneth Leech has turned used coffee cups into brilliant art exhibits. After a cup is used by someone, ④ she paints a unique design on it and hangs it with many other painted cups in front of a window or pretty background. ⑤ These works from Leech and Deininger are not only pleasing to the eye, but they also naturally provoke an interest in environmental conservation in people.

17

다음 글의 밑줄 친 단어의 영영풀이로 적절하지 않은 것은?

When artists add their own ⓐ creative touches, things that most people consider junk are reborn as beautiful works of art. The giant pictures made from ⓑ trash by environmental artist Tom Deininger are one of a kind. Up close, these brightly colored creations look like a mixed-up ⓒ mess of broken plastic, unwanted toys, and bent wire—all things that cannot be recycled. From farther away, however, they appear to ⓓ blend together into marvelous landscapes or other paintings. There is also an artist who shows that even disposable cups can be reused as artistic ⓔ material. For years, Gwyneth Leech has turned used coffee cups into brilliant art exhibits. After a cup is used by someone, she paints a unique design on it and hangs it with many other painted cups in front of a window or pretty background. These works from Leech and Deininger are not only pleasing to the eye, but they also naturally provoke an interest in environmental conservation in people.

① ⓐ: using the ability or imagination to make or think of something original
② ⓑ: things that are no longer useless and unwanted
③ ⓒ: a very dirty or disordered state or condition
④ ⓓ: to mix with something in an attractive or effective way
⑤ ⓔ: a substance from which something is made or can be created

18

다음 글의 빈칸 (A), (B)에 들어갈 말로 가장 적절한 것은?

When artists add their own creative touches, things that most people consider junk are reborn as beautiful works of art. The giant pictures made from trash by environmental artist Tom Deininger _____(A)_____ one of a kind. Up close, these brightly colored creations look like a mixed-up mess of broken plastic, unwanted toys, and bent wire—all things that cannot be recycled. From farther away, however, they appear to blend together into marvelous landscapes or other paintings. There is also an artist who shows that even disposable cups can be reused as artistic material. For years, Gwyneth Leech has turned used coffee cups into brilliant art exhibits. After a cup is used by someone, she paints a unique design on _____(B)_____ and hangs it with many other painted cups in front of a window or pretty background. These works from Leech and Deininger are not only pleasing to the eye, but they also naturally provoke an interest in environmental conservation in people.

	(A)		(B)		(A)		(B)
①	is	–	it	②	is	–	them
③	are	–	it	④	are	–	them
⑤	are	–	itself				

19

다음 글의 밑줄 친 부분 중, 어법상 틀린 것을 찾아 바르게 고치시오. (단, 본문에 있는 단어로 고칠 것)

When artists add their own creative touches, things ① that most people consider junk are reborn as beautiful works of art. The giant pictures made from trash by environmental artist Tom Deininger ② are one of a kind. Up close, these brightly colored creations look like a mixed-up mess of broken plastic, unwanted toys, and bent wire—all things ③ whose cannot be recycled. From farther away, however, they appear ④ to blend together into marvelous landscapes or other paintings. There is also an artist who shows that even disposable cups can be reused as artistic material. For years, Gwyneth Leech ⑤ has turned used coffee cups into brilliant art exhibits. After a cup is used by someone, she paints a unique design on it and hangs it with many other painted cups in front of a window or pretty background. These works from Leech and Deininger are not only pleasing to the eye, but they also naturally provoke an interest in environmental conservation in people.

(　　) _____ → _____

20

다음 중, 밑줄 친 부분의 쓰임이 〈보기〉와 다른 것은?

> 〈보기〉 Up close, these brightly colored creations look like a mixed-up mess of broken plastic, unwanted toys, and bent wire—all things that cannot be recycled.

① A puppy called Milo was found with its leg caught in a net.
② Teenagers influenced by their peers become easy targets for SNS advertisements.
③ Trust established between parents and children is stronger than that in any other relationship.
④ A brave citizen overpowered a bank robber in the act of threatening bankers with a gun.
⑤ People living in developed countries are more likely to suffer from sleep disorders.

21

다음 글의 밑줄 친 부분 중, 문맥상 낱말의 쓰임이 적절하지 않은 것은?

When artists add their own creative touches, things that most people consider ① junk are reborn as beautiful works of art. The giant pictures made from trash by environmental artist Tom Deininger are one of a kind. Up close, these brightly colored creations look like a mixed-up ② harmony of broken plastic, unwanted toys, and bent wire—all things that cannot be recycled. From farther away, however, they appear to ③ blend together into marvelous landscapes or other paintings. There is also an artist who shows that even ④ disposable cups can be reused as artistic material. For years, Gwyneth Leech has turned used coffee cups into brilliant art ⑤ exhibits. After a cup is used by someone, she paints a unique design on it and hangs it with many other painted cups in front of a window or pretty background. These works from Leech and Deininger are not only pleasing to the eye, but they also naturally provoke an interest in environmental conservation in people.

22

다음 글의 밑줄 친 ⓐ~ⓔ와 바꿔 쓸 수 없는 것은?

When artists add their own creative touches, things that most people consider junk are reborn as beautiful works of art. The giant pictures made from ⓐ trash by environmental artist Tom Deininger are one of a kind. Up close, these brightly colored creations look like a mixed-up mess of ⓑ broken plastic, unwanted toys, and bent wire—all things that cannot be recycled. From farther away, however, they appear to ⓒ blend together into marvelous landscapes or other paintings. There is also an artist who shows that even ⓓ disposable cups can be reused as artistic material. For years, Gwyneth Leech has turned used coffee cups into brilliant art exhibits. After a cup is used by someone, she paints a unique design on it and hangs it with many other painted cups in front of a window or pretty background. These works from Leech and Deininger are not only ⓔ pleasing to the eye, but they also naturally provoke an interest in environmental conservation in people.

① ⓐ: garbage   ② ⓑ: shattered
③ ⓒ: plug   ④ ⓓ: throwaway
⑤ ⓔ: pleasurable

23

다음 글의 밑줄 친 부분의 우리말 해석이 바르지 않은 것은?

When artists add their own creative touches, things that most people consider junk are reborn as beautiful works of art. ① The giant pictures made from trash by environmental artist Tom Deininger are one of a kind. Up close, these brightly colored creations look like a mixed-up mess of broken plastic, unwanted toys, and ② bent wire—all things that cannot be recycled. From farther away, however, they ③ appear to blend together into marvelous landscapes or other paintings. There is also an artist who shows that even disposable cups can be reused as artistic material. For years, Gwyneth Leech has turned used coffee cups into ④ brilliant art exhibits. After a cup is used by someone, she paints a unique design on it and hangs it with many other painted cups in front of a window or pretty background. These works from Leech and Deininger are ⑤ not only pleasing to the eye, but they also naturally provoke an interest in environmental conservation in people.

① 쓰레기로 만들어진 거대한 그림들
② 휘어진 선
③ 보기 좋게 조합되도록 나타난다
④ 멋진 미술 전시품들
⑤ 눈을 즐겁게 할 뿐만 아니라

24

다음 글의 (A), (B), (C)의 각 네모 안에서 어법상 알맞은 말로 바르게 연결된 것은?

When artists add their own creative touches, things that most people consider junk are reborn as beautiful works of art. The giant pictures made from trash by environmental artist Tom Deininger are one of a kind. Up close, these brightly colored creations (A) look / look like a mixed-up mess of broken plastic, unwanted toys, and bent wire—all things that cannot be recycled. From farther away, however, they appear to (B) blend / blending together into marvelous landscapes or other paintings. There is also an artist who shows that even disposable cups can be reused as artistic material. For years, Gwyneth Leech has turned used coffee cups into brilliant art exhibits. After a cup is used by someone, she paints a unique design on it and hangs it with many other painted cups in front of a window or pretty background. These works from Leech and Deininger are not only (C) pleasing / pleased to the eye, but they also naturally provoke an interest in environmental conservation in people.

	(A)	(B)	(C)
①	look	– blending	– pleasing
②	look	– blend	– pleased
③	look like	– blend	– pleased
④	look like	– blend	– pleasing
⑤	look like	– blending	– pleased

25

다음 문장의 밑줄 친 우리말을 주어진 〈조건〉에 맞게 영작하시오.

When artists add their own creative touches, things that most people consider junk 아름다운 예술작품들로 다시 태어난다.

〈조건〉
1. reborn, work of art, beautiful, as를 이용할 것
2. 필요시 어법에 맞게 어형을 바꿔 쓸 것
3. 총 7단어로 쓸 것

26

다음 중, 괄호 안에 주어진 단어를 올바른 형태로 바꾸지 <u>않은</u> 것은?

When artists add their own creative touches, things that most people consider junk ① _____ (be) reborn as beautiful works of art. The giant pictures ② _____ (make) from trash by environmental artist Tom Deininger are one of a kind. Up close, these brightly colored creations ③ _____ (look) like a mixed-up mess of broken plastic, unwanted toys, and bent wire—all things that cannot be recycled. For years, Gwyneth Leech ④ _____ (turn) used coffee cups into brilliant art exhibits. After a cup ⑤ _____ (use) by someone, she paints a unique design on it and hangs it with many other painted cups in front of a window or pretty background.

① are   ② made
③ look   ④ has been turned
⑤ is used

27

다음 글의 밑줄 친 부분 중, 문맥상 적절하지 <u>않은</u> 것은?

When artists add their own creative touches, things that most people ① <u>think</u> junk are reborn as beautiful works of art. The giant pictures ② <u>created</u> from trash by environmental artist Tom Deininger are one of a kind. Up close, these brightly colored creations look like a mixed-up mess of broken plastic, unwanted toys, and bent wire—all things that cannot be ③ <u>reused</u>. From farther away, however, they appear to ④ <u>mix</u> together into marvelous landscapes or other paintings. There is also an artist who shows that even disposable cups can be reused as artistic material. For years, Gwyneth Leech has ⑤ <u>put</u> used coffee cups into brilliant art exhibits. After a cup is used by someone, she paints a unique design on it and hangs it with many other painted cups in front of a window or pretty background. These works from Leech and Deininger are not only pleasing to the eye, but they also naturally provoke an interest in environmental conservation in people.

28

다음 글의 밑줄 친 우리말을 〈보기〉의 단어를 모두 활용해 영작하시오. (7단어)

〈보기〉 someone, cup, by, use, after, a

For years, Gwyneth Leech has turned used coffee cups into brilliant art exhibits. 컵이 누군가에 의해 사용된 후, she paints a unique design on it and hangs it with many other painted cups in front of a window or pretty background. These works from Leech and Deininger are not only pleasing to the eye, but they also naturally provoke an interest in environmental conservation in people.

29

다음 글의 (A), (B), (C)의 각 네모 안에서 어법상 알맞은 말로 바르게 연결된 것은?

Up close, these brightly (A) coloring / colored creations look like a mixed-up mess of broken plastic, unwanted toys, and bent wire—all things that cannot be recycled. From farther away, however, they appear to blend together into marvelous landscapes or other paintings. There is also an artist who shows that even disposable cups can be reused as artistic material. For years, Gwyneth Leech has turned (B) using / used coffee cups into brilliant art exhibits. After a cup is used by someone, she paints a unique design on it and hangs it with many other (C) painting / painted cups in front of a window or pretty background. These works from Leech and Deininger are not only pleasing to the eye, but they also naturally provoke an interest in environmental conservation in people.

	(A)	(B)	(C)
①	coloring	using	painting
②	coloring	used	painting
③	colored	using	painted
④	colored	used	painting
⑤	colored	used	painted

30

다음 글의 밑줄 친 부분 중, 같은 의미로 바꿔 쓸 수 <u>없는</u> 것은?

When artists add their own creative touches, ⓐ things that most people consider junk are reborn as beautiful works of art. The giant pictures ⓑ made from trash by environmental artist Tom Deininger are one of a kind. Up close, these brightly colored creations look like a mixed-up mess of broken plastic, unwanted toys, and bent wire— all things that cannot be recycled. From farther away, however, they appear to blend together into marvelous landscapes or other paintings. There is also an artist ⓒ who shows that even disposable cups can be reused as artistic material. For years, Gwyneth Leech has turned used coffee cups into brilliant art exhibits. ⓓ After a cup is used by someone, she paints a unique design on it ⓔ and hangs it with many other painted cups in front of a window or pretty background. These works from Leech and Deininger are not only pleasing to the eye, but they also naturally provoke an interest in environmental conservation in people.

① ⓐ: what most people consider
② ⓑ: which are made
③ ⓒ: showing that
④ ⓓ: A cup being used
⑤ ⓔ: hung

본문[4]

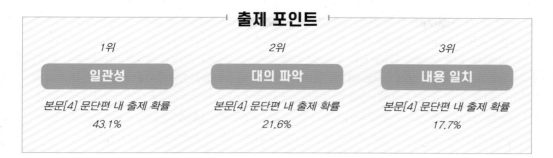

출제 포인트

1위	2위	3위
일관성	**대의 파악**	**내용 일치**
본문[4] 문단편 내 출제 확률 43.1%	본문[4] 문단편 내 출제 확률 21.6%	본문[4] 문단편 내 출제 확률 17.7%

● 일관성

이 문단에서는 일관성 문제가 43.1%로 가장 많이 출제되었다. 본문에서는 Deininger의 작품 설명에서 작품을 가까이에서 봤을 때의 모습과 멀리서 봤을 때의 감상을 역접 관계를 나타내는 연결어 however를 사용하여 대조적으로 제시했다는 점을 기억하자. 또한, 부사 also를 사용하여 Deininger의 작품처럼 쓰레기로 예술작품을 만드는 Leech에 대한 정보를 추가적으로 제시했다는 점도 함께 기억하자.

> **Q. 다음 글의 흐름으로 보아, 주어진 문장이 들어가기에 가장 적절한 곳은?**
>
> > From farther away, however, they appear to blend together into marvelous landscapes or other paintings.
>
> When artists add their own creative touches, things that most people consider junk are reborn as beautiful works of art. The giant pictures made from trash by environmental artist Tom Deininger are one of a kind. (①) Up close, these brightly colored creations look like a mixed-up mess of broken plastic, unwanted toys, and bent wire—all things that cannot be recycled. (②) There is also an artist who shows that even disposable cups can be reused as artistic material. (③) For years, Gwyneth Leech has turned used coffee cups into brilliant art exhibits. (④) After a cup is used by someone, she paints a unique design on it and hangs it with many other painted cups in front of a window or pretty background. (⑤) These works from Leech and Deininger are not only pleasing to the eye, but they also naturally provoke an interest in environmental conservation in people.

정답 ②

② 앞 문장은 그림을 가까이 보면, 쓰레기들이 뒤섞인 것처럼 보인다는 내용이며, ② 다음 문장은 일회용 컵을 재사용하여 예술작품을 만든 다른 예시를 제시하고 있다. 주어진 문장의 they는 ② 앞 문장의 these brightly colored creations를 가리키고, 멀리서 보면, 그것들은 보기 좋게 조합된 것처럼 보인다는 내용을 담고 있으므로, 역접 관계를 나타내는 연결어 however가 있는 주어진 문장이 들어가기에 가장 적절한 곳은 ②이다.

● 대의 파악

이 문단에서는 대의 파악 문제가 21.6%로 두 번째로 많이 출제되었다. 사람들이 쓰레기라고 여기는 물건에 Tom Deininger와 Gwyneth Leech와 같은 예술가들의 창의적 솜씨가 더해져서 예술작품으로 다시 태어나고, 이러한 업사이클 작품들은 사람들에게 즐거움뿐만 아니라 환경 보존에 대한 관심을 유발한다는 내용의 글이다. 글의 키워드인 upcycle, creative 등을 활용한 선지가 출제되므로, 키워드 creative의 유의어인 inventive, imaginative와 같은 어휘를 함께 알아두자.

> **Q. 다음 글의 제목으로 가장 적절한 것은?**
>
> When artists add their own creative touches, things that most people consider junk are reborn as beautiful works of art. The giant pictures made from trash by

environmental artist Tom Deininger are one of a kind. Up close, these brightly colored creations look like a mixed-up mess of broken plastic, unwanted toys, and bent wire—all things that cannot be recycled. From farther away, however, they appear to blend together into marvelous landscapes or other paintings. There is also an artist who shows that even disposable cups can be reused as artistic material. For years, Gwyneth Leech has turned used coffee cups into brilliant art exhibits. After a cup is used by someone, she paints a unique design on it and hangs it with many other painted cups in front of a window or pretty background. These works from Leech and Deininger are not only pleasing to the eye, but they also naturally provoke an interest in environmental conservation in people.

① Artists: The Worst Garbage Handlers
② Why Is Garbage Welcomed at Art Shows?
③ Artists Sensitive to the Litter Problem
④ Recycling: A Way to Make Artists Satisfied
⑤ No Longer Rubbish, But Things with Artistic Value

정답 ⑤
사람들이 쓰레기라고 여기는 물건에 예술가들의 창의적 솜씨가 더해져서 예술작품으로 다시 태어난다는 내용의 글이다. 따라서, 글의 제목으로 가장 적절한 것은 ⑤ '더 이상 쓰레기가 아닌, 예술적 가치가 있는 사물들'이다.
① 예술가: 쓰레기를 가장 못 다루는 사람들
② 왜 쓰레기는 예술 전시회에서 환영받는가?
③ 쓰레기 문제에 대해 예민한 예술가들
④ 재활용: 예술가를 만족시키는 방법

● 내용 일치

이 문단에서는 내용 일치 유형이 17.7%로, 세 번째로 많이 출제되었다. 내용 일치 문제를 풀 때는, 기본적으로 본문의 내용을 충실히 숙지해야 한다. 본문에 Tom Deininger의 작품과 Gwyneth Leech의 작품이 소개되었으므로, 각각의 예술작품의 재료와 특징, 예술작품의 효과 등을 확실히 알아두도록 하자.

문장1	When artists add their own creative touches, things that most people consider junk are reborn as beautiful works of art.	14.0%
문장2	The giant pictures made from trash by environmental artist Tom Deininger are one of a kind.	7.0%
문장3	Up close, these brightly colored creations look like a mixed-up mess of broken plastic, unwanted toys, and bent wire—all things that cannot be recycled.	20.9%
문장4	From farther away, however, they appear to blend together into marvelous landscapes or other paintings.	14.0%
문장5	There is also an artist who shows that even disposable cups can be reused as artistic material.	4.7%
문장6	For years, Gwyneth Leech has turned used coffee cups into brilliant art exhibits.	16.3%
문장7	After a cup is used by someone, she paints a unique design on it and hangs it with many other painted cups in front of a window or pretty background.	9.3%
문장8	These works from Leech and Deininger are not only pleasing to the eye, but they also naturally provoke an interest in environmental conservation in people.	14.0%

정답

1	F	2	T	3	F
4	F	5	F	6	F
7	F	8	T	9	T
10	F	11	T	12	T
13	F	14	F	15	F
16	T				

(9) Deininger의 작품들은 가까이에서 보면 지저분한 쓰레기 더미처럼 보인다.

Q. 글의 내용과 일치하면 T, 일치하지 않으면 F에 표시하시오.

(1) Deininger의 작품들은 자세히 보면 재활용품이 질서정연하게 섞여 있는 것처럼 보인다. (T / F)

(2) Gwyneth Leech는 전시품을 만들기 위해 사용된 컵을 사용한다. (T / F)

(3) 예술가들은 쓰레기를 미적 가치가 있는 예술작품이라고 여긴다. (T / F)

(4) Deininger의 작품들은 멀리서 보면 다른 그림들이 뒤섞인 것처럼 보인다. (T / F)

(5) Leech와 Deininger는 사람들에게 환경에 관한 의식을 심어주기 위해 작품들을 만든다. (T / F)

(6) Leech는 사용된 컵에 유리창 또는 예쁜 배경을 그려 넣는다. (T / F)

(7) 환경에 관심이 있는 Tom Deininger가 만든 거대한 조각상은 이 세상에 둘도 없는 것이다. (T / F)

(8) 일회용 컵을 재료로 예술작품을 만든 예술가가 있다. (T / F)

(9) Deininger's works look like an untidy collection of garbage up close. (T / F)

(10) Gwyneth Leech purchases many cups to make her artworks. (T / F)

(11) Trash is transformed into an object of artistic value thanks to artists' creativity. (T / F)

(12) From a distance, Deininger's works come across as harmonious things. (T / F)

(13) Fascinating works by Leech and Deininger deliver a warning message about the environment. (T / F)

(14) Leech paints unique cups on windows or on a pretty background. (T / F)

(15) Tom Deininger makes paintings of the environment, such as trash. (T / F)

(16) Gwyneth Leech uses a cup made to be thrown away after use in her work. (T / F)

(10) Gwyneth Leech는 그녀의 작품을 만들기 위해 많은 컵을 구입한다.

(11) 쓰레기는 예술가들의 창의성 덕분에 예술적 가치가 있는 물건으로 탈바꿈한다.

(12) 멀리서 보면 Deininger의 작품들은 조화로워 보인다.

(13) Leech와 Deininger의 매혹적인 작품들은 환경에 대한 경고 메시지를 전달한다.

(14) Leech는 창문이나 예쁜 배경에 독특한 컵을 그린다.

(15) Tom Deininger는 쓰레기와 같은 환경의 그림을 그린다.

(16) Gwyneth Leech는 사용한 후 버려지도록 만들어진 컵을 자신의 작품에 사용한다.

● 요약

이 문단에서는 요약 유형이 13.9% 출제되었다. 예술가 Tom Deininger와 Gwyneth Leech의 작품이 공통으로 시사하는 바가 요약문으로 출제될 가능성이 높으므로, 마지막 문장 These works ~.를 분명하게 이해하고, provoke an interest의 유사 표현들을 숙지하도록 하자.

Q. 다음 글의 내용을 한 문장으로 요약하고자 한다. 빈칸 (A), (B)에 들어갈 단어를 본문에서 찾아 쓰시오. (필요시 어형 변화 가능)

When artists add their own creative touches, things that most people consider junk are reborn as beautiful works of art. The giant pictures made from trash by environmental artist Tom Deininger are one of a kind. Up close, these brightly colored creations look like a mixed-up mess of broken plastic, unwanted toys, and bent wire—all things that cannot be recycled. From farther away, however, they appear to blend together into marvelous landscapes or other paintings. There is also an artist who shows that even disposable cups can be reused as artistic material. For years, Gwyneth Leech has turned used coffee cups into brilliant art exhibits. After a cup is used by someone, she paints a unique design on it and hangs it with many other painted cups in front of a window or pretty background. These works from Leech and Deininger are not only pleasing to the eye, but they also naturally provoke an interest in environmental conservation in people.

| Leech and Deininger used their _____ (A) _____ to transform the useless into remarkable artwork, thereby influencing people's _____ (B) _____ awareness. |

(A) _____ (B) _____

정답

(A) creativity
(B) environmental

예술가들이 쓰레기에 그들의 창의적인 손길을 더해 아름다운 예술작품으로 다시 탄생시킨다는 내용의 글이다. 특히 Deininger와 Leech의 작품들은 보는 즐거움뿐만 아니라 사람들이 환경 보존에 관심을 갖도록 만든다고 했으므로, 빈칸 (A)에는 creativity가, (B)에는 environmental이 들어가는 것이 가장 적절하다.

01

다음 글의 흐름으로 보아, 주어진 문장이 들어가기에 가장 적절한 곳은?

> There is also an artist who shows that even disposable cups can be reused as artistic material.

When artists add their own creative touches, things that most people consider junk are reborn as beautiful works of art. The giant pictures made from trash by environmental artist Tom Deininger are one of a kind. (①) Up close, these brightly colored creations look like a mixed-up mess of broken plastic, unwanted toys, and bent wire—all things that cannot be recycled. (②) From farther away, however, they appear to blend together into marvelous landscapes or other paintings. (③) For years, Gwyneth Leech has turned used coffee cups into brilliant art exhibits. (④) After a cup is used by someone, she paints a unique design on it and hangs it with many other painted cups in front of a window or pretty background. (⑤) These works from Leech and Deininger are not only pleasing to the eye, but they also naturally provoke an interest in environmental conservation in people.

02

다음 글을 읽고 알 수 있는 내용으로 적절하지 <u>않은</u> 것은?

When artists add their own creative touches, things that most people consider junk are reborn as beautiful works of art. The giant pictures made from trash by environmental artist Tom Deininger are one of a kind. Up close, these brightly colored creations look like a mixed-up mess of broken plastic, unwanted toys, and bent wire—all things that cannot be recycled. From farther away, however, they appear to blend together into marvelous landscapes or other paintings. There is also an artist who shows that even disposable cups can be reused as artistic material. For years, Gwyneth Leech has turned used coffee cups into brilliant art exhibits. After a cup is used by someone, she paints a unique design on it and hangs it with many other painted cups in front of a window or pretty background. These works from Leech and Deininger are not only pleasing to the eye, but they also naturally provoke an interest in environmental conservation in people.

① 예술가들의 손길로 쓰레기는 예술작품으로 다시 태어날 수 있다.
② Tom Deininger가 쓰레기로 만든 거대한 그림은 가까이에서 보면 재활용품들로 뒤섞인 것처럼 보인다.
③ Tom Deininger의 작품은 보는 사람과의 거리에 따라 다른 느낌을 준다.
④ Gwyneth Leech는 일회용컵에 그림을 그려서 유리창이나 예쁜 배경 앞에 매달아 놓는다.
⑤ 사람들은 Gwyneth Leech의 작품을 보고서 환경 보존에 대해 관심이 생긴다.

03

다음 글의 제목으로 가장 적절한 것은?

When artists add their own creative touches, things that most people consider junk are reborn as beautiful works of art. The giant pictures made from trash by environmental artist Tom Deininger are one of a kind. Up close, these brightly colored creations look like a mixed-up mess of broken plastic, unwanted toys, and bent wire—all things that cannot be recycled. From farther away, however, they appear to blend together into marvelous landscapes or other paintings. There is also an artist who shows that even disposable cups can be reused as artistic material. For years, Gwyneth Leech has turned used coffee cups into brilliant art exhibits. After a cup is used by someone, she paints a unique design on it and hangs it with many other painted cups in front of a window or pretty background. These works from Leech and Deininger are not only pleasing to the eye, but they also naturally provoke an interest in environmental conservation in people.

① Artists' Roles in Raising Fund for Their Works
② Who Takes the Lead in Environmental Pollution?
③ Interpretations of Works Made from Trash Vary!
④ Clever Ideas: From the Worthless to an Artistic Creation
⑤ Art Shows: The Most Popular Environmental Campaign

04

주어진 글 다음에 이어질 글의 순서로 가장 적절한 것은?

When artists add their own creative touches, things that most people consider junk are reborn as beautiful works of art. The giant pictures made from trash by environmental artist Tom Deininger are one of a kind.

(A) After a cup is used by someone, she paints a unique design on it and hangs it with many other painted cups in front of a window or pretty background. These works from Leech and Deininger are not only pleasing to the eye, but they also naturally provoke an interest in environmental conservation in people.

(B) Up close, these brightly colored creations look like a mixed-up mess of broken plastic, unwanted toys, and bent wire—all things that cannot be recycled. From farther away, however, they appear to blend together into marvelous landscapes or other paintings.

(C) There is also an artist who shows that even disposable cups can be reused as artistic material. For years, Gwyneth Leech has turned used coffee cups into brilliant art exhibits.

① (A) – (C) – (B)　　　② (B) – (A) – (C)
③ (B) – (C) – (A)　　　④ (C) – (A) – (B)
⑤ (C) – (B) – (A)

05

다음 글의 주제로 가장 적절한 것은?

When artists add their own creative touches, things that most people consider junk are reborn as beautiful works of art. The giant pictures made from trash by environmental artist Tom Deininger are one of a kind. Up close, these brightly colored creations look like a mixed-up mess of broken plastic, unwanted toys, and bent wire—all things that cannot be recycled. From farther away, however, they appear to blend together into marvelous landscapes or other paintings. There is also an artist who shows that even disposable cups can be reused as artistic material. For years, Gwyneth Leech has turned used coffee cups into brilliant art exhibits. After a cup is used by someone, she paints a unique design on it and hangs it with many other painted cups in front of a window or pretty background. These works from Leech and Deininger are not only pleasing to the eye, but they also naturally provoke an interest in environmental conservation in people.

① positive effects of environmental pollution on artists
② the importance of proper distance in appreciating a work
③ a chemical process that converts waste into art materials
④ a recycling competition among artists
⑤ a way to add new value to what has been thrown away

06

다음 글의 내용을 한 문장으로 요약하고자 한다. 빈칸 (A), (B)에 들어갈 말로 가장 적절한 것은?

When artists add their own creative touches, things that most people consider junk are reborn as beautiful works of art. The giant pictures made from trash by environmental artist Tom Deininger are one of a kind. Up close, these brightly colored creations look like a mixed-up mess of broken plastic, unwanted toys, and bent wire—all things that cannot be recycled. From farther away, however, they appear to blend together into marvelous landscapes or other paintings. There is also an artist who shows that even disposable cups can be reused as artistic material. For years, Gwyneth Leech has turned used coffee cups into brilliant art exhibits. After a cup is used by someone, she paints a unique design on it and hangs it with many other painted cups in front of a window or pretty background. These works from Leech and Deininger are not only pleasing to the eye, but they also naturally provoke an interest in environmental conservation in people.

Artists make use of what has been _____(A)_____
such as throwaway products in a(n) _____(B)_____
manner in order to create art pieces.

	(A)	(B)
①	distributed	user-friendly
②	distributed	earth-friendly
③	discarded	computer-friendly
④	discarded	eco-friendly
⑤	abandoned	family-friendly

다음 글의 내용과 일치하지 <u>않는</u> 것은?

When artists add their own creative touches, things that most people consider junk are reborn as beautiful works of art. The giant pictures made from trash by environmental artist Tom Deininger are one of a kind. Up close, these brightly colored creations look like a mixed-up mess of broken plastic, unwanted toys, and bent wire—all things that cannot be recycled. From farther away, however, they appear to blend together into marvelous landscapes or other paintings. There is also an artist who shows that even disposable cups can be reused as artistic material. For years, Gwyneth Leech has turned used coffee cups into brilliant art exhibits. After a cup is used by someone, she paints a unique design on it and hangs it with many other painted cups in front of a window or pretty background. These works from Leech and Deininger are not only pleasing to the eye, but they also naturally provoke an interest in environmental conservation in people.

① Tom Deininger는 사람들이 쓰레기라고 여기는 사물들에 그의 창의성을 더했다.
② 멀리서 보면, Tom Deininger의 거대한 창작물은 서로 잘 어우러지는 것처럼 보인다.
③ Gwyneth Leech는 수년간 일회용 커피컵을 예술적 재료로 사용해 왔다.
④ Gwyneth Leech는 그녀가 쓴 커피컵에 독특한 디자인을 그린 후 다른 컵들과 함께 전시한다.
⑤ Tom Deininger와 Gwyneth Leech의 작품들을 감상하는 것은 우리의 눈을 즐겁게 하는 일이다.

다음 글의 요지로 가장 적절한 것은?

When artists add their own creative touches, things that most people consider junk are reborn as beautiful works of art. The giant pictures made from trash by environmental artist Tom Deininger are one of a kind. Up close, these brightly colored creations look like a mixed-up mess of broken plastic, unwanted toys, and bent wire—all things that cannot be recycled. From farther away, however, they appear to blend together into marvelous landscapes or other paintings. There is also an artist who shows that even disposable cups can be reused as artistic material. For years, Gwyneth Leech has turned used coffee cups into brilliant art exhibits. After a cup is used by someone, she paints a unique design on it and hangs it with many other painted cups in front of a window or pretty background. These works from Leech and Deininger are not only pleasing to the eye, but they also naturally provoke an interest in environmental conservation in people.

① 관람객들은 적절한 거리에서 예술작품을 감상해야 한다.
② 환경 문제는 예술작품에서 가장 흔히 다루는 주제이다.
③ 예술가들 사이에서 재활용품은 훌륭한 미술 재료로 여겨진다.
④ 예술가들은 일회용품 사용에 대한 대중들의 의식을 높이고자 노력한다.
⑤ 예술가들은 쓸모없는 것을 가지고 창의적으로 예술작품을 만들어낸다.

09

다음 글의 내용을 한 문장으로 요약하고자 한다. 빈칸 (A), (B)에 들어갈 말로 가장 적절한 것은?

When artists add their own creative touches, things that most people consider junk are reborn as beautiful works of art. The giant pictures made from trash by environmental artist Tom Deininger are one of a kind. Up close, these brightly colored creations look like a mixed-up mess of broken plastic, unwanted toys, and bent wire—all things that cannot be recycled. From farther away, however, they appear to blend together into marvelous landscapes or other paintings. There is also an artist who shows that even disposable cups can be reused as artistic material. For years, Gwyneth Leech has turned used coffee cups into brilliant art exhibits. After a cup is used by someone, she paints a unique design on it and hangs it with many other painted cups in front of a window or pretty background. These works from Leech and Deininger are not only pleasing to the eye, but they also naturally provoke an interest in environmental conservation in people.

Waste or used items are ___(A)___ into works of art by artists, which make people ___(B)___ with the environment.

	(A)		(B)
①	upcycled	–	satisfied
②	upcycled	–	concerned
③	recycled	–	pleased
④	recycled	–	disappointed
⑤	put	–	delighted

10

다음 글에서 전체 흐름과 관계 없는 문장은?

When artists add their own creative touches, things that most people consider junk are reborn as beautiful works of art. The giant pictures made from trash by environmental artist Tom Deininger are one of a kind. Up close, these brightly colored creations look like a mixed-up mess of broken plastic, unwanted toys, and bent wire—all things that cannot be recycled. ① Breaking these things into fragments prevents the garbage disposal from being jammed. ② From farther away, however, they appear to blend together into marvelous landscapes or other paintings. ③ There is also an artist who shows that even disposable cups can be reused as artistic material. ④ For years, Gwyneth Leech has turned used coffee cups into brilliant art exhibits. ⑤ After a cup is used by someone, she paints a unique design on it and hangs it with many other painted cups in front of a window or pretty background. These works from Leech and Deininger are not only pleasing to the eye, but they also naturally provoke an interest in environmental conservation in people.

기타 연습 문제

1회 등장 포인트

● look like + 명사

> Up close, these brightly colored creations look like a mixed-up mess of broken plastic, unwanted toys, and bent wire—all things that cannot be recycled.

● 부사 brightly

> Up close, these brightly colored creations look like a mixed-up mess of broken plastic, unwanted toys, and bent wire—all things that cannot be recycled.

● 수 일치

> For years, Gwyneth Leech has turned used coffee cups into brilliant art exhibits.

> These works from Leech and Deininger are not only pleasing to the eye, but they also naturally provoke an interest in environmental conservation in people.

● 능동태

> These works from Leech and Deininger are not only pleasing to the eye, but they also naturally provoke an interest in environmental conservation in people.

01

다음 글의 밑줄 친 부분 중, 어법상 어색한 것은?

When artists add their own creative touches, things that most people consider junk are reborn as beautiful works of art. The giant pictures made from trash by environmental artist Tom Deininger are one of a kind. Up close, these ① brightly colored creations ② look like a mixed-up mess of broken plastic, unwanted toys, and bent wire— all things that cannot be recycled. From farther away, however, they appear to blend together into marvelous landscapes or other paintings. There is also an artist who shows that even disposable cups can be reused as artistic material. For years, Gwyneth Leech ③ has turned used coffee cups into brilliant art exhibits. After a cup is used by someone, she paints a unique design on it and hangs it with many other painted cups in front of a window or pretty background. These works from Leech and Deininger ④ is not only pleasing to the eye, but they also naturally ⑤ provoke an interest in environmental conservation in people.

● ⟨appear to-v⟩ ↔ ⟨it appears that ~⟩

> From farther away, however, they appear to blend together into marvelous landscapes or other paintings.

02

다음 문장의 밑줄 친 부분을 주어진 〈조건〉에 맞게 바꿔 쓰시오.

From farther away, however, it appears that they blend together into marvelous landscapes or other paintings.

> 〈조건〉 – to부정사를 활용할 것
> – 총 5단어로 작성할 것

● 수동태

> Up close, these brightly colored creations look like a mixed-up mess of broken plastic, unwanted toys, and bent wire—all things that cannot be recycled.

● **not only[just/simply/merely] A, but (also) B**

> These works from Leech and Deininger are not only pleasing to the eye, but they also naturally provoke an interest in environmental conservation in people.

03

다음 글의 (A), (B), (C)의 각 네모 안에서 어법에 적절한 것끼리 짝지은 것은?

When artists add their own creative touches, things that most people consider junk are reborn as beautiful works of art. The giant pictures made from trash by environmental artist Tom Deininger are one of a kind. Up close, these brightly colored creations look like a mixed-up mess of broken plastic, unwanted toys, and bent wire—all things that cannot (A) recycle / be recycled . From farther away, however, they appear to blend together into marvelous landscapes or other paintings. There is also an artist who shows that even disposable cups can be reused as artistic material. For years, Gwyneth Leech has (B) turned / been turned used coffee cups into brilliant art exhibits. After a cup is used by someone, she paints a unique design on it and hangs it with many other painted cups in front of a window or pretty background. These works from Leech and Deininger are not only pleasing to the eye, but they also naturally (C) provoke / to provoke an interest in environmental conservation in people.

	(A)		(B)		(C)
①	recycle	–	been turned	–	to provoke
②	recycle	–	turned	–	provoke
③	be recycled	–	been turned	–	provoke
④	be recycled	–	turned	–	to provoke
⑤	be recycled	–	turned	–	provoke

● 어휘 **reborn**

> When artists add their own creative touches, things that most people consider junk are reborn as beautiful works of art.

● 어휘 **up close, unwanted**

> Up close, these brightly colored creations look like a mixed-up mess of broken plastic, unwanted toys, and bent wire—all things that cannot be recycled.

● 어휘 **landscape**

> From farther away, however, they appear to blend together into marvelous landscapes or other paintings.

04

다음 글의 밑줄 친 부분 중, 문맥상 어색한 것은?

When artists add their own creative touches, things that most people consider junk are ① reborn as beautiful works of art. The giant pictures made from trash by environmental artist Tom Deininger are one of a kind. ② In distance, these brightly colored creations look like a mixed-up mess of broken plastic, ③ unwanted toys, and bent wire—all things that cannot be recycled. From farther away, however, they appear to blend together into marvelous ④ landscapes or other paintings. There is also an artist who shows that even disposable cups can be ⑤ reused as artistic material. For years, Gwyneth Leech has turned used coffee cups into brilliant art exhibits. After a cup is used by someone, she paints a unique design on it and hangs it with many other painted cups in front of a window or pretty background. These works from Leech and Deininger are not only pleasing to the eye, but they also naturally provoke an interest in environmental conservation in people.

● 어휘 **turn**

> For years, Gwyneth Leech has turned used coffee cups into brilliant art exhibits.

● 어휘 unique

After a cup is used by someone, she paints a unique design on it and hangs it with many other painted cups in front of a window or pretty background.

● 어휘 environmental

These works from Leech and Deininger are not only pleasing to the eye, but they also naturally provoke an interest in environmental conservation in people.

05

다음 글의 (A), (B), (C)의 각 네모 안에서 문맥상 적절한 것끼리 짝지은 것은?

When artists add their own creative touches, things that most people consider junk are reborn as beautiful works of art. The giant pictures made from trash by environmental artist Tom Deininger are one of a kind. Up close, these brightly colored creations look like a mixed-up mess of broken plastic, unwanted toys, and bent wire—all things that cannot be recycled. From farther away, however, they appear to blend together into marvelous landscapes or other paintings. There is also an artist who shows that even disposable cups can be reused as artistic material. For years, Gwyneth Leech has (A) turned / tuned used coffee cups into brilliant art exhibits. After a cup is used by someone, she paints a (B) conventional / unique design on it and hangs it with many other painted cups in front of a window or pretty background. These works from Leech and Deininger are not only pleasing to the eye, but they also naturally provoke an interest in (C) environmental / historical conservation in people.

	(A)	(B)	(C)
①	turned	conventional	historical
②	turned	unique	historical
③	turned	unique	environmental
④	tuned	unique	historical
⑤	tuned	conventional	environmental

● 목적

06

다음 글의 목적으로 가장 적절한 것은?

When artists add their own creative touches, things that most people consider junk are reborn as beautiful works of art. The giant pictures made from trash by environmental artist Tom Deininger are one of a kind. Up close, these brightly colored creations look like a mixed-up mess of broken plastic, unwanted toys, and bent wire—all things that cannot be recycled. From farther away, however, they appear to blend together into marvelous landscapes or other paintings. There is also an artist who shows that even disposable cups can be reused as artistic material. For years, Gwyneth Leech has turned used coffee cups into brilliant art exhibits. After a cup is used by someone, she paints a unique design on it and hangs it with many other painted cups in front of a window or pretty background. These works from Leech and Deininger are not only pleasing to the eye, but they also naturally provoke an interest in environmental conservation in people.

① to guide you through recycling
② to promote an exhibition of upcycling
③ to encourage you to pick up trash
④ to introduce examples of upcycled art
⑤ to complain about the waste disposal

● 함축적 의미 These works

These works from Leech and Deininger are not only pleasing to the eye, but they also naturally provoke an interest in environmental conservation in people.

문장에서 These works는 Leech와 Deininger가 만든 것이라는 점을 유추할 수 있다. 또한, 본문에서 Leech와 Deininger가 만든 작품들은 모두 쓰레기로 만든 예술작품이기 때문에, 이 내용도 함축적 의미로 선지에 나올 수 있다는 점을 유의하자.

출제 포인트 89.3% 정복!

리딩
본문[5]

10.5% 확률로 본문[5]에서 출제

★★
As you can see, creative thinking has the power to make many
★★★
positive changes to the environment. By giving old products more

value, we can lessen the amount of waste in a way that is even more

eco-friendly than recycling. So what would you say to Jamie now as

he decides what to do with his cans? Perhaps he could upcycle them

to make lanterns, toys, or sculptures for his friends and family. The

options are endless, and all he needs is a little creativity to think of
★
them. In the same way, stop and think before you throw something out.

Who knows? Maybe you can turn that trash into treasure.

일관성 〈출제 1위 유형〉

본문[5]는 삽입, 순서, 무관한 문장 고르기 문제로 출제될 가능성이 높다. 글의 흐름은 아래와 같으니 정확히 파악해두자. 환경에 있어서 많은 긍정적 변화를 가져오는 창의적인 생각 → 재활용보다 더 친환경적인 방식의 업사이클링 → 업사이클링의 예시 → 약간의 창의력으로 끝없이 많은 선택의 업사이클링 → 쓰레기를 보물로 바꿀 가능성의 여지가 있음

대의 파악 〈출제 2위 유형〉

제목이나 주제 등을 묻는 문제에서는, 글의 전체 내용을 포괄할 수 있는 내용을 골라야 한다. '업사이클링을 통해 쓰레기를 줄이는 방법'이나 '사용한 제품을 쓰레기를 줄이며 창의적으로 가치 있는 제품으로 탈바꿈하기'와 같은 내용이 답이 될 수 있으니, 중심내용을 잘 파악해두자.

내용 일치 〈출제 3위 유형〉

내용 일치 유형 문제를 풀 때에는 선지와 글의 내용을 하나씩 대조해서 확인한다. 특히, 낡은 제품에 더 많은 가치를 부여하여 친환경적으로 쓰레기를 줄이는 upcycling(업사이클링)을 recycling(재활용)으로 바꿔 글의 내용에 일치하지 않는 보기로 출제될 가능성이 높다는 점을 명심하자.

출제 1위 문장 ★★★

By giving old products more value, we can lessen the amount of waste in a way that is even more eco-friendly than recycling.

[주격관계대명사 that] 출제 1위 (문장편-문장2 → p.166)
[어휘 lessen] 출제 2위 (문장편-문장2 → p.166)
[전치사+동명사] 출제 3위 (문장편-문장2 → p.167)

출제 2위 문장 ★★

As you can see, creative thinking has the power to make many positive changes to the environment.

[빈칸 many positive changes to the environment] 출제 1위 (문장편-문장1 → p.164)
[to부정사의 형용사적 용법 – 명사 수식] 출제 2위 (문장편-문장1 → p.164)

출제 3위 문장 ★

The options are endless, and all he needs is a little creativity to think of them.

[수 일치] 출제 1위 (문장편-문장5 → p.171)
[어휘 endless] 출제 2위 (문장편-문장5 → p.171)
[어휘 creativity] 출제 3위 (문장편-문장5 → p.171)

문장1

> **As you can see, creative thinking has the power** <u>**to make many**</u>
> <u>**positive changes to the environment.**</u>
>
> 빈칸 many ~ environment
>
> to부정사 형용사적 용법
> – 명사 수식

출제 포인트

1위	*2위*
빈칸 many positive changes to the environment	**to부정사의 형용사적 용법 – 명사 수식**
문장 내 출제 확률 52.4% *본문[5] 문장편 내 출제 확률 12.1%*	*문장 내 출제 확률 28.6%* *본문[5] 문장편 내 출제 확률 6.6%*

● 빈칸 many positive changes to the environment

이 문장에서 출제가 된다면 52.4%의 확률로 창의적인 생각이 어떤 힘을 가지고 있는지 묻는 빈칸 문제가 나올 수 있다. 특히, 어휘 positive가 들어가는 것을 묻는 문제도 나올 수 있으므로 '환경에 있어서의 긍정적인 변화'라는 키워드를 잘 기억해두자. 또한, positive 대신 positively를 사용한 문장으로 변형되어 나올 수도 있다. 여기서 changes는 명사로 쓰였으므로, 명사를 수식하기 위해서는 부사 positively가 아닌 형용사 positive를 써야 한다는 것을 기억하자.

> **Q. 다음 빈칸에 들어갈 말을 〈보기〉에서 골라 쓰시오.**
>
> 〈보기〉 aggressive / negative / contemporary / positive / relics / traditions / changes / passive / environment / culture
>
> As you can see, creative thinking has the power to make many _____(A)_____ to the _____(B)_____. By giving old products more value, we can lessen the amount of waste in a way that is even more eco-friendly than recycling. So what would you say to Jamie now as he decides what to do with his cans? Perhaps he could upcycle them to make lanterns, toys, or sculptures for his friends and family. The options are endless, and all he needs is a little creativity to think of them. In the same way, stop and think before you throw something out. Who knows? Maybe you can turn that trash into treasure.
>
> (A) _____ (2단어)   (B) _____ (1단어)

정답

(A) positive changes
(B) environment

낡은 제품에 더 많은 가치를 부여하여 재활용보다도 훨씬 더 친환경적인 방법으로 쓰레기를 줄일 수 있다는 내용을 고려할 때, 환경에 있어서 긍정적인 변화를 가져오는 힘을 가지고 있다는 내용이 글의 흐름상 적절하다.

● to부정사의 형용사적 용법 – 명사 수식

문장1에서 출제될 가능성은 2.7%이다. 이 문장에서 출제가 된다면 28.6%의 확률로 to부정사의 형용사적 용법(명사 수식)과 관련된 어법 문제가 나올 수 있다. 여기서 to make는 명사 the power를 수식하여 '~하는'의 의미를 가진다. 또한, to make는 주격관계대명사 that이나 which를 사용한 절의 형태로 변형되어 나올 수 있다. 선행사(the power)가 사물이므로 who는 적절하지 않으며, 선행사를 포함하는 관계대명사 what도 쓸 수 없다는 점에 유의하자.

Q. 다음 밑줄 친 부분을 같은 의미에 해당하는 2단어로 변형하여 쓰시오.

As you can see, creative thinking has the power <u>which can make</u> many positive changes to the environment. By giving old products more value, we can lessen the amount of waste in a way that is even more eco-friendly than recycling. So what would you say to Jamie now as he decides what to do with his cans? Perhaps he could upcycle them to make lanterns, toys, or sculptures for his friends and family. The options are endless, and all he needs is a little creativity to think of them. In the same way, stop and think before you throw something out. Who knows? Maybe you can turn that trash into treasure.

_____

정답 to make

선행사 the power를 수식하는 관계대명사절을 형용사적 용법의 to부정사를 사용해서 바꿔 쓸 수 있다.

● 수 일치

이 문장에서 출제가 된다면 9.5%의 확률로 수 일치에 대한 문제가 나올 수 있다. 주어가 creative thinking이므로 단수동사 has가 쓰였다. 또한, creative thinking이 to think creatively, thinking creatively 등으로 변형되어 나올 수 있다. 이와 같이 변형한 형태에서도 주어가 to부정사구 또는 동명사구이므로 단수 취급하여 단수동사를 써야 하는 것을 유의하자.

Q. 다음 글의 밑줄 친 부분 중, 어법상 옳지 <u>않은</u> 것은?

As you can see, to creatively think ① <u>have</u> the power to make many positive changes to the environment. By giving old products more value, we can lessen the amount of waste in a way ② <u>that</u> is even more eco-friendly than recycling. So what would you say to Jamie now as he decides ③ <u>what</u> to do with his cans? Perhaps he could upcycle them to make lanterns, toys, or sculptures for his friends and family. The options are endless, and all he needs ④ <u>is</u> a little creativity to think of them. In the same way, stop and think before you throw something out. Who knows? Maybe you can turn ⑤ <u>that</u> trash into treasure.

정답 ①

① to부정사구가 주어인 경우 단수 취급하므로 단수동사 has가 되어야 한다.

오답

② a way를 선행사로 하는 주격관계대명사
③ decides의 목적어 역할을 하는 〈의문사+to부정사〉
④ 단수 취급하는 주어 all과 수 일치
⑤ trash를 수식하는 지시형용사

출제 포인트 91.1% 정복!

문장2   문장 출제 확률: 3.6% (총 771개의 출제 포인트 중 28회 출현, 46개 문장 중 10위)

전치사+동명사   줄이다

By giving old products more value, we can lessen the amount of waste in a way that is even more eco-friendly than recycling.

주격관계대명사

	1위	2위	3위
	주격관계대명사 that	어휘 lessen	전치사 + 동명사
	문장 내 출제 확률 35.7%	문장 내 출제 확률 28.6%	문장 내 출제 확률 17.9%
	본문[5] 문장편 내 출제 확률 11.0%	본문[5] 문장편 내 출제 확률 8.8%	본문[5] 문장편 내 출제 확률 5.5%

● 주격관계대명사 that

문장2에서 출제될 가능성은 3.6%이다. 이 문장에서 출제가 된다면 35.7%의 확률로 주격관계대명사의 형태를 묻는 어법 문제가 나올 수 있다. 관계대명사 who, that, which는 선행사를 필요로 하는데, 이 문장에서 선행사가 a way이므로 which나 that이 와야 하고, 관계대명사 that이 이끄는 절의 동사는 선행사의 수에 일치시키므로 is가 쓰였다.

Q. 다음 글의 ⓐ~ⓔ 중, 어법상 어색한 문장을 바르게 고쳐 문장 전체를 쓰시오. (단, 한 단어만 고칠 것)

ⓐ Creative thinking has the power to make many positive changes to the environment. ⓑ By giving old products more value, we can lessen the amount of waste in a way what is even more eco-friendly than recycling. So what would you say to Jamie now as he decides what to do with his cans? ⓒ Perhaps he could upcycle them to make lanterns, toys, or sculptures for his friends and family. ⓓ The options are endless, and all he needs is a little creativity to think of them. In the same way, stop and think before you throw something out. Who knows? ⓔ Maybe you can turn that trash into treasure.

어색한 문장 기호: _____

고쳐 쓰기: _____

● 어휘 lessen

이 문장에서 출제가 된다면 28.6%의 확률로 lessen에 대한 어휘 문제가 나올 수 있다. 낡은 제품에 더 많은 가치를 부여함으로써 재활용보다 훨씬 더 친환경적인 방식으로 쓰레기의 양을 '줄일' 수 있다는 점을 꼭 기억해야 한다. 유의어 decrease, reduce, cut down on 등이나, 반의어 increase, boost 등으로 변형되어 나올 수 있으니 이러한 어휘들도 함께 잘 알아두자.

Q. 다음 글의 밑줄 친 부분 중, 문맥상 낱말의 쓰임이 적절하지 <u>않은</u> 것은?

As you can see, creative thinking has the power to make many ① positive changes to the environment. By giving old products more value, we can ② boost the amount of waste in a way that is even more eco-friendly than recycling. So what would you say to Jamie now as he decides what to do with his cans? Perhaps he could ③ upcycle them to make lanterns, toys, or sculptures for his friends and family. The options are endless, and all he needs is a little ④ creativity to think of them. In the same way, stop and think before you throw something out. Who knows? Maybe you can ⑤ turn that trash into treasure.

● 전치사＋동명사

이 문장에서 출제가 된다면 17.9%의 확률로 〈전치사＋동명사〉 형태를 묻는 어법 문제가 나올 수 있다. 전치사 뒤에는 명사구(동명사)만 올 수 있다. 또한, 〈전치사＋동명사〉의 의미를 이해하는지 확인하는 문제가 나올 수 있으므로, 여러 전치사구의 의미를 기억해두자. 〈by＋동명사〉는 '~함으로써', 〈on＋동명사〉는 '~하자마자', 〈in＋동명사〉는 '~할 때, ~하는 데 있어서'라는 의미이다.

Q. 다음 글의 밑줄 친 부분 중, 어법상 적절하지 <u>않은</u> 것은?

    As you can see, creative thinking has the power ① <u>to make</u> many positive changes to the environment. By ② <u>give</u> old products more value, we can lessen the amount of waste in a way that ③ <u>is</u> even more eco-friendly than recycling. So what would you say to Jamie now as he decides what to do with his cans? Perhaps he could upcycle them to make lanterns, toys, or sculptures for his friends and family. The options are endless, and all he needs is a ④ <u>little</u> creativity to think of them. In the same way, stop and think before you throw something out. Who knows? Maybe you can turn that trash ⑤ <u>into</u> treasure.

정답 ②

전치사 by 뒤에 동사를 쓰려면 동명사 형태가 되어야 하므로, giving이 적절하다.

오답

① the power를 수식하는 형용사적 용법의 to부정사

③ 관계대명사절의 주어 역할을 하는 선행사 a way에 수 일치하여 단수동사 is

④ 셀 수 없는 명사 앞에 쓰이는 (a) little

⑤ 'A를 B로 바꾸다'의 의미인 〈turn A into B〉

● 비교급 강조

이 문장에서 출제가 된다면 14.3%의 확률로 비교급 강조에 대해 묻는 어법 문제가 출제될 수 있다. 비교급을 강조하는 부사로 much, (by) far, still, even, a lot, way(비격식) 등이 있다. 단, very는 형용사와 부사의 원급을 강조하고, 비교급을 수식할 수 없다는 점을 유의하자.

Q. 다음 문장에서 밑줄 친 부분과 바꿔 쓸 수 있는 것을 〈보기〉에서 <u>모두</u> 골라 쓰시오.

> 〈보기〉 single / too / simply / still / far / a lot / very / just / much

By giving old products more value, we can lessen the amount of waste in a way that is <u>even</u> more eco-friendly than recycling.

_____

정답

still, far, a lot, much

비교급을 강조하는 부사로 much, (by) far, still, even, a lot 등이 있다. single, simply는 최상급을 강조하는 부사이며, too, very, just는 원급을 강조하는 부사이다.

출제 포인트 93.6% 정복!

문장3

접속사 as 부사 역할 – 시간(~할 때)

So what would you say to Jamie now <u>as</u> he decides <u>what to do</u> with his cans?

의문사+to부정사

┤ **출제 포인트** ├

공동 1위	공동 1위
접속사 as 부사 역할 – 시간	**의문사+to부정사**
문장 내 출제 확률 50.0%	문장 내 출제 확률 50.0%
본문[5] 문장편 내 출제 확률 2.2%	본문[5] 문장편 내 출제 확률 2.2%

● 접속사 as 부사 역할 – 시간

문장3에서 출제될 가능성은 0.5%이다. 이 문장에서 출제가 된다면 50.0%의 확률로 시간을 나타내는 접속사 as에 대해 묻는 어법 문제가 나올 수 있다. 부사절을 이끄는 접속사 as와 전치사 as의 쓰임을 명확히 구별할 수 있어야 한다. 접속사 as는 뒤에 주어와 동사를 포함하는 절이 와야 하는 반면, 전치사 as는 뒤에 명사 형태가 온다는 점을 꼭 유의하자. 또한, as가 '~할 때'라는 의미로 쓰이는 경우, 접속사 when으로도 바꿔 쓸 수 있다는 점을 기억하자. 문장1의 As는 '~하듯'의 의미인 부사절을 이끄는 접속사로 쓰인 것도 함께 알아두자.

정답 ③
전치사 at은 뒤에 주어 (he)+동사(decides)의 절이 올 수 없으므로, 접속사 as나 when으로 고쳐야 한다.

오답
① '~하듯'의 의미인 접속사
② 선행사 a way에 수 일치
④ 목적을 나타내는 부사적 용법의 to부정사
⑤ 주어 all은 단수 취급하므로 단수동사로 수 일치

> **Q. 다음 글의 밑줄 친 부분 중, 어법상 적절하지 <u>않은</u> 것은?**
>
> ① <u>As</u> you can see, creative thinking has the power to make many positive changes to the environment. By giving old products more value, we can lessen the amount of waste in a way that ② <u>is</u> even more eco-friendly than recycling. So what would you say to Jamie now ③ <u>at</u> he decides what to do with his cans? Perhaps he could upcycle them ④ <u>to make</u> lanterns, toys, or sculptures for his friends and family. The options are endless, and all he needs ⑤ <u>is</u> a little creativity to think of them. In the same way, stop and think before you throw something out. Who knows? Maybe you can turn that trash into treasure.

● 의문사+to부정사

이 문장에서 출제가 된다면 마찬가지로 50.0%의 확률로 〈의문사+to부정사〉에 대한 어법 문제가 출제될 수 있다. 〈의문사+to부정사〉는 주어, 목적어, 보어 역할을 하는데, 목적어로 많이 쓰인다. 또한, what to do를 절의 형태인 〈what+주어+should+동사원형〉으로 변형하여 나올 수 있다는 점을 유의하자.

정답

what to do with his cans
동사 decides의 목적어로 〈what+to부정사〉 형태나 〈what+주어+should+동사원형〉 형태로 쓸 수 있다. 6단어로 영작하라고 했으므로, what to do with his cans로 써야 한다.

> **Q. 다음 글의 밑줄 친 우리말을 6단어로 영작하시오.**
>
> As you can see, creative thinking has the power to make many positive changes to the environment. By giving old products more value, we can lessen the amount of waste in a way that is even more eco-friendly than recycling. So what would you say to Jamie now as he decides <u>그가 그의 캔들을 가지고 무엇을 해야 할지를</u>? Perhaps

he could upcycle them to make lanterns, toys, or sculptures for his friends and family. The options are endless, and all he needs is a little creativity to think of them. In the same way, stop and think before you throw something out. Who knows? Maybe you can turn that trash into treasure.

문장4

문장 출제 확률: 1.2%

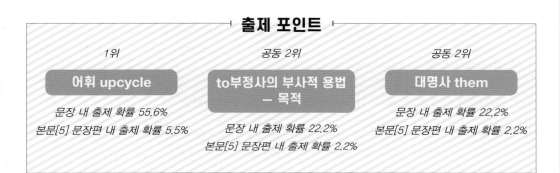

Perhaps he could upcycle them to make lanterns, toys, or sculptures for his friends and family.

출제 포인트

1위	공동 2위	공동 2위
어휘 upcycle	to부정사의 부사적 용법 – 목적	대명사 them
문장 내 출제 확률 55.6%	문장 내 출제 확률 22.2%	문장 내 출제 확률 22.2%
본문[5] 문장편 내 출제 확률 5.5%	본문[5] 문장편 내 출제 확률 2.2%	본문[5] 문장편 내 출제 확률 2.2%

● 어휘 upcycle

문장4에서 출제될 가능성은 1.2%이다. 이 문장에서 출제가 된다면 55.6%의 확률로 upcycle에 대한 어휘 문제가 나올 수 있다. 특히, recycle과 비교하여 나올 수 있다는 점을 유의하자.

Q. 다음 글의 (A), (B), (C)의 각 네모 안에서 문맥에 맞는 낱말로 가장 적절한 것은?

As you can see, creative thinking has the power to make many positive changes to the environment. By giving old products more value, we can (A) reduce / increase the amount of waste in a way that is even more eco-friendly than recycling. So what would you say to Jamie now as he decides what to do with his cans? Perhaps he could (B) recycle / upcycle them to make lanterns, toys, or sculptures for his friends and family. The options are (C) limitless / limited , and all he needs is a little creativity to think of them. In the same way, stop and think before you throw something out. Who knows? Maybe you can turn that trash into treasure.

	(A)	(B)	(C)		(A)	(B)	(C)
①	reduce	– recycle	– limitless	②	increase	– recycle	– limited
③	reduce	– upcycle	– limitless	④	increase	– upcycle	– limitless
⑤	reduce	– upcycle	– limited				

정답 ③
(A) 낡은 제품에 더 많은 가치를 부여함으로써 재활용보다 더 친환경적인 방식으로 버려지는 쓰레기의 양을 '줄일(reduce)' 수 있다는 내용이 자연스럽다.
increase: 늘리다
(B) 음료수 캔으로 랜턴, 장난감, 혹은 조각품을 만드는 것은 캔을 '업사이클(upcycle)'하는 것에 해당한다.
recycle: 재활용하다
(C) 음료수 캔으로 랜턴, 장난감, 조각품 등을 만들 수 있다고 했으므로, 선택할 수 있는 것은 '무한하다(limitless)'는 것을 알 수 있다.
limited: 제한된

169

● to부정사의 부사적 용법 – 목적

이 문장에서 출제가 된다면 22.2%의 확률로, 목적을 나타내는 부사적 용법의 to부정사에 관한 어법 문제가 나올 수 있다. 부사적 용법의 to부정사는 문장의 필수 성분(주어, 동사, 목적어, 보어)을 갖춘 문장에서 수식어로 쓰인다. 이 문장에서 to make는 '만들기 위해서'라는 목적을 나타낸다. 목적을 표현하는 〈in order＋to부정사〉나 〈so as＋to부정사〉 형태로도 바뀌어 출제될 수 있다는 점을 유의하자.

정답 making → to make
'만들기 위해'라는 의미를 나타내려면 목적을 나타내는 부사적 용법의 to부정사를 써야 한다.

> **Q. 다음 문장의 우리말 해석과 일치하도록 어색한 부분을 찾아 고쳐 쓰시오. (단, 2단어로 쓸 것)**
>
> Perhaps he could upcycle them making lanterns, toys, or sculptures for his friends and family.
>
> (아마도 그는 그의 친구와 가족을 위해 랜턴, 장난감 또는 조각품을 만들기 위해 그것들을 업사이클할 수 있다.)
>
> _____ → _____

● 대명사 them

이 문장에서 출제가 된다면 22.2%의 확률로 대명사 them에 대한 지칭 문제가 나올 수 있다. 이 문장에서 them은 바로 앞 문장에서 언급된 his cans를 가리킨다. 이 문장의 lanterns, toys, sculptures가 모두 복수명사이므로 them이 가리키는 것을 혼동하지 않도록 유의하자.

정답 his cans
'캔들로 무엇을 할지 결정하려는 Jamie는 그것들로 랜턴, 장난감, 조각품을 만들 수 있다'는 내용이 되어야 자연스럽다. 따라서, them은 앞 문장의 his cans임을 알 수 있다.

> **Q. 다음 글의 밑줄 친 them이 가리키는 것을 본문에서 찾아 쓰시오.**
>
> So what would you say to Jamie now as he decides what to do with his cans? Perhaps he could upcycle them to make lanterns, toys, or sculptures for his friends and family.
>
> _____

기출의 94.8% 점령

문장5

문장 출제 확률: 2.5%

끝이 없는   창의성
The options are endless, and all he needs is a little creativity to think of them.

출제 포인트

공동 1위	공동 1위	3위
수 일치	**어휘 endless**	**어휘 creativity**
문장 내 출제 확률 36.8%	문장 내 출제 확률 36.8%	문장 내 출제 확률 26.3%
본문[5] 문장편 내 출제 확률 7.7%	본문[5] 문장편 내 출제 확률 7.7%	본문[5] 문장편 내 출제 확률 5.5%

● 수 일치

문장5에서 출제될 가능성은 2.5%이다. 이 문장에서 출제가 된다면 36.8%의 확률로 수 일치에 대한 어법 문제가 나올 수 있다. 부정대명사 all이 주어 자리에서 관계사가 이끄는 절의 수식을 받는 경우 단수 취급하므로 단수동사로 수 일치시켜야 한다. 팝 가수 머라이어 캐리의 노래 중 하나인 "All (that) I want for Christmas Is You"를 연상하는 것도 좋은 방법이다. all이 '모든'이라는 뜻을 의미한다는 이유로 복수동사로 쓰면 안 된다는 점을 유의하자.

> **Q. 다음 문장에서 어법상 옳지 <u>않은</u> 부분을 찾아 바르게 고쳐 쓰시오.**
>
> The options are endless, and all he needs are a little creativity to think of them.
>
> ＿＿＿＿＿＿ → ＿＿＿＿＿＿

정답 are → is

and 뒤에 이어지는 절에서 관계사절 he needs의 수식을 받는 all이 주어이므로, 단수 취급하여 are을 is로 고쳐야 한다.

● 어휘 endless

역시 36.8%의 확률로 endless에 대한 어휘 문제가 나올 수 있다. 약간의 창의성만 있다면 업사이클할 방법이 '끝없이 많다'는 의미로 endless가 쓰였다. 유의어로 infinite, unlimited, limitless, countless 등이 있으며, 반의어로는 restrictive, limited, finite 등이 있다. endless가 유의어나 반의어로 변형되어 나올 수 있으니 반드시 숙지하자.

> **Q. 다음 빈칸에 들어갈 수 <u>없는</u> 것을 <u>모두</u> 고르시오.**
>
> So what would you say to Jamie now as he decides what to do with his cans? Perhaps he could upcycle them to make lanterns, toys, or sculptures for his friends and family. The options are ＿＿＿＿＿＿, and all he needs is a little creativity to think of them. In the same way, stop and think before you throw something out. Who knows? Maybe you can turn that trash into treasure.
>
> ① countless ② limited ③ unlimited ④ restrictive ⑤ endless

정답 ②, ④

빈칸 뒤에서 '약간의 창의성만 발휘하면 많은 것들을 생각해낼 수 있다'고 했으므로, 업사이클할 수 있는 선택지가 '많다'는 의미가 되어야 자연스럽다. 따라서 빈칸에 들어갈 수 없는 것은 ② limited(한정된), ④ restrictive(제한하는)이다.
① 셀 수 없는
③ 무제한의
⑤ 끝이 없는

● 어휘 creativity

이 문장에서 출제가 된다면 26.3%의 확률로 creativity에 대한 어휘 문제가 나올 수 있다. 약간의 창의성만 있으면 업사이클할 것으로 선택할 수 있는 것이 끝이 없다는 글의 흐름상 creativity가 쓰였다. creativity는 '창의성'이라는 의미로, 유의어 imagination, inventiveness, originality, innovation, 반의어 tradition, convention, stereotype도 함께 기억하자.

> **Q. 다음 글의 빈칸 (A), (B)에 들어갈 말을 〈보기〉에서 골라 쓰시오.**
>
> | 〈보기〉 use / creativity / end / upcycle / throw away |
>
> So what would you say to Jamie now as he decides what to do with his cans? Perhaps he could ＿＿(A)＿＿ them to make lanterns, toys, or sculptures for his friends and family. The options are limitless, and all he needs is a little ＿＿(B)＿＿ to think of them. In the same way, stop and think before you throw something out. Who knows? Maybe you can turn that trash into treasure.
>
> (A) ＿＿＿＿＿＿ (B) ＿＿＿＿＿＿

정답
(A) upcycle (B) creativity

(A) 바로 앞 문장에서 Jamie가 캔으로 무엇을 하기로 결정할지 묻고, 다음 문장에서 그가 랜턴, 장난감, 또는 조각상을 만들어낼 것이라고 했다. 따라서 빈칸 (A)에 들어갈 말로 가장 적절한 것은 upcycle이다.
(B) 바로 앞에서 선택할 수 있는 것은 끝이 없다고 했고, 약간의 '빈칸'만 발휘하면 될 뿐이라고 하였다. 또 다음 문장에서 같은 방식으로 무언가를 버리기 전에 잠시 멈추어 '생각'해보라고 하고 있다. 따라서 빈칸 (B)에 들어갈 말로 가장 적절한 것은 creativity이다.

출제 포인트 96.6% 정복!

문장6

In the same way, stop and think before you throw something out.

이 문장은 출제 빈도가 낮기 때문에 문장편 최중요 포인트에서는 제외된다.

문장7

Who knows?

이 문장은 출제 빈도가 낮기 때문에 문장편 최중요 포인트에서 제외된다.

문장8

문장 출제 확률: 0.9%

turn A into B: A를 B로 바꾸다

Maybe you can __turn__ that trash __into__ treasure.

함축된 의미: 가치 있는 것

출제 포인트

공동 1위	공동 1위
turn A into B	**어휘 treasure**
출제 확률 28.6%	문장 내 출제 확률 28.6%
본문[5] 문장편 내 출제 확률 2.2%	본문[5] 문장편 내 출제 확률 2.2%

● **turn A into B**

문장8에서 출제될 가능성은 0.9%이다. 이 문장에서 출제가 된다면 28.6%의 확률로 〈turn A into B〉에 관한 어법 문제가 나올 수 있다. 동사 turn은 전치사 into와 함께 쓰여 '~을 …로 바꾸다'라는 의미를 나타낸다. 비슷한 의미인 〈change A into B〉나 〈transform A into B〉, 〈convert A into B〉로 변형되어 나올 수 있으니 함께 알아두자. 또한, 〈turn A into B〉의 표현에서 A와 B의 대상에 유의하자.

> Q. 다음 글의 밑줄 친 (A)~(E) 중, 어법상 틀린 부분이 있는 것의 기호를 쓰고 문장 전체를 바르게 고쳐 쓰시오.
>
> (A) As you can see, creative thinking has the power to make many positive changes to the environment. (B) By giving old products more value, we can lessen the amount of waste in a way that is even more eco-friendly than recycling.

(C) So what would you say to Jamie now as he decides what to do with his cans? Perhaps he could upcycle them to make lanterns, toys, or sculptures for his friends and family. (D) The options are endless, and all he needs is a little creativity to think of them. In the same way, stop and think before you throw something out. Who knows? (E) Maybe you can be transformed that trash into treasure.

(   ) → _____

정답

(E) Maybe you can transform that trash into treasure.

뒤에 목적어 that trash가 온 것으로 보아 능동태 문장이 되어야 한다. 따라서 be transformed를 transform으로 고쳐 문장을 다시 써야 한다.

● 어휘 treasure

이 문장에서 출제가 된다면 28.6%의 확률로 어휘 treasure에 관한 문제가 나올 수 있다. 물건을 버리기 전에 그것을 보물로 바꿀 수도 있다는 내용으로, 여기서는 보물(금은보화)이 아닌 '보물처럼 가치 있는 것'으로 이해해야 한다. '소중한'이라는 의미의 precious, valuable, invaluable, priceless 등으로, 또는 '가치 없는'이라는 맥락의 valueless, trivial, minor, frivolous 등으로 표현이 바뀌어 나올 수 있으므로 유의하자.

Q. 다음 글의 밑줄 친 부분 중, 문맥상 낱말의 쓰임이 적절하지 않은 것은?

As you can see, creative thinking has the power to make many ① positive changes to the environment. By giving old products more value, we can ② lessen the amount of waste in a way that is even more eco-friendly than recycling. So what would you say to Jamie now as he decides what to do with his cans? Perhaps he could ③ upcycle them to make lanterns, toys, or sculptures for his friends and family. The options are ④ endless, and all he needs is a little creativity to think of them. In the same way, stop and think before you throw something out. Who knows? Maybe you can turn that trash into something ⑤ minor.

정답 ⑤

낡은 제품에 더 많은 가치를 부여함으로써 재활용보다 훨씬 더 친환경적으로 쓰레기의 양을 줄일 수 있다는 내용을 고려할 때, 그 쓰레기를 '중요한 무언가'로 바꿀 수도 있다는 내용이 문맥상 적절하다. 따라서, minor(중요하지 않은, 하찮은)가 아닌 precious(중요한)와 같은 말이 적절하다.

출제 포인트 97% 정복!

01

다음 글의 밑줄 친 부분 중, 어법상 어색한 것은?

As you can see, creative thinking has the power ① to make many positive changes to the environment. By ② giving old products more value, we can lessen the amount of waste in a way ③ what is even more eco-friendly than recycling. So what would you say to Jamie now as he decides what to do with his cans? Perhaps he could upcycle them ④ to make lanterns, toys, or sculptures for his friends and family. The options are endless, and all he needs ⑤ is a little creativity to think of them. In the same way, stop and think before you throw something out. Who knows? Maybe you can turn that trash into treasure.

02

다음 글의 괄호 안에 주어진 말을 바르게 배열하여 문장을 완성하시오. (단, 필요시 단어를 변형하되, 단어를 추가하지 않을 것)

As you can see, creative thinking has the power to make many positive changes to the environment. By giving old products more value, we can lessen the amount of waste (much / that / than / be / recycle / a way / in / even / eco-friendly). So what would you say to Jamie now as he decides what to do with his cans? Perhaps he could upcycle them to make lanterns, toys, or sculptures for his friends and family. The options are endless, and all he needs is a little creativity to think of them. In the same way, stop and think before you throw something out. Who knows? Maybe you can turn that trash into treasure.

_____

03

다음 글의 (A), (B), (C)의 각 네모 안에서 문맥에 맞는 낱말로 가장 적절한 것은?

As you can see, (A) creative / stereotypical thinking has the power to make many positive changes to the environment. By giving old products more value, we can (B) increase / decrease the amount of waste in a way that is even more eco-friendly than recycling. So what would you say to Jamie now as he decides what to do with his cans? Perhaps he could (C) recycle / upcycle them to make lanterns, toys, or sculptures for his friends and family. The options are endless, and all he needs is a little creativity to think of them. In the same way, stop and think before you throw something out. Who knows? Maybe you can turn that trash into treasure.

	(A)	(B)	(C)
①	creative	– increase	– recycle
②	creative	– increase	– upcycle
③	creative	– decrease	– upcycle
④	stereotypical	– increase	– recycle
⑤	stereotypical	– decrease	– upcycle

04

다음 글의 밑줄 친 부분 중, 문맥상 낱말의 쓰임이 적절하지 않은 것은?

As you can see, ① creative thinking has the power to make many positive changes to the environment. By giving old products more value, we can ② double the amount of waste in a way that is even more eco-friendly than recycling. So what would you say to Jamie now as he decides what to do with his cans? Perhaps he could upcycle them to make lanterns, toys, or sculptures for his friends and family. The options are ③ limitless, and all he needs is a little creativity to think of them. In the same way, stop and think before you ④ throw something out. Who knows? Maybe you can turn that trash into ⑤ treasure.

05

다음 글의 밑줄 친 부분 중, 어법상 <u>틀린</u> 것은?

As you can see, creative thinking has the power ① to make many positive changes to the environment. By giving old products more value, we can lessen the amount of waste in a way that is ② very more eco-friendly than recycling. So what would you say to Jamie now as he decides what to do with his cans? Perhaps he could ③ upcycle them to make lanterns, toys, or sculptures for his friends and family. The options are endless, and all he needs is a little creativity to think of ④ them. In the same way, ⑤ stop and think before you throw something out. Who knows? Maybe you can turn that trash into treasure.

06

다음 글의 (A), (B), (C)의 각 네모 안에서 문맥에 맞는 낱말끼리 짝지어진 것은?

As you can see, creative thinking has the power to make many (A) negative / positive changes to the environment. By giving (B) new / old products more value, we can lessen the amount of waste in a way that is even more eco-friendly than recycling. So what would you say to Jamie now as he decides what to do with his cans? Perhaps he could upcycle them to make lanterns, toys, or sculptures for his friends and family. The options are (C) finite / endless , and all he needs is a little creativity to think of them. In the same way, stop and think before you throw something out. Who knows? Maybe you can turn that trash into treasure.

	(A)	(B)	(C)
①	negative	– new	– endless
②	negative	– old	– finite
③	negative	– new	– finite
④	positive	– old	– endless
⑤	positive	– new	– finite

07

다음 글의 밑줄 친 부분 중, 어법상 옳지 <u>않은</u> 것은?

As you can see, creative thinking has the power ① makes many positive changes to the environment. By giving old products more value, we can lessen the amount of waste in a way ② that is even more eco-friendly than recycling. So what would you say to Jamie now as he decides what ③ to do with his cans? Perhaps he could upcycle them to make lanterns, toys, or sculptures for his friends and family. The options are endless, and all he needs is a ④ little creativity to think of them. In the same way, stop and think before you throw something out. Who knows? Maybe you can turn ⑤ that trash into treasure.

08

다음 글의 밑줄 친 ⓐ~ⓔ 중, 어법상 <u>어색한</u> 문장을 찾아, 〈조건〉에 맞게 고쳐 쓰시오.

〈조건〉	– 어색한 부분만이 아닌 문장 전체를 다시 쓸 것
	– 새로운 단어를 추가하지 않을 것

ⓐ As you can see, thinking creatively have the power to make many positive changes to the environment. ⓑ By giving old products more value, we can lessen the amount of waste in a way that is even more eco-friendly than recycling. So what would you say to Jamie now as he decides what to do with his cans? ⓒ Perhaps he could upcycle them to make lanterns, toys, or sculptures for his friends and family. ⓓ The options are endless, and all he needs is a little creativity to think of them. ⓔ In the same way, stop and think before you throw something out. Who knows? Maybe you can turn that trash into treasure.

(   ) _____

_____

09

다음 글의 밑줄 친 부분 중, 문맥상 낱말의 쓰임이 적절하지 않은 것은?

As you can see, creative thinking has the power to make many ① positive changes to the environment. By giving old products more value, we can ② cut down the amount of waste in a way that is even more eco-friendly than recycling. So what would you say to Jamie now as he decides what to do with his cans? Perhaps he could ③ upcycle them to make lanterns, toys, or sculptures for his friends and family. The options are ④ restrictive, and all he needs is a little creativity to think of them. In the same way, stop and think before you throw something out. Who knows? Maybe you can turn that trash into ⑤ treasure.

10

다음 빈칸에 들어갈 말로 가장 적절한 것은?

As you can see, creative thinking has the power to make many positive changes to the environment. By giving old products more value, we can lessen the amount of waste in a way that is even more eco-friendly than recycling. So what would you say to Jamie now as he decides what to do with his cans? Perhaps he could upcycle them to make lanterns, toys, or sculptures for his friends and family. The options are endless, and all he needs is _____. In the same way, stop and think before you throw something out. Who knows? Maybe you can turn that trash into treasure.

① to learn how to make recycled products
② many valueless items to be recycled
③ a little time to collect antiques
④ eco-friendly materials
⑤ a little creativity to think them up

11

다음 글의 밑줄 친 부분 중, 어법상 어색한 것은?

As you can see, creative thinking has the power to make many positive changes to the environment. By ① giving old products more value, we can lessen the amount of waste in a way that is even more eco-friendly than recycling. So what would you say to Jamie now as he decides ② what to do with his cans? Perhaps he could upcycle them ③ to make lanterns, toys, or sculptures for his friends and family. The options are endless, and all he needs ④ are a little creativity to think of them. In the same way, stop and think before you throw something out. Who knows? Maybe you can turn ⑤ that trash into treasure.

12

다음 글의 흐름에 맞게 글의 빈칸을 완성하기 위해 〈보기〉에 주어진 단어를 모두 한 번씩 사용하여 바르게 영작하시오. (단, 필요시 형태 변형 가능하나 단어 추가 불가능)

〈보기〉 a little creativity / be / to / he / all / think of / need / them

As you can see, creative thinking has the power to make many positive changes to the environment. By giving old products more value, we can lessen the amount of waste in a way that is even more eco-friendly than recycling. So what would you say to Jamie now as he decides what to do with his cans? Perhaps he could upcycle them to make lanterns, toys, or sculptures for his friends and family. The options are endless, and _____ _____. In the same way, stop and think before you throw something out. Who knows? Maybe you can turn that trash into treasure.

_____

13

다음 글의 (A), (B), (C)의 각 네모 안에서 문맥에 맞는 낱말끼리 짝지어진 것은?

As you can see, (A) conventional / creative thinking has the power to make many positive changes to the environment. By giving old products more value, we can lessen the amount of waste in a way that is even more eco-friendly than recycling. So what would you say to Jamie now as he decides what to do with his cans? Perhaps he could upcycle them to make lanterns, toys, or sculptures for his friends and family. The options are (B) limited / endless , and all he needs is a little creativity to think of them. In the (C) same / different way, stop and think before you throw something out. Who knows? Maybe you can turn that trash into treasure.

	(A)	(B)	(C)
①	conventional	– limited	– same
②	conventional	– limited	– different
③	conventional	– endless	– same
④	creative	– limited	– same
⑤	creative	– endless	– same

14

다음 빈칸에 들어갈 말로 가장 적절한 것은?

As you can see, creative thinking has the power to make many positive changes to the environment. By giving old products more value, we can lessen the amount of waste in a way that is even more eco-friendly than recycling. So what would you say to Jamie now as he decides what to do with his cans? Perhaps he could upcycle them to make lanterns, toys, or sculptures for his friends and family. The options are endless, and _____ is all that he needs. In the same way, stop and think before you throw something out. Who knows? Maybe you can turn that trash into treasure.

① the most enjoyable time to develop his hobby
② a decision to decrease the amount of trash
③ a little imagination to come up with them
④ creative thought to make trendy items
⑤ a new approach to making profitable products

15

다음 빈칸에 들어갈 말로 가장 적절한 것은?

As you can see, creative thinking has the power _____.
By giving old products more value, we can lessen the amount of waste in a way that is even more eco-friendly than recycling. So what would you say to Jamie now as he decides what to do with his cans? Perhaps he could upcycle them to make lanterns, toys, or sculptures for his friends and family. The options are endless, and all he needs is a little creativity to think of them. In the same way, stop and think before you throw something out. Who knows? Maybe you can turn that trash into treasure.

① to make a lot of advantageous environmental changes
② to guide a variety of art shows
③ to cultivate a new perspective on works of art
④ to warn us about the exhaustion of natural resources
⑤ to show the negative results of single-use products

본문[5]

출제 포인트

1위	2위	3위
일관성	대의 파악	내용 일치
본문[5] 문단편 내 출제 확률 43.5%	본문[5] 문단편 내 출제 확률 21.7%	본문[5] 문단편 내 출제 확률 17.4%

● 일관성

이 문단에서는 일관성 유형이 43.5%로 가장 많이 출제되었다. 주어진 문장의 인과 관계, 연결사, 관사, 대명사 등이 글의 흐름을 찾는 단서가 될 수 있다. '창의적인 생각은 환경에 많은 긍정적인 변화'를 가져오고, 그 구체적인 방법으로, '사용된 제품에 더 많은 가치를 부여하여 재활용보다 더 친환경적인 방식으로 쓰레기를 줄일 수 있다'는 내용이 이어지고 있다. 흐름과 무관한 문장 문제에서 '환경 보존 방법', '제품 거래' 등에 관한 내용이 나올 수 있다.

정답 ②

주어진 문장에서 'Jamie가 음료수 캔으로 무엇을 할 수 있을지'에 대한 물음을 던졌으므로, 캔으로 업사이클할 수 있는 예시가 이어지는 ⓑ에 들어가는 것이 글의 흐름상 적절하다.

> **Q. 다음 글의 흐름으로 보아, 주어진 문장이 들어가기에 가장 적절한 곳은?**
>
> So what would you say to Jamie now as he decides what to do with his cans?
>
> As you can see, creative thinking has the power to make many positive changes to the environment. (ⓐ) By giving old products more value, we can lessen the amount of waste in a way that is even more eco-friendly than recycling. (ⓑ) Perhaps he could upcycle them to make lanterns, toys, or sculptures for his friends and family. (ⓒ) The options are endless, and all he needs is a little creativity to think of them. (ⓓ) In the same way, stop and think before you throw something out. (ⓔ) Who knows? Maybe you can turn that trash into treasure.
>
> ① ⓐ   ② ⓑ   ③ ⓒ   ④ ⓓ   ⑤ ⓔ

● 대의 파악

이 문단에서는 대의 파악 유형이 21.7%로 두 번째로 많이 출제되었다. 업사이클링을 통해 쓰레기를 줄이는 방법과, 사용한 제품을 창의적으로 새롭게 만드는 내용을 포괄하여야 제목이 될 수 있다. 창의적이고 친환경적인 방식으로 쓰레기의 양을 줄일 수 있다는 내용과, 그 결과로 지구를 더 나은 환경으로 만든다는 내용이 주제나 요지가 될 수 있다. 본문에서 언급하는 업사이클링의 취지를 잘못 설명하거나 부분적인 내용이 오답으로 제시될 수 있다는 점을 유의하자.

정답 ②

업사이클링을 통해 제품을 새롭게 변형하여 쓰레기의 양을 줄일 수 있다는 내용을 고려할 때, 글의 제목으로 가장 적절한 것은 ② '업사이클링을 통한 쓰레기 감소 방안'이다.

> **Q. 다음 글의 제목으로 가장 적절한 것은?**
>
> As you can see, creative thinking has the power to make many positive changes to the environment. By giving old products more value, we can lessen the amount of waste in a way that is even more eco-friendly than recycling. So what would you say to Jamie now as he decides what to do with his cans? Perhaps he could upcycle them to make lanterns, toys, or sculptures for his friends and family. The

options are endless, and all he needs is a little creativity to think of them. In the same way, stop and think before you throw something out. Who knows? Maybe you can turn that trash into treasure.

① How to Use Lanterns That Can Contribute to Environmental Conservation
② Measures to Reduce Waste through Upcycling
③ The Power That Turns Creativity into Reality
④ How to Generate Profits through Garbage
⑤ A New Trend in Creating Art Pieces

① 환경 보존에 기여할 수 있는 랜턴 사용법
③ 창의성을 현실로 바꾸는 힘
④ 쓰레기를 통해 이익을 발생시키는 방법
⑤ 예술작품을 만드는 새로운 경향

● 내용 일치

이 문단에서는 내용 일치 유형이 17.4%로 세 번째로 많이 출제되었다. 내용 일치 여부 문제를 풀기 위해서는 글의 세부적인 내용에 유의해야 하며, 문제의 보기와 해당 지문의 내용이 정확히 일치하는지 반드시 확인해야 한다. 특히, 낡은 제품에 더 많은 가치를 부여하여 친환경적으로 쓰레기를 줄이는 방식인 upcycling(업사이클링)을 recycling(재활용)으로 바꾼 내용이 오답 선지로 출제될 가능성이 높으므로, 혼동하지 않아야 한다.

문장1	As you can see, creative thinking has the power to make many positive changes to the environment.	16.7%
문장2	By giving old products more value, we can lessen the amount of waste in a way that is even more eco-friendly than recycling.	66.7%
문장3	So what would you say to Jamie now as he decides what to do with his cans?	0.0%
문장4	Perhaps he could upcycle them to make lanterns, toys, or sculptures for his friends and family.	0.0%
문장5	The options are endless, and all he needs is a little creativity to think of them.	0.0%
문장6	In the same way, stop and think before you throw something out.	16.7%
문장7	Who knows?	0.0%
문장8	Maybe you can turn that trash into treasure.	0.0%

Q. 글의 내용과 일치하면 T, 일치하지 않으면 F에 표시하시오.

(1) 낡은 제품에 더 많은 가치를 부여하는 업사이클링을 통해 친환경적인 방식으로 쓰레기의 양을 줄일 수 있다. (T / F)
(2) 창의적인 생각이 업무 환경에 있어서 긍정적인 변화를 가져오는 힘을 가질 수 있다. (T / F)
(3) It can be helpful to lessen the amount of trash by using eco-friendly products. (T / F)
(4) Creative ideas have the power that brings the environmental advantages. (T / F)
(5) In the same way, you need to stop and think before collecting used items. (T / F)
(6) Recycling is a way that transforms trash into treasure. (T / F)

(3) 친환경 제품을 사용하여 쓰레기의 양을 줄이는 것은 유익할 수 있다.
(4) 창의적인 생각은 환경에 대한 이점을 가져오는 힘을 가지고 있다.
(5) 같은 방식으로, 사용된 물건을 수집하기 전에 멈춰서 생각할 필요가 있다.
(6) 재활용은 쓰레기를 보물로 바꾸는 방식이다.

출제 포인트 98.8% 정복!

01

다음 글의 흐름으로 보아, 주어진 문장이 들어가기에 가장 적절한 곳은?

> So what would you say to Jamie now as he decides what to do with his cans?

After a cup is used by someone, she paints a unique design on it and hangs it with many other painted cups in front of a window or pretty background. (①) These works from Leech and Deininger are not only pleasing to the eye, but they also naturally provoke an interest in environmental conservation in people. (②)

As you can see, creative thinking has the power to make many positive changes to the environment. (③) By giving old products more value, we can lessen the amount of waste in a way that is even more eco-friendly than recycling. (④) Perhaps he could upcycle them to make lanterns, toys, or sculptures for his friends and family. (⑤) The options are endless, and all he needs is a little creativity to think of them. In the same way, stop and think before you throw something out. Who knows? Maybe you can turn that trash into treasure.

02

다음 글에 관한 내용으로 적절하지 않은 것은?

As you can see, creative thinking has the power to make many positive changes to the environment. By giving old products more value, we can lessen the amount of waste in a way that is even more eco-friendly than recycling. So what would you say to Jamie now as he decides what to do with his cans? Perhaps he could upcycle them to make lanterns, toys, or sculptures for his friends and family. The options are endless, and all he needs is a little creativity to think of them. In the same way, stop and think before you throw something out. Who knows? Maybe you can turn that trash into treasure.

① It is possible that things thrown away can be transformed into valuable ones.
② Small daily necessaries can also be upcycled.
③ Creative ideas have the power to bring positive changes into the environment.
④ It is necessary to have a second thought before throwing things away.
⑤ It is recommended to give away toys that are no longer needed to friends or neighbors.

03

다음 글의 제목으로 가장 적절한 것은?

As you can see, creative thinking has the power to make many positive changes to the environment. By giving old products more value, we can lessen the amount of waste in a way that is even more eco-friendly than recycling. So what would you say to Jamie now as he decides what to do with his cans? Perhaps he could upcycle them to make lanterns, toys, or sculptures for his friends and family. The options are endless, and all he needs is a little creativity to think of them. In the same way, stop and think before you throw something out. Who knows? Maybe you can turn that trash into treasure.

① Distinguishing between Recycling and Upcycling
② Creative Thinking: A Tool That Can Be Valuable for Survival
③ The Reason Why We Should Recycle Wasted Materials
④ Repurpose Used Items with a Little Creativity
⑤ Keeping Updated about Reusable Energy Developments

04

주어진 글 다음에 이어질 글의 순서로 가장 적절한 것은?

When artists add their own creative touches, things that most people consider junk are reborn as beautiful works of art.

(A) There is also an artist who shows that even disposable cups can be reused as artistic material. For years, Gwyneth Leech has turned used coffee cups into brilliant art exhibits. After a cup is used by someone, she paints a unique design on it and hangs it with many other painted cups in front of a window or pretty background. These works from Leech and Deininger are not only pleasing to the eye, but they also naturally provoke an interest in environmental conservation in people.

(B) The giant pictures made from trash by environmental artist Tom Deininger are one of a kind. Up close, these brightly colored creations look like a mixed-up mess of broken plastic, unwanted toys, and bent wire—all things that cannot be recycled. From farther away, however, they appear to blend together into marvelous landscapes or other paintings.

(C) As you can see, creative thinking has the power to make many positive changes to the environment. By giving old products more value, we can lessen the amount of waste in a way that is even more eco-friendly than recycling. So what would you say to Jamie now as he decides what to do with his cans? Perhaps he could upcycle them to make lanterns, toys, or sculptures for his friends and family. The options are endless, and all he needs is a little creativity to think of them. In the same way, stop and think before you throw something out. Who knows? Maybe you can turn that trash into treasure.

① (A) – (B) – (C)
② (B) – (A) – (C)
③ (B) – (C) – (A)
④ (C) – (A) – (B)
⑤ (C) – (B) – (A)

05

다음 글의 요지로 가장 적절한 것은?

As you can see, creative thinking has the power to make many positive changes to the environment. By giving old products more value, we can lessen the amount of waste in a way that is even more eco-friendly than recycling. So what would you say to Jamie now as he decides what to do with his cans? Perhaps he could upcycle them to make lanterns, toys, or sculptures for his friends and family. The options are endless, and all he needs is a little creativity to think of them. In the same way, stop and think before you throw something out. Who knows? Maybe you can turn that trash into treasure.

① The possibilities for upcycling are limitless.
② To bring a new life into discarded items, it's important to consider social norms.
③ Recycling helps you to prepare for potential environmental disasters.
④ By staying creative, we all can upcycle and benefit the environment.
⑤ The goal of upcycling is to preserve items.

06

다음 글에서 전체 흐름과 관계 없는 문장은?

As you can see, creative thinking has the power to make many positive changes to the environment. ① By giving old products more value, we can lessen the amount of waste in a way that is even more eco-friendly than recycling. ② People think that the way is adaptable for a new work environment. ③ So what would you say to Jamie now as he decides what to do with his cans? ④ Perhaps he could upcycle them to make lanterns, toys, or sculptures for his friends and family. ⑤ The options are endless, and all he needs is a little creativity to think of them. In the same way, stop and think before you throw something out. Who knows? Maybe you can turn that trash into treasure.

07

다음 글의 내용과 일치하지 <u>않은</u> 것은?

As you can see, creative thinking has the power to make many positive changes to the environment. By giving old products more value, we can lessen the amount of waste in a way that is even more eco-friendly than recycling. So what would you say to Jamie now as he decides what to do with his cans? Perhaps he could upcycle them to make lanterns, toys, or sculptures for his friends and family. The options are endless, and all he needs is a little creativity to think of them. In the same way, stop and think before you throw something out. Who knows? Maybe you can turn that trash into treasure.

① 버려진 물건이 가치 있는 것으로 바뀔 가능성이 있다.
② 재활용보다 더 친환경적인 방법으로 쓰레기의 양을 줄일 수 있다.
③ 창의적인 사고를 통해 환경에 긍정적인 영향을 줄 수 있다.
④ 낡은 제품에 더 많은 가치를 부여함으로써 경제 발전에 이바지할 수 있다.
⑤ 쓰레기를 버리기 전에 가치 있는 물건이 될 수 있는지 멈춰서 생각해 봐야 한다.

08

다음 글의 흐름으로 보아, 주어진 문장이 들어가기에 가장 적절한 곳은?

By giving old products more value, we can lessen the amount of waste in a way that is even more eco-friendly than recycling.

After a cup is used by someone, she paints a unique design on it and hangs it with many other painted cups in front of a window or pretty background. (①) These works from Leech and Deininger are not only pleasing to the eye, but they also naturally provoke an interest in environmental conservation in people. (②)

As you can see, creative thinking has the power to make many positive changes to the environment. (③) So what would you say to Jamie now as he decides what to do with his cans? (④) Perhaps he could upcycle them to make lanterns, toys, or sculptures for his friends and family. (⑤) The options are endless, and all he needs is a little creativity to think of them. In the same way, stop and think before you throw something out. Who knows? Maybe you can turn that trash into treasure.

09

다음 글의 주제로 가장 적절한 것은?

  As you can see, creative thinking has the power to make many positive changes to the environment. By giving old products more value, we can lessen the amount of waste in a way that is even more eco-friendly than recycling. So what would you say to Jamie now as he decides what to do with his cans? Perhaps he could upcycle them to make lanterns, toys, or sculptures for his friends and family. The options are endless, and all he needs is a little creativity to think of them. In the same way, stop and think before you throw something out. Who knows? Maybe you can turn that trash into treasure.

① decreasing the amount of waste by using the used products at least several times before throwing them away
② reducing the amount of waste by reusing discarded products with creative thinking to make the Earth greener
③ preserving the environment by separating materials that are recycled
④ saving natural resources by shutting down coal power plants
⑤ donating used things to help the developing countries

10

다음 글에서 전체 흐름과 관계 <u>없는</u> 문장은?

  As you can see, creative thinking has the power to make many positive changes to the environment. By giving old products more value, we can lessen the amount of waste in a way that is even more eco-friendly than recycling. ① So what would you say to Jamie now as he decides what to do with his cans? ② Perhaps he could upcycle them to make lanterns, toys, or sculptures for his friends and family. ③ It is more likely that people prefer upcycled products to recycled products. ④ The options are endless, and all he needs is a little creativity to think of them. ⑤ In the same way, stop and think before you throw something out. Who knows? Maybe you can turn that trash into treasure.

기타 연습 문제

본문[5] 1회 등장 포인트

● 어휘 creative, changes

As you can see, creative thinking has the power to make many positive changes to the environment.

● 어휘 before, 일반동사 명령문, 구동사 throw out

In the same way, stop and think before you throw something out.

01

다음 글의 (A), (B), (C)의 각 네모 안에서 문맥에 맞는 낱말로 가장 적절한 것은?

As you can see, (A) imaginative / obsolete thinking has the power to make many positive changes to the environment. By giving old products more value, we can lessen the amount of waste in a way that is even more eco-friendly than recycling. So what would you say to Jamie now as he decides what to do with his cans? Perhaps he could upcycle them to make lanterns, toys, or sculptures for his friends and family. The options are endless, and all he needs is a little (B) fact / creativity to think of them. In the same way, stop and think (C) before / after you throw something out. Who knows? Maybe you can turn that trash into treasure.

	(A)	(B)	(C)
①	imaginative	– fact	– before
②	imaginative	– fact	– after
③	imaginative	– creativity	– before
④	obsolete	– fact	– before
⑤	obsolete	– creativity	– after

● 빈칸 trash, 지시형용사 that

Maybe you can turn that trash into treasure.

02

다음 글의 빈칸 (A), (B), (C)에 각각 들어갈 말을 〈보기〉에서 골라 쓰시오. (단, 한 번씩만 사용할 것)

〈보기〉 recycle / tradition / trash / challenges / mount / decrease / changes / governments / creativity

As you can see, creative thought has the power to make many advantageous _____(A)_____ to the environment. By giving old products more value, we can lessen the amount of waste in a way that is even more eco-friendly than recycling. So what would you say to Jamie now as he decides what to do with his cans? Perhaps he could upcycle them to make lanterns, toys, or sculptures for his friends and family. The options are endless, and all he needs is a little _____(B)_____ to think of them. In the same way, stop and think before you throw something out. Who knows? Maybe you can turn that _____(C)_____ into treasure.

(A) _____

(B) _____

(C) _____

● 문장 변형

동사 make를 사용하여 make the Earth far greener와 같이 5형식 문장으로 변형되어 문제가 나올 수 있다는 점을 유의하자.

By giving old products more value, we can lessen the amount of waste in a way that is even more eco-friendly than recycling.

03

다음 글의 밑줄 친 부분 중, 어법상 어색한 것은?

As you can see, creative thinking has the power to make many positive changes to the environment. By giving old products more value, we can lessen the amount of waste and make the Earth ① far greener. So what would you say to Jamie now as he decides ② what to do with his cans? Perhaps he could upcycle them to make lanterns, toys, or sculptures for his friends and family. The options are endless, and all he needs is a little creativity to think of them.

In the same way, stop and ③ thinking before you ④ throw something out. Who knows? Maybe you can turn ⑤ that trash into treasure.

● 함축된 의미 **treasure**

> **Maybe you can turn that trash into treasure.**

treasure가 내포하는 의미를 묻는 문제가 출제될 수 있다. 이 본문에서 treasure는 우리가 사전적 정의로 알고 있는 금은보화를 가리키는 보물의 의미가 아닌 가치 있는 것으로 이해해야 한다.

● 요약

이 문단에서 글을 요약하는 문제가 출제될 수 있다. 글의 중심 내용이 주로 요약한 문장으로 나온다. 이 문장에서 글의 핵심은 우리가 낡은 물건을 업사이클하여 쓰레기의 양을 줄이는 데 필요로 하는 것은 약간의 창의성이라는 내용이다. With a little creativity, it is possible for us to upcycle old items, which can help reduce the amount of waste 등과 같이 약간의 창의력으로 쓰레기를 줄일 수 있다는 부분이 변형되어 나올 수 있다는 점을 유의하자.

04

다음 글을 한 문장으로 요약하고자 한다. 빈칸 (A), (B)에 들어갈 말로 가장 적절한 것을 고르시오.

As you can see, creative thinking has the power to make many positive changes to the environment. By giving old products more value, we can lessen the amount of waste in a way that is even more eco-friendly than recycling. So what would you say to Jamie now as he decides what to do with his cans? Perhaps he could upcycle them to make lanterns, toys, or sculptures for his friends and family. The options are endless, and all he needs is a little creativity to think of them. In the same way, stop and think before you throw something out. Who knows? Maybe you can turn that trash into treasure.

We can _____(A)_____ the volume of waste by using a little _____(B)_____ to think of upcycling old things.

	(A)	(B)
①	increase	– imagination
②	decrease	– creativity
③	maximize	– motivation
④	keep	– inspiration
⑤	reduce	– expectation

본문
핵심 분석

1

from A to B: A에서 B로
FROM TRASH **TO** TREASURE
= waste, garbage, litter, rubbish

2

days (X) for(X)   S   V1   O   V2
Every day during lunch, Jamie enjoys a soft drink and has a
O   to-v 형용사적 용법   V   S
decision (to make): What should he do with the empty can?

3

S   V   V' 명령문 O'
Many people would answer, "Recycle it!"
= the empty can

4

S   V   SC
Obviously, recycling is good for many reasons.
= Of course, Certainly

5

the amount of: ~의 양   throwing (X)
S   V1   O   과거분사   V2
We can reduce **the amount of** trash (thrown away), use **less**
O 비교급+than: ~보다 더 …하게 to-v 부사적 용법 〈목적〉 V3
energy **than** we would to make new products, and conserve
O   (use)
natural resources by recycling.

6

S   V   SC   to-v 형용사적 용법
However, recycling is not a perfect way (to manage waste).

7

S   V   O   to-v 부사적 용법 〈목적〉
It still requires large amounts of energy to purify used resources
= Recycling   using (X)
and convert them into new products.
(to)   = used resources

★
주제문

What about v-ing :   · try to-v: 노력하다
~하는 건 어때?   · try v-ing: 시험삼아 해보다
8 So, what about trying to creatively reuse, or "upcycle," them
creatively reusing (X)   = used resources
instead?

9

= Upcycling   S   V 현재진행   SC   = as[because]
This new approach is becoming more popular since it is
비교급 강조   = upcycling
even more environmentally friendly than recycling.
very (X) much, still, a lot, far (O)

10

S   V   SC
What's more, it can also be fun!
= In addition   = upcycling
Moreover
Furthermore

11

V   S   간접의문문: 의문사+주어+동사
Here are some inspiring examples of [how people have
inspired (X)   how have people (X)
creatively upcycled old, used things].

1 쓰레기에서 보물로

2 매일 점심을 먹을 때, Jamie는 청량음료를 마시고 결정을 해야 한다. 이 빈 캔을 가지고 무엇을 해야 할까?

3 많은 사람들이 "재활용 해!"라고 말할 것이다.

4 분명히 여러 가지 이유에서 재활용은 좋다.

5 재활용을 함으로써 버려지는 쓰레기 양을 줄이고, 새 제품을 만드는 데 쓰는 것보다 적은 에너지를 사용하며 천연자원을 절약할 수 있다.

6 하지만, 재활용이 쓰레기를 처리하는 완벽한 방법은 아니다.

7 재활용은 여전히 사용된 자원을 정화시키고 새 제품으로 바꾸기 위해 많은 양의 에너지를 필요로 한다.

8 그렇다면, 대신 창의적인 재사용, 즉 업사이클을 시도해보는 것은 어떨까?

9 이 새로운 접근법은 재활용보다 훨씬 더 환경친화적이기 때문에 점점 인기를 얻고 있다.

10 게다가 재미있기까지 할 수 있다!

11 여기 사람들이 오래된 중고 물건들을 어떻게 창의적으로 업사이클했는지를 보여주는 몇몇 고무적인 사례들이 있다.

Words and Phrases

- trash **n.** 쓰레기
- make a decision 결정하다
- empty **a.** 텅 빈
- recycle **v.** 재활용하다
- obviously **ad.** 분명히, 명백하게
- reduce **v.** 줄이다
- throw away ~을 버리다
- conserve **v.** 아끼다, 절약하다
- natural resource 천연자원
- manage **v.** 처리하다
- require **v.** 필요로 하다
- purify **v.** 정화시키다
- convert A into B A를 B로 바꾸다
- instead **ad.** 대신에
- approach **n.** 접근법
- environmentally friendly 환경친화적인
- what's more 게다가
- inspiring **a.** 고무적인
- example **n.** 예, 예시

업사이클링으로, Freitag 형제는 쓰레기를 가방으로 재사용했고, Kyle Parsons는 낡은 오토바이 타이어를 샌들 밑창으로 탈바꿈시키고 있음

1 Through upcycling, a seemingly useless object can be transformed into something completely different (that is useful for everyday life).
→ useful
조동사 + 수동태
S   V
주격관계대명사
completely different something (X)
→ useless

2 What do you think can be done with old truck tarps, car seat belts, and bicycle inner tubes?
V   S   조동사 + 수동태

3 Individually, these things look like trash, but with a little imagination the Freitag brothers, Markus and Daniel, repurpose them for something totally new: very strong bags.
S1   V1   little (X), a few (X)
S2   V2
O
totally new something (X)

4 These bags are perfect for bicyclists (going to work every day in all kinds of weather).
S   V   SC   현재분사
gone (X)   days(X)

5 Similarly, a man (named Kyle Parsons) and his partners have been creatively reusing old motorcycle tires from Bali, Indonesia.
S1   과거분사   S2   V   현재완료 진행
naming (X)   O

- a number of: 많은
- the number of: ~의 수
The shocking number of (X)

6 A shocking number of tires get thrown away there every year, and they are a serious environmental problem since they cannot decompose or be recycled.
S1   V1   get p.p.: ~해지다
throwing (X)   SC   years (X)
S2   V2
= tires   수동태   = as[because]
(cannot)

7 To solve this problem, Parsons and his team are turning them into sandal bottoms.
to-v 부사적 용법 〈목적〉   S1   S2   V 현재진행   O
= tires

8 They then use canvas and natural materials to make the other sandal parts.
S   V   O1   O2   to-v 부사적 용법 〈목적〉
= Parsons and his team

9 What a great reuse of resources!
What 감탄문: What + (a/an) + 형용사 + 명사 (+ 주어 + 동사)!

1 업사이클링을 통해, 겉보기에는 쓸모없는 물건도 일상 생활에 유용한 완전히 다른 것으로 탈바꿈될 수 있다.

2 낡은 트럭 방수포, 자동차 안전 벨트, 그리고 자전거 타이어의 안쪽 튜브를 가지고 무엇을 할 수 있다고 생각하는가?

3 개별적으로 보면 이것들은 쓰레기처럼 보일 수 있지만, Markus와 Daniel이라는 Freitag 형제는 약간의 상상력으로 이것들을 완전히 새로운 것으로 바꾼다. 매우 튼튼한 가방이 바로 그것이다.

4 이 가방들은 어떤 날씨에도 매일 일하러 가는 자전거 이용자들에게 완벽하다.

5 이와 유사하게, Kyle Parsons라는 남자와 그의 동업자들은 인도네시아 발리에서 나오는 낡은 오토바이 타이어를 창의적으로 재사용해오고 있다.

6 그곳에서 매년 엄청난 수의 타이어들이 버려지고, 그것들은 분해되거나 재활용될 수 없기 때문에 심각한 환경 문제이다.

7 이 문제를 해결하고자, Parsons와 그의 팀은 타이어를 샌들 밑창으로 탈바꿈시키고 있다.

8 그런 다음 그들은 샌들의 다른 부분들을 만들기 위해 캔버스와 천연 재료들을 활용한다.

9 얼마나 훌륭한 자원 재활용인가!

Words and Phrases

- through prep. ~를 통해
- seemingly ad. 겉보기에
- useless a. 쓸모없는
- object n. 물건
- transform A into B A를 B로 변형시키다
- completely ad. 완전히
- useful a. 유용한
- tarp n. 방수포
- individually ad. 개별적으로
- imagination n. 상상력
- repurpose v. 다른 목적에 맞게 고치다
- totally ad. 완전히
- similarly ad. 유사하게
- shocking a. 매우 놀랄 만한
- serious a. 심각한
- environmental a. 환경의
- decompose v. 분해되다
- solve v. 해결하다
- bottom n. 바닥
- natural material 천연 재료

본문3 업사이클링을 통해 오래된 건물도 재사용할 수 있으며, 이는 업사이클링이 환경뿐만 아니라 유산도 보호할 수 있음을 보여줌

★
주제문
1
even, still, a lot, far (O)
very (X)
Along with small everyday items, much bigger things can also
조동사+수동태   주격관계대명사   조동사+수동태
be upcycled—even old buildings (that cannot be used for their
use(X) = old buildings'
original purpose anymore).
= any longer

2
S   V   IO   DO
The German government showed us an excellent example of
주격관계대명사
this with a former steel plant (that closed in 1985).
= 건물처럼 큰 것도 업사이클될 수 있다는 것   has closed (X)

3
Rather than destroy the plant's buildings or abandon the entire
S   V   O to-v 명사적 용법   abandoning (X)
facility, they decided to give it new meaning as a series of useful
= German government giving (X) = the former steel plant
public structures.

4
S   V1   O   V2
Many of the buildings kept their original shapes, but received
O1   O2   현재분사
extra equipment and new designs in their surrounding areas.
surrounded (X)

5
S   V   SC
For instance, old gas tanks became pools for divers.

6
S   V 수동태
Concrete walls of iron storage towers were turned into ideal
training fields for rock climbers.

7
V S   O   S'   V'
Can you believe [a building for melting metal is now a viewing
SC' (that)
platform with a gorgeous 360-degree view]?
360-degrees (X)

8
S   V   SC
The final result is the Landscape Park Duisburg Nord.

9
S V   O   과거분사
It has almost 570 acres of land (filled with gardens, cycling
= The Landscape Park Duisburg Nord   filling (X)
paths, and pretty lights at night, in addition to its creatively
과거분사   in addition (X)
repurposed buildings).
repurposing (X)

10
접속사 that
S V   O 가S'V' SC' 진S' to-v 명사적 용법
This park proves [that it's possible to preserve the heritage of a
place **as well as** the environment].
not only the environment but also the heritage of a place (O)

---

1 작은 일상 물품들과 더불어, 훨씬 더 커다란 것들도 업사이클될 수 있다. 원래 용도로 더는 사용될 수 없는 오래된 건물들조차도 말이다.

2 독일 정부는 1985년도에 문을 닫은 옛 철강 공장으로 우리에게 이것의 훌륭한 예를 보여주었다.

3 공장 건물을 부수거나 전체 시설을 버려두기보다, 그들은 일련의 유용한 공공 구조물로서 그것에게 새로운 의미를 부여하기로 결정했다.

4 건물의 많은 부분이 원래 모습을 유지했으나 주변 부지에 추가 설비가 설치되고 새로운 디자인이 입혀졌다.

5 예를 들면, 오래된 가스탱크는 다이버들을 위한 풀이 되었다.

6 철을 저장하는 타워들의 콘크리트 벽은 암벽등반가들을 위한 이상적인 훈련장으로 바뀌었다.

7 금속을 녹이기 위한 건물이 이제는 360도의 멋진 경치를 보여주는 전망대라는 것을 믿을 수 있겠는가?

8 그 최종 결과물이 뒤스부르크 환경 공원이다.

9 이는 창의적으로 개조된 건물들 이외에도 정원, 자전거 길, 밤에 빛나는 멋진 조명으로 가득 찬 대략 570에이커 크기의 땅이다.

10 이 공원은 환경뿐만 아니라 어떤 장소의 유산도 보호할 수 있다는 것을 증명한다.

Words and Phrases

- government n. 정부
- former a. 이전의
- steel plant 철강 공장
- rather than ~ 대신에, ~라기 보다는
- destroy v. 파괴하다
- abandon v. 버리다, 유기하다
- entire a. 전체의
- facility n. 시설
- a series of 일련의
- structure n. 구조물
- extra a. 추가의
- equipment n. 설비
- storage n. 저장
- turn A into B A를 B로 바꾸다
- ideal a. 이상적인
- melt v. 녹이다
- gorgeous a. 멋진
- degree n. (각도의 단위인) 도
- filled with ~로 가득 찬
- in addition to ~뿐만 아니라
- prove v. 증명하다
- preserve v. 보존하다
- heritage n. 유산
- B as well as A A뿐만 아니라 B도

본문4 | 대부분의 사람들이 쓰레기로 여기던 사물들을 예술가들이 업사이클링을 통해서 예술 작품으로 다시 태어나게 함

★주제문

1 When artists add their own creative touches, things (that most people consider junk) are reborn as beautiful works of art.

S 목적격관계대명사
V 수동태
is (X)

1 예술가들이 그들의 창의적인 손길을 더할 때, 대부분의 사람들이 쓰레기로 여기던 사물들이 아름다운 예술작품으로 다시 태어난다.

2 The giant pictures (made from trash by environmental artist Tom Deininger) are one of a kind.

= huge, enormous, vast S 과거분사
making (X)
V SC
is (X)

2 환경 예술가 Tom Deininger에 의해 쓰레기로 만들어진 거대한 그림들은 매우 독특하다.

3 Up close, these brightly colored creations look like a mixed-up mess of broken plastic, unwanted toys, and bent wire—all things (that cannot be recycled).

S V
coloring (X)
주격관계대명사 조동사+수동태
recycle (X)

3 가까이 보면, 밝게 색칠된 이 작품들은 조각난 플라스틱과 버려진 장난감, 휘어진 선 등 모두 재활용될 수 없는 것들이 섞여 있는 것처럼 보인다.

4 From farther away, however, they appear to blend together into marvelous landscapes or other paintings.

≠ further (정도가 더 먼) S V SC
it appears[seems] that they blend (O)

4 하지만 멀리서 보면, 그들은 보기 좋게 조합되어, 놀라운 풍경 혹은 여타 그림들처럼 보인다.

5 There is also an artist (who shows [that even disposable cups can be reused as artistic material]).

V S 주격관계대명사 접속사 that
that(O)
조동사+수동태

5 일회용 컵이 예술적 재료로 재사용될 수 있다는 것을 보여주는 또 다른 예술가가 있다.

6 For years, Gwyneth Leech has turned used coffee cups into brilliant art exhibits.

S V 현재완료 〈계속〉 O
During (X)

6 수년간, Gwyneth Leech는 사용된 커피 컵을 멋진 미술 전시품으로 바꿔왔다.

7 After a cup is used by someone, she paints a unique design on it and hangs it with many other painted cups (in front of a window or pretty background).

수동태 S V1 O
V2 O
=the used cup

7 컵이 누군가에 의해 사용된 후, 그녀는 컵에 독특한 디자인을 그리고, 유리창이나 예쁜 배경 앞에 그림이 그려진 다른 많은 컵들과 함께 이것을 매달아 놓는다.

8 These works (from Leech and Deininger) are not only pleasing to the eye, but they also naturally provoke an interest in environmental conservation in people.

S1 V1 SC
is (X) O pleased (X)
S2 V2

8 Leech와 Deininger의 전시품들은 눈을 즐겁게 할 뿐만 아니라, 자연스럽게 환경 보존에 대한 사람들의 관심을 유발한다.

Words and Phrases

- creative **a.** 창의적인
- touch **n.** 손길
- consider **v.** 여기다
- junk **n.** 쓰레기
- reborn **v.** 다시 태어나다
- one of a kind 독특한 사람[것]
- creation **n.** 창작품, 예술품
- look like ~처럼 보이다
- mess **n.** 엉망인 상태
- bent **a.** 구부러진
- appear to-v ~하는 것처럼 보이다
- blend **v.** 섞이다
- marvelous **a.** 놀라운
- landscape **n.** 풍경
- disposable **a.** 일회용의, 사용 후 버리는
- artistic material 예술 재료
- exhibit **n.** 전시물
- unique **a.** 독특한
- hang **v.** 걸다, 매달다
- in front of ~의 앞에
- background **n.** 배경
- pleasing **a.** 즐겁게 하는
- naturally **ad.** 자연적으로
- provoke **v.** 유발하다

본문5 업사이클링을 통한 창의적인 생각은 환경에 많은 긍정적 변화를 가져오는 힘이 있음

★
주제문
1 As you can see, creative thinking has the power (to make many

positive changes to the environment).
S   V   O   to-v 형용사적 용법

by v-ing: By giving more value to
~함으로써   old products (O)
2 **By giving** old products more value, we can lessen the amount
S   V   O
of waste in a way (that is even **more** eco-friendly **than** recycling).
주격관계대명사
very (X)
much, still, a lot, far (O)

O   V   S   S'   V'   O'
3 So what would you say to Jamie now as he decides what to do
what he should do (O)
with his cans?

S   V   O   to-v 부사적 용법 〈목적〉
4 Perhaps he could upcycle them to make lanterns, toys, or
= his cans
sculptures for his friends and family.
to, of (X)

S1   V1   SC   S2   V2   SC
5 The options are endless, and all (he needs) is a little creativity
to-v 형용사적 용법   (목적격관계대명사)   are (X)   little (X)
(to think of them).   a few (X)
= the options

명령문
V1   V2   S'   V'   O'
6 In the same way, stop and think before you throw something
= Likewise, Similarly
out.

S   V   S   V   O
7 Who knows? Maybe you can turn that trash into treasure.
= Nobody knows.

---

1 당신도 볼 수 있듯, 창의적인 생각은 환경에 있어서 많은 긍정적 변화를 가져오는 힘이 있다.

2 낡은 제품에 더 많은 가치를 부여함으로써 우리는 재활용보다 훨씬 더 친환경적인 방식으로 쓰레기의 양을 줄일 수 있다.

3 자, 그렇다면 이제 음료수 캔으로 무엇을 할지 결정하려는 Jamie에게 뭐라고 말하겠는가?

4 아마도 그는 친구와 가족을 위한 랜턴, 장난감, 혹은 조각품을 만들기 위해 캔들을 업사이클할 수 있을 것이다.

5 선택할 수 있는 것은 끝이 없으며, 그가 필요한 것은 그것들에 대해 생각해 볼 약간의 창의성뿐이다.

6 똑같은 방식으로, 여러분도 무언가를 버리기 전 잠시 멈추어 생각해 보라.

7 누가 알겠는가? 당신이 쓰레기를 보물로 변화시킬지.

Words and Phrases

- positive **a.** 긍정적인
- environment **n.** 환경
- product **n.** 제품
- value **n.** 가치
- lessen **v.** 줄이다
- amount **n.** 양
- eco-friendly **a.** 친환경적인
- perhaps **ad.** 아마도
- sculpture **n.** 조각품
- option **n.** 선택지
- endless **a.** 끝없는
- creativity **n.** 창의력
- in the same way 같은 방식으로
- throw out ~을 버리다

기타 본문

a: Using recycling bins is a great way to save the Earth. Everyone should separate things that can be recycled from their trash and put them in the bins.

b: If we creatively reuse the things thrown away, we can make the Earth greener by reducing trash and saving more energy.

c: Reusing items several times before throwing them away cuts down on the amount of waste we produce. It saves you money, too.

출제 1위 문장 ★★★

If we creatively reuse the things thrown away, we can make the Earth greener by reducing trash and saving more energy.

형용사 vs. 부사

형용사는 명사를 수식할 수 있는 반면에, 부사는 동사, 형용사, 부사와 문장 전체를 수식할 수 있다. 이 문장에서 부사 creatively가 동사 reuse를 수식한다.

과거분사

과거분사는 '(대상)이 ~된', '~(해)진'이라는 의미이다. 현재분사와 과거분사의 구분 문제를 풀기 위해서는 수식을 받는 대상과 분사의 관계가 능동인지, 수동인지를 구분해야 한다는 점을 명심하자.

동명사 병렬

등위접속사 and, so, but이 나올 때는 병렬구조를 파악하는 문제가 나올 확률이 높다. 문장은 '쓰레기를 줄이고 에너지를 절약함으로써 지구를 더 푸르게 만들 수 있다'라는 의미로 전치사 by에 이어지는 동명사 reducing과 saving이 and로 병렬 연결되어 있다.

출제 2위 문장 ★★

Using recycling bins is a great way to save the Earth.

동명사의 수 일치

동명사는 문장에서 주어, 목적어, 보어 자리에 올 수 있는 명사 역할을 할 수 있다. 동명사가 문장에서 주어 자리에 올 때는 단수 취급하여 동사 또한 3인칭 단수형으로 쓴다.

해석

a: 분리수거함을 이용하는 것은 지구를 구하는 훌륭한 방법이야. 모든 사람들이 쓰레기로부터 재활용될 수 있는 것들을 분리하여 그것들을 수거함 속에 넣어야 해.

b: 만일 우리가 버려진 물건들을 창의적으로 재사용한다면, 쓰레기를 줄이고 더 많은 에너지를 절약함으로써 지구를 더 푸르게 할 수 있을 거야.

c: 물건을 버리기 전에 여러 번 재사용하는 것은 우리가 만들어내는 쓰레기의 양을 줄여줘. 그것을 통해 돈도 아낄 수 있어.

Inside Culture 적중 MAPPING

이것만 알아도 맞힌다!

a. This beautiful bookshop used to be a theater featuring magnificent paintings on its ceiling. In 2000, it was repurposed. The cinema seating was removed, and rows of bookshelves were installed in place of the original balconies and floors. The red stage curtains, theater boxes, and many other architectural details still remain, making this building a historic and luxurious place.

b. This museum is housed in a former power station. **After it closed down in 1981, the government decided to transform it into a museum instead of destroying it.** Now this museum holds the national collection of modern British artwork and is famous for its modern and contemporary art.

c. The aquarium was founded in 1984 on the site of a former fish canning factory. ★★★ **After the fishing industry collapsed, a team decided to reuse this building but still retain its historic character.** Now, it holds thousands of plants and animals, with more than 600 species on display, and is enjoyed by both residents and tourists.

대의 파악 〈출제 1위 유형〉

글에서 세 건물이 언급되기 때문에, 이러한 건물들의 공통점을 아우를 수 있는 내용이 무엇인지 파악하는 문제가 나올 확률이 높다. 본문의 내용을 충분히 파악하지 않고 단순히 '환경 보호'라는 큰 주제만 생각한다면 오답 선지를 고를 수 있으니 유의하도록 하자.

내용 일치 〈출제 2위 유형〉

주어진 글에서는 역사적 가치를 보존하면서도 새롭고 흥미롭게 변한 건물 세 가지 사례를 소개하고 있다. 각 건물의 특성이 다르기 때문에, 본문을 읽고 핵심을 정리하는 것이 중요하다. 특히, 세 건물 모두 변형한 점과 보존한 점이 공존하기 때문에, 어떤 요소는 유지하고 어떤 요소는 바꿨는지를 구별해서 파악해두는 것이 중요하다.

출제 1위 문장 ★★★

After the fishing industry collapsed, a team decided to reuse this building but still retain its historic character.

---

to부정사 병렬

decided의 목적어 to reuse와 (to) retain이 등위접속사 but으로 병렬 연결된 구조이다.

어휘 retain

이 문장에서 retain 대신에 사용할 수 있는 동사는 maintain, preserve, sustain, conserve 등이다. 이와 같은 단어로 변형되어 출제될 수 있기 때문에 함께 기억하자. 또한, 반대되는 뜻을 지닌 destroy, degrade, deteriorate, decompose와 같은 단어는 올 수 없으니 유의하자.

출제 2위 문장 ★★

After it closed down in 1981, the government decided to transform it into a museum instead of destroying it.

전치사+동명사

전치사 다음에 동사를 쓰려면, 동사를 동명사 형태로 써야 한다. to부정사는 올 수 없다는 것을 기억하자.

해석

a. 이 멋진 서점은 천장에 장엄한 그림들을 특징으로 하는 극장이었다. 2000년에 이는 다른 용도로 개조되었다. 영화 좌석은 제거되고, 기존의 발코니와 바닥 자리에 책장들이 줄줄이 설치되었다. 빨간 무대 커튼, 극장 칸막이 특별석, 그리고 많은 다른 건축적 세부사항들이 여전히 남아 이 건물을 역사적이고 호화로운 장소로 만들어주고 있다.

b. 이 박물관은 예전 발전소에 자리하고 있다. 발전소가 1981년 문을 닫은 후, 정부는 이를 파괴하는 대신 박물관으로 바꾸기로 결정했다. 현재 이 박물관은 국가 소유의 현대 영국 미술품을 보유하고 있으며, 근현대 미술로 유명하다.

c. 이 수족관은 1984년 예전 생선 통조림 공장터에 설립되었다. 어업이 붕괴된 후, 어느 팀에서 이 건물을 재사용하되 여전히 역사적 특징은 유지하기로 결정했다. 현재 이 수족관은 수천의 동식물을 보유하고 있으며 600여 종 이상이 전시되어 있고 주민과 관광객 모두에게 즐거움을 준다.

01

다음 글의 빈칸에 알맞은 말을 괄호 안의 동사를 활용하여 올바른 형태로 쓰시오.

Using recycling bins _____(be) a great way to save the Earth. Everyone should separate things that can be recycled from their trash and put them in the bins.

02

다음 글의 밑줄 친 부분을 어법상 바르게 고친 것으로 적절하지 <u>않은</u> 것은?

① <u>Use</u> recycling bins is a great way to save the Earth. Everyone should separate things that can ② <u>recycle</u> from their trash and put them in the bins. If we creatively reuse the things ③ <u>throw</u> away, we can make the Earth greener by reducing trash and ④ <u>save</u> more energy. Reusing items several times before throwing them away ⑤ <u>cut</u> down on the amount of waste we produce.

① → Using	② → be recycled
③ → throwing	④ → saving
⑤ → cuts	

03

다음 글에서 밑줄 친 부분 중, 어법상 적절하지 <u>않은</u> 것은?

This beautiful bookshop used ① <u>to be</u> a theater featuring magnificent paintings on its ceiling. In 2000, it was repurposed. The cinema seating was removed, and rows of bookshelves ② <u>were installed</u> in place of the original balconies and floors. The red stage curtains, theater boxes, and many other architectural details still remain, ③ <u>making</u> this building a historic and luxurious place.

This museum is housed in a former power station. After it closed down in 1981, the government decided to transform it into a museum instead of ④ <u>to destroy</u> it. Now this museum holds the national collection of modern British artwork and ⑤ <u>is</u> famous for its modern and contemporary art.

04

다음 글의 괄호에서 어법상 옳은 것은?

The aquarium was founded in 1984 on the site of a former fish canning factory. After the fishing industry collapsed, a team decided to reuse this building but still (retain / retaining) its historic character. Now, it holds thousands of plants and animals, with more than 600 species on display, and is enjoyed by both residents and tourists.

05

다음 글에서 밑줄 친 부분 중, 어법상 적절하지 <u>않은</u> 것은?

Using recycling bins ① <u>is</u> a great way to save the Earth. Everyone should separate things that can be recycled from their trash and ② <u>put</u> them in the bins. If we ③ <u>creatively</u> reuse the things thrown away, we can make the Earth greener by reducing trash and ④ <u>to save</u> more energy. Reusing items several times before ⑤ <u>throwing</u> them away cuts down on the amount of waste we produce.

06

다음 글의 빈칸에 알맞은 말을 괄호 안의 동사를 활용하여 올바른 형태로 쓰시오.

The aquarium was founded in 1984 on the site of a former fish canning factory. After the fishing industry collapsed, a team decided _____ (reuse) this building but still retain its historic character. Now, it holds thousands of plants and animals, with more than 600 species on display, and is enjoyed by both residents and tourists.

07

다음 글의 밑줄 친 부분 중, 문맥상 낱말의 쓰임이 어색한 것은?

This museum is housed in a former power station. After it closed down in 1981, the government decided to ① change it into a museum instead of demolishing it. Now this museum ② contains the national collection of modern British artwork and is famous for its modern and contemporary art. The aquarium was ③ established in 1984 on the site of a former fish canning factory. After the fishing industry collapsed, a team decided to reuse this building but still ④ destroy its historic character. Now, it holds thousands of plants and animals, with more than 600 species on display, and is ⑤ loved by both residents and tourists.

08

주어진 문장 다음에 이어질 글의 순서로 적절한 것은?

I went to Puruum Art Hall to see an exhibition titled "Upcycle the World."

(A) More than a hundred items were on display, so it took me two hours to see everything.

(B) I saw accessories, blankets, and furniture. I liked the earrings made from used bottle caps the most, so I bought a pair!

(C) It is definitely worth visiting alone or with your friends. You will be able to find various items designed in an eco-friendly way!

① (A) – (C) – (B)   ② (B) – (A) – (C)
③ (B) – (C) – (A)   ④ (C) – (A) – (B)
⑤ (C) – (B) – (A)

09

다음 글의 내용과 일치하지 않는 것은?

This beautiful bookshop used to be a theater featuring magnificent paintings on its ceiling. In 2000, it was repurposed. The cinema seating was removed, and rows of bookshelves were installed in place of the original balconies and floors. The red stage curtains, theater boxes, and many other architectural details still remain, making this building a historic and luxurious place.

This museum is housed in a former power station. After it closed down in 1981, the government decided to transform it into a museum instead of destroying it. Now this museum holds the national collection of modern British artwork and is famous for its modern and contemporary art.

The aquarium was founded in 1984 on the site of a former fish canning factory. After the fishing industry collapsed, a team decided to reuse this building but still retain its historic character. Now, it holds thousands of plants and animals, with more than 600 species on display, and is enjoyed by both residents and tourists.

① 과거에 서점은 멋진 천장 그림이 특징인 극장이었다.
② 서점은 영화 좌석을 방문객이 이용할 수 있게 남겨두었다.
③ 박물관은 국가 소유의 현대 영국 미술품을 전시하고 있다.
④ 수족관은 어업이 붕괴되기 이전에 생선 통조림 공장이었다.
⑤ 수족관은 수천 종의 동식물을 보유하고 있다.

10

다음 글의 필자의 주장과 일치하는 견해로 적절한 것은?

This beautiful bookshop used to be a theater featuring magnificent paintings on its ceiling. In 2000, it was repurposed. The cinema seating was removed, and rows of bookshelves were installed in place of the original balconies and floors. The red stage curtains, theater boxes, and many other architectural details still remain, making this building a historic and luxurious place.

This museum is housed in a former power station. After it closed down in 1981, the government decided to transform it into a museum instead of destroying it. Now this museum holds the national collection of modern British artwork and is famous for its modern and contemporary art.

The aquarium was founded in 1984 on the site of a former fish canning factory. After the fishing industry collapsed, a team decided to reuse this building but still retain its historic character. Now, it holds thousands of plants and animals, with more than 600 species on display, and is enjoyed by both residents and tourists.

① A: Everyone should separate things that can be recycled from their trash and put them in the bins.

② B: Reusing items several times before throwing them away cuts down on the amount of waste we produce.

③ C: Reusing items several times before throwing them away saves you money.

④ D: If you creatively reuse the things thrown away, we can make the Earth greener by reducing trash and saving more energy.

⑤ E: Children should have many opportunities to experience recycling with their parents.

Listen & Speak

Listen & Speak 1 적중 MAPPING

이것만 알아도 대화문 맞힌다!

[Listen & Speak 1]

B: Hey, Michelle. What are you looking at?

G: It's an advertisement for a handy new product: a flexible power strip.

B: I[1]'ve never heard of that kind of thing. How can a power strip be flexible?

G: Well, it is divided into sections [2]so that it can be bent into different shapes.

B: Oh, I see. Maybe that will[3] make it easier to fit it in small places.

G: That's right. Isn't [4]it amazing how one small change can improve a product so much?

B: Definitely. It is a clever invention.

남: 안녕, Michelle. 무엇을 보고 있니?
여: 편리한 신제품에 대한 광고야. 구부러지는 멀티탭이래.
남: 그런 물건은 들어본 적 없는데. 어떻게 멀티탭이 구부러질 수 있지?
여: 음, 그것은 다른 모양으로 구부러질 수 있도록 여러 부분으로 나누어져 있어.
남: 아, 알겠다. 아마 그렇게 되면 작은 공간에 들어가기가 더 쉽겠구나.
여: 맞아. 작은 변화 하나가 제품을 이렇게 많이 개선할 수 있다는 게 놀랍지 않니?
남: 물론이야. 기발한 발명품이구나.

핵심 의사소통기능 – 가능성 정도 표현하기

√ "Maybe[Perhaps/Probably] it[that] will ~"은 '아마도 ~일 것이다'라는 의미로, 어떤 일에 대한 가능성을 이야기한다.

√ "It is likely[possible/probable] that ~", "Chances are (that) ~"으로도 말할 수 있다. 이때, maybe, perhaps, probably는 '아마도', likely는 '~할 것 같은', possible은 '가능성 있는', probable은 '있을 것 같은'이라는 뜻이라는 것도 함께 알아두자.

집중!

· 가능성을 말하는 표현이기 때문에 주로 미래시제와 함께 쓰인다.
· "I'm sure ~"처럼 강한 확신을 나타내는 표현과 구분하자.

출제 포인트 1

√ 남자는 Michelle이 보고 있는 상품에 대해 들어본 적이 있다. (불일치)
√ 멀티탭은 여러 부분으로 나뉘어 있기 때문에 구부러질 수 있다. (일치)

출제 포인트 2

1) have never heard
경험을 나타내는 현재완료가 부정어 never와 함께 쓰여 '~해본 적이 (전혀) 없다'의 의미를 나타낸다.

2) so that it can be bent
〈so that+주어+can+동사원형〉의 형태로, '주어가 ~할 수 있도록'이라는 목적을 나타낸다. 주어 it은 a power strip(멀티탭)을 가리키며, 멀티탭은 구부러지는 것이므로 수동태 be bent가 쓰였다.

3) make it easier to fit
〈동사(make)+가목적어(it)+목적격 보어(easier)+진목적어(to fit)〉 형태의 5형식 문장이다. 여기서 fit은 '~에 맞다'라는 의미로 뒤에 오는 it은 멀티탭을 가리킨다.

4) 가주어 it
it은 의문사절 how one small change ~ so much를 대신하는 가주어이다.

[Use It]

G: Here are those cool stairs I was telling you about.
B: Wow, it's been designed to look just like piano keys.
G: Isn't it neat? It even plays notes when you step on it.
B: Yeah, it's amazing! Who came up with this idea?
G: Well, it's part of a new project taking place throughout the city.
B: What is the project's goal? To make our surroundings more beautiful?
G: It's more than just that. These creative designs can actually change people's behavior.
B: How do they do that?
G: After the stairs were installed, many people started walking on them instead of riding the escalator.
B: That's really great. Maybe other cities will copy this creative idea!
G: That would be wonderful!

여: 여기에 내가 너에게 이야기하던 멋진 계단이 있어.
남: 와, 마치 피아노 건반처럼 보이도록 디자인되었구나.
여: 멋지지 않니? 심지어 밟으면 음을 연주하기도 해.
남: 그래, 대단하다! 누가 이 아이디어를 생각해냈지?
여: 음, 이건 도시 전역에서 진행되고 있는 새 프로젝트의 일부야.
남: 그 프로젝트의 목표가 뭔데? 우리 환경을 더 아름답게 만드는 것?
여: 그 이상이야. 이 창의적인 디자인들은 실제로 사람들의 행동을 변화시킬 수 있어.
남: 어떻게 그렇게 하지?
여: 계단이 설치된 후, 많은 사람들이 에스컬레이터를 타는 대신 계단 위로 걷기 시작했어.
남: 정말 훌륭하다. 어쩌면 다른 도시들도 이 창의적인 생각을 따라 하겠는걸!
여: 그러면 멋지겠다!

[Listen & Speak 2]

B: Wow, this village has murals everywhere! I've never seen a place like this!

G: I'm glad you like it! There are ¹⁾even more murals in the rest of the village.

B: That's great. But why were they painted?

G: This ²⁾used to be a lifeless village. But recently, artists decided to paint lots of pictures ³⁾to raise the residents' spirits.

B: The residents ⁴⁾must have been very pleased.

G: You can say that again. Thanks to these murals, this village has become a wonderful place to live and a popular tourist attraction.

B: It seems to me that the artists breathed new life into this area.

남: 와, 이 마을은 곳곳에 벽화가 있네! 이런 곳은 본 적이 없어!

여: 네가 좋아하니 기쁘다! 이 마을의 다른 곳에도 훨씬 더 많은 벽화들이 있어.

남: 멋지구나. 그런데 왜 이것들이 그려진 거지?

여: 이곳은 생기 없는 마을이었어. 그런데 최근에 예술가들이 주민들의 사기를 높이기 위해 많은 그림을 그리기로 결정했지.

남: 주민들이 분명 아주 기뻐했겠다.

여: 정말 그래. 이 벽화들 덕분에 이 마을은 살기에 멋진 곳이 되었고 인기 있는 관광지가 되었어.

남: 예술가들이 이 지역에 새 생명을 불어넣은 것 같구나.

핵심 의사소통기능 – 의견 표현하기

√ "It seems to me that ~"은 '내 생각에는 ~인 것 같다'라는 의미로, 자신의 의견을 상대방에게 말하는 표현이다.

√ "I think[believe/feel] (that) ~"이나 "In my opinion[view], ~" 등으로도 말할 수 있다.

집중!

• 동사 seem(~인 것 같다) 대신에 비슷한 의미의 동사 appear을 쓸 수 있다.

출제 포인트 1

√ 두 사람이 보고 있는 벽화는 이 마을 유일한 벽화이다. (불일치)

√ 예술가들이 마을에 벽화를 그린 것은 관광객을 유치하기 위함이었다. (불일치)

출제 포인트 2

1) even more
even은 '훨씬'의 의미로, 뒤에 오는 비교급 more를 강조한다. even 대신 much, still, far, a lot으로 바꿀 수 있다.

2) used to be 과거의 상태
〈used to+동사원형〉은 '~하곤[이곤] 했다'라는 의미로, 과거의 습관이나 상태를 나타낸다. 아래 표현들과 비교해서 정확히 알아두자.
〈be used to-v〉~하는 데 사용되다
〈be used to v-ing〉~하는 데 익숙하다

3) to raise
to raise는 '높이기 위해서'라는 의미로, 목적을 나타내는 to부정사이다. 앞의 동사 decided의 목적어로 쓰인 to paint와 쓰임을 구분하자.

4) must have been
〈must have p.p.〉는 '~했음에 틀림없다'라는 뜻으로, 과거에 대한 강한 추측을 나타낸다.

[Use It]

There is an advertisement that shows an elephant standing in an open plain. It is surrounded by vertical black bars; it seems to be trapped in a cage. Below these black bars, there is a series of numbers. What looks like a cage at first glance is actually a barcode, something you see on many of the products you buy every day. This shocking advertisement symbolizes a very real threat to the lives of the elephants — illegal wild animal trade. When people see this advertisement, some will be reminded that buying and selling wild elephants is a serious crime, and maybe others will even be inspired to help solve this problem. In this way, creative ideas can have a powerful effect on people's thoughts.

탁 트인 들판에 서 있는 코끼리를 보여주는 광고가 있다. 그 코끼리는 검은색 세로 막대기에 둘러싸여 있다. 그것은 우리에 갇혀 있는 듯하다. 이 검은 막대기들 아래에 일련의 숫자들이 있다. 첫눈에는 우리처럼 보인 것이 실제로는 당신이 매일 사는 제품 다수에서 볼 수 있는 바코드인 것이다. 이 충격적인 광고는 야생동물 불법 거래라는, 코끼리의 생명에 대한 매우 실제적인 위협을 상징한다. 이 광고를 보았을 때, 어떤 사람들은 야생 코끼리를 사고파는 것이 심각한 범죄라는 것을 다시 한번 깨닫게 될 것이며, 또 어쩌면 다른 사람들은 이 문제를 해결하는 데에 도움을 주도록 고무될 수도 있다. 이런 식으로 창의적 아이디어들은 사람들의 생각에 강력한 영향을 미칠 수 있다.

[01~03]

다음 대화문을 읽고, 물음에 답하시오.

> B: Hey, Michelle. What are you looking at?
>
> G: It's an advertisement for a ① handy new product: a flexible power strip.
>
> B: I'ⓐ ve never heard of that kind of thing. How can a power strip be ② flexible?
>
> G: Well, it is divided into ③ sections ⓑ so that it can ⓒ be bent into different shapes.
>
> B: Oh, I see. Maybe that will make it ④ more difficult ⓓ to fit it in small places.
>
> G: That's right. ⓔ Aren't they amazing how one small change can ⑤ improve a product so much?
>
> B: Definitely. It is a clever invention.

01

위 대화의 내용과 일치하지 않는 것은?

① The man hasn't seen before the product Michelle is looking at.
② The bending power strip is separated into several parts.
③ The flexible power strip is suitable for placing in a high place.
④ Michelle admires that one little change can greatly enhance the product.
⑤ The man thinks the bending power strip is ingenious.

02

위 대화의 밑줄 친 ①~⑤ 중, 문맥상 적절하지 않은 것은?

①   ②   ③   ④   ⑤

03

위 대화의 밑줄 친 ⓐ~ⓔ 중, 어법상 적절하지 않은 것을 찾아 기호를 쓰고 바르게 고치시오.

(   ) _____ → _____

[04~06]

다음 대화문을 읽고, 물음에 답하시오.

> B: Wow, this village has murals everywhere! I've never seen a place like this!
>
> G: I'm glad you like it! There are ① even more murals in the rest of the village.
>
> B: That's great. But why were they painted?
>
> G: This ② used to be a lifeless village. But recently, artists decided to paint lots of pictures ③ to raise the residents' spirits.
>
> B: The residents ④ must have been very pleased.
>
> G: _____ again. Thanks to these murals, this village has become a wonderful place to live and a popular tourist attraction.
>
> B: It seems to me ⑤ which the artists breathed new life into this area.

04

위 대화의 빈칸에 동의를 나타내는 말이 되도록 문장을 완성하시오. (단, 4단어로 쓸 것)

_____ again.

05

위 대화 내용과 일치하지 않는 것은?

① 마을의 다른 곳에는 훨씬 많은 벽화들이 있다.
② 마을은 이전에 생기 없는 마을이었다.
③ 관광객을 유치하기 위해서 예술가들이 벽화를 그렸다.
④ 벽화가 그려진 마을은 살기 좋은 곳이 되었다.
⑤ 예술가들 덕분에 마을에 새 생명이 불어넣어졌다.

06

위 대화의 밑줄 친 부분 중, 어법상 적절하지 않은 것은?

①   ②   ③   ④   ⑤

07

다음 대화문을 한 문장으로 요약하고자 한다. 빈칸 (A), (B)에 들어갈 말로 가장 적절한 것은?

> G: Here are those cool stairs I was telling you about.
>
> B: Wow, it's been designed to look just like piano keys.
>
> G: Isn't it neat? It even plays notes when you step on it.
>
> B: Yeah, it's amazing! Who came up with this idea?
>
> G: Well, it's part of a new project taking place throughout the city.
>
> B: What is the project's goal? To make our surroundings more beautiful?
>
> G: It's more than just that. These creative designs can actually change people's behavior.
>
> B: How do they do that?
>
> G: After the stairs were installed, many people started walking on them instead of riding the escalator.
>
> B: That's really great. Maybe other cities will copy this creative idea!
>
> G: That would be wonderful!

Stairs like piano keys not only made the _____(A)_____ more beautiful but also had people _____(B)_____ on them.

	(A)		(B)
①	offices	–	dance
②	buildings	–	dance
③	buildings	–	walk
④	surroundings	–	walk
⑤	surroundings	–	sleep

08

다음 글의 밑줄 친 (A), (B)와 같은 쓰임으로 사용된 것끼리 바르게 연결된 것은?

　There is an advertisement (A) that shows an elephant standing in an open plain. It is surrounded by vertical black bars; it seems to be trapped in a cage. Below these black bars, there is a series of numbers. What looks like a cage at first glance is actually a barcode, something you see on many of the products you buy every day. This shocking advertisement symbolizes a very real threat to the lives of the elephants — illegal wild animal trade. When people see this advertisement, some will be reminded (B) that buying and selling wild elephants is a serious crime, and maybe others will even be inspired to help solve this problem. In this way, creative ideas can have a powerful effect on people's thoughts.

---

a. It was surprising that she didn't show up to the meeting.
b. I knew that we would meet again.
c. He tried to explain that understanding mathematics is not difficult.
d. As far as I know, he is a man that learns a lot from mistakes.

	(A)		(B)
①	a	–	b
②	b	–	c
③	b	–	d
④	d	–	a
⑤	d	–	b

Grammar
&
Vocabulary

이 단원의 핵심 문법

√ 명사를 수식하는 과거분사(구)

√ 주격관계대명사

01

다음 중, 단어의 영영풀이가 <u>어색한</u> 것은?

① reduce: to make something smaller or less in size, amount, etc.
② inspire: to make someone want to do something
③ object: a thing that you can see and touch that is not alive
④ imagination: a way of thinking about something
⑤ decompose: to be destroyed slowly by nature process

02

다음 중, 어법상 <u>어색한</u> 부분이 있는 문장 두 개를 골라 기호를 쓰고 <u>어색한</u> 부분을 바르게 고치시오.

> ⓐ I bought a cell phone case made of wood.
> ⓑ I want to buy some items designing in an eco-friendly way.
> ⓒ It is a new phone that is really sensational these days.
> ⓓ My sister is a hairdresser who she is very popular.

(1) (　　) ＿＿＿＿＿＿ → ＿＿＿＿＿＿

(2) (　　) ＿＿＿＿＿＿ → ＿＿＿＿＿＿

03

다음 (A), (B) 각 문장의 밑줄 친 우리말에 맞게 주어진 단어를 활용하여 문장을 완성하시오. (필요시 단어의 형태를 변형하여 쓰되, 단어를 추가하지 않을 것)

(A) I like the phrase 그 책 커버에 쓰인. (book, the, on, cover, write)
(B) The wall 빨간색으로 칠해진 is my favorite place in the town. (red, paint, in)

04

다음 중, 단어의 영영풀이가 <u>어색한</u> 것은?

① manage: to be in control of an office, shop, team, etc.
② convert: to change into a different form
③ transform: to change spoken or written words into another language
④ original: being the first or existing at the beginning
⑤ gorgeous: very beautiful or attractive

05

다음 〈보기〉에 주어진 말을 〈조건〉에 맞게 알맞게 배열하여 완전한 문장을 쓰시오.

> 〈보기〉 of / the works / the writer / I / make / like / most / by

> 나는 그 작가가 쓴 대부분의 작품을 좋아한다.

> 〈조건〉 – 주어진 단어를 모두 한 번씩만 사용할 것
>   – 필요시 단어를 변형하되, 추가하지 않을 것

＿＿＿＿＿＿＿＿＿＿＿＿＿＿＿＿＿

＿＿＿＿＿＿＿＿＿＿＿＿＿＿＿＿＿

06

다음 밑줄 친 부분 중, 어법상 <u>어색한</u> 것은?

① There are so many ideas <u>using</u> to make life comfortable.
② Wounds <u>caused</u> by words cannot be removed.
③ I went to an exhibition <u>named</u> "Let's Change the World."
④ You can find various works <u>designed</u> by famous artists there.
⑤ She really hates bugs <u>flying</u> in the kitchen.

07

다음 중, 관계대명사를 사용하여 두 문장을 한 문장으로 올바르게 바꾼 것은?

① She lived in a house. + The house has a large garden.
→ She lived in a house which having a large garden.

② The teacher gave me some examples of math problems. + The math problems are very difficult.
→ The teacher gave me some examples of math problems which is very difficult.

③ Did you finish your work? + The work is due tomorrow.
→ Did you finish your work that is due tomorrow?

④ He likes the picture of the children. + The picture was taken by his girlfriend.
→ He likes the picture of children that were taken by his girlfriend.

⑤ I rescued a young boy. + The young boy fell into water.
→ I rescued a young boy whom fell into water.

08

다음은 어떤 단어에 대한 사전의 내용이다. 빈칸 ⓐ, ⓑ에 공통으로 들어갈 낱말로 가장 적절한 것은?

ⓐ_____ : (adjective)
something that is made to be thrown away after it is used once
ex) Buying ⓑ_____ items is not good for the environment.

① original   ② disposable
③ pleasing   ④ ordinary
⑤ marvelous

09

다음 주어진 두 문장을 〈조건〉에 맞게 한 문장으로 연결하시오.

The researcher has studied tigers. They were cared for by people when they were young.

〈조건〉 – 관계대명사를 사용할 것
        – that을 사용하지 말 것

_____

_____

10

다음 글의 (A), (B), (C)의 각 네모 안에서 문맥에 맞는 낱말로 가장 적절한 것은?

There is an advertisement that shows an elephant standing in an open plain. It is surrounded by vertical black bars; it seems to be (A) trapped / built in a cage. Below these black bars, there is a series of numbers. What looks like a cage at first glance is actually a barcode, something you see on many of the products that you buy every day. This shocking advertisement (B) symbolizes / causes a very real threat to the lives of the elephants— (C) legal / illegal wild animal trade. When people see this advertisement, some will be reminded that buying and selling wild elephants is a serious crime, and maybe others will even be inspired to help solve this problem.

	(A)	(B)	(C)
①	trapped	symbolizes	legal
②	trapped	symbolizes	illegal
③	trapped	causes	legal
④	built	symbolizes	legal
⑤	built	causes	illegal

시험 문제 미리보기

01

다음 중, 단어의 영영풀이가 바르지 <u>않은</u> 것은?

① purify: to remove impurities or pollutants from something
② transform: to convert into another form, substance, or state
③ preserve: to maintain something in its original or existing state
④ abandon: to leave something completely, usually without intending to return
⑤ decompose: to create or put together something by combining various parts or elements

02

다음 대화문의 흐름으로 보아, 주어진 문장이 들어가기에 가장 적절한 곳은?

> You can say that again.

B: Wow, this village has murals everywhere! I've never seen a place like this! (①)
G: I'm glad you like it! There are even more murals in the rest of the village.
B: That's great. But why were they painted? (②)
G: This used to be a lifeless village. But recently, artists decided to paint lots of pictures to raise the residents' spirits.
B: (③) The residents must have been very pleased.
G: (④) Thanks to these murals, this village has become a wonderful place to live and a popular tourist attraction.
B: It seems to me that the artists breathed new life into this area. (⑤)

①   ②   ③   ④   ⑤

[03~04]

다음 글을 읽고, 물음에 답하시오.

Through upcycling, a seemingly useless object can be transformed into something completely different ① <u>that</u> is useful for everyday life. What do you think can be done with old truck tarps, car seat belts, and bicycle inner tubes? Individually, these things ② <u>look trashy,</u> but with a little imagination the Freitag brothers, Markus and Daniel, repurpose them for something totally new: very strong bags. These bags are perfect for bicyclists ③ <u>who go</u> to work every day in all kinds of weather. Similarly, a man named Kyle Parsons and his partners have been ④ <u>creative</u> reusing old motorcycle tires from Bali, Indonesia. A shocking number of tires get thrown away there every year, which are a serious environmental problem since they cannot decompose or be recycled. ⑤ <u>In order to solve</u> this problem, Parsons and his team are turning them into sandal bottoms. They then use canvas and natural materials to make the other sandal parts. What a great reuse of resources!

03

윗글의 제목으로 가장 적절한 것은?

① The Effects of Using Upcycled Products
② The Importance of Recycling Resources
③ Upcycling: The Rebirth of Useless Products
④ Technology Used in Making Old Things New
⑤ The Various Ways to Solve Environmental Problems

04

윗글의 밑줄 친 부분 중, 어법상 적절하지 <u>않은</u> 것은?

①   ②   ③   ④   ⑤

[05~07]

다음 글을 읽고, 물음에 답하시오.

Along with small everyday items, much bigger things can also be upcycled—even old buildings that cannot be used for their original purpose anymore. The German government showed us an excellent example of this with a former steel plant that closed in 1985. Rather than (A) build / destroy the plant's buildings or abandon the entire facility, they decided to give it new meaning as a series of useful public structures. Many of the buildings (B) kept / lost their original shapes, but received extra equipment and new designs in their surrounding areas. For instance, old gas tanks became pools for divers. Concrete walls of iron storage towers were turned into ideal training fields for rock climbers. Can you believe a building for melting metal is now a viewing platform with a gorgeous 360-degree view? The final result is the Landscape Park Duisburg Nord. It has almost 570 acres of land filled with gardens, cycling paths, and pretty lights at night, in addition to its creatively repurposed buildings. This park proves that it's (C) possible / impossible to preserve the heritage of a place as well as the environment.

05

윗글의 (A), (B), (C)의 각 네모 안에 들어갈 말로 바르게 짝 지어진 것은?

	(A)		(B)		(C)
①	build	–	kept	–	possible
②	build	–	lost	–	impossible
③	destroy	–	lost	–	possible
④	destroy	–	kept	–	possible
⑤	destroy	–	kept	–	impossible

06

윗글의 내용과 일치하지 않는 것은?

① 작은 일상적인 물건들뿐만 아니라 건물과 같은 큰 것들도 업사이클될 수 있다.

② 독일 정부는 문을 닫은 철강 공장을 유용한 공공 구조물로 바꿨다.

③ 추가 설비를 설치하고 디자인을 새롭게 입힘으로써 철강 공장은 완전히 탈바꿈되었다.

④ 철을 저장하는 타워들의 콘크리트 벽들은 암벽 등반가들을 위한 훈련장이 되었다.

⑤ 뒤스부르크 환경 공원은 환경뿐만 아니라 어떤 장소의 유산도 보호할 수 있다는 것을 보여준다.

07

윗글의 주제로 가장 알맞은 것은?

① why old buildings should be upcycled in the suburbs

② how to upcycle relatively new public structures

③ shapes and material as a necessary part of design

④ conflicting interests between divers and rock climbers

⑤ the way the German government upcycled the old plant

08

다음 글의 밑줄 친 부분 중, 문맥상 낱말의 쓰임이 어색한 것은?

This museum is housed in a former power station. After it closed down in 1981, the government decided to ① transform it into a museum instead of destroying it. Now this museum ② holds the national collection of modern British artwork and is famous for its modern and contemporary art.

The aquarium was ③ founded in 1984 on the site of a former fish canning factory. After the fishing industry collapsed, a team decided to reuse this building but still ④ destroy its historic character. Now, it holds thousands of plants and animals, with more than 600 species on display, and is ⑤ enjoyed by both residents and tourists.

09

다음 밑줄 친 부분 중, 어법상 적절하지 <u>않은</u> 것은?

① I gave him a chair <u>made</u> of plastic.
② There is a bottle <u>filling</u> with orange juice.
③ The old man <u>called</u> the legend played his last game.
④ No one knows where the treasure <u>hidden</u> in the castle is.
⑤ That cathedral <u>built</u> in 12C is famous for the statue in its yard.

[10~12]

다음 글을 읽고, 물음에 답하시오.

When artists add their own creative touches, things that most people consider junk are reborn as beautiful works of art. <u>The giant pictures make from trash by environmental artist Tom Deininger are one of a kind.</u> (①) Up close, these brightly colored creations look like a mixed-up mess of broken plastic, unwanted toys, and bent wire—all things that cannot be recycled. (②) From farther away, however, they appear to blend together into marvelous landscapes or other paintings. (③) For years, Gwyneth Leech has turned used coffee cups into brilliant art exhibits. (④) After a cup is used by someone, she paints a unique design on it and hangs it with many other painted cups in front of a window or pretty background. (⑤) These works from Leech and Deininger are not only pleasing to the eye, but they also naturally provoke an interest in environmental conservation in people.

10

윗글에서 주어진 문장이 들어가기에 가장 적절한 곳은?

> Also, there is an artist who shows that even disposable cups can be reused as artistic material.

①   ②   ③   ④   ⑤

11

윗글의 내용과 일치하지 <u>않는</u> 것은?

① Inventive approaches to rubbish by artists result in unique artwork.
② A closer look reveals that Tom Deininger's pictures look like a collection of worthless things.
③ Comments on Tom Deininger's work depend on where one looks at Tom Deininger's work.
④ Gwyneth Leech paints the used cups and hangs them in front of the window to dry them.
⑤ Works of art created by Leech and Deininger attract attention to the environmental issue.

12

윗글의 밑줄 친 문장에서 어법상 틀린 부분을 찾아 바르게 고쳐 쓰시오.

_____ → _____

[13~15]

다음 글을 읽고, 물음에 답하시오.

As you can see, creative thinking has the power ① to make many positive changes to the environment. By ② giving old products more value, we can lessen the amount of waste in a way ③ that is even more eco-friendly than recycling. So what would you say to Jamie now as he decides what to do with his cans? Perhaps he could upcycle them ④ make lanterns, toys, or sculptures for his friends and family. The options are endless, and all he needs is a little creativity ⑤ to think of them. In the same way, stop and think before you throw something out. Who knows? Maybe you can turn that trash into (A) treasure.

13

윗글의 밑줄 친 부분 중, 어법상 옳지 <u>않은</u> 것은?

①   ②   ③   ④   ⑤

14

윗글의 밑줄 친 (A) treasure가 될 수 있는 것은?

① creative thinking   ② recycling
③ the environment   ④ a toy
⑤ his family

15

윗글의 내용을 다음과 같이 한 문장으로 요약하고자 한다. 빈칸 (A), (B)에 들어갈 말로 가장 적절한 것은?

> All we need is a little _____(A)_____ to think of upcycling old things and _____(B)_____ the amount of waste.

       (A)   (B)
① imagination – increase
② creativity   – decrease
③ motivation – measure
④ inspiration   – keep
⑤ imitation   – reduce

[16~18]

다음 글을 읽고, 물음에 답하시오.

Every day during lunch, Jamie enjoys a soft drink and has a decision to make: What should he do with the empty can? Many people would answer, "Recycle it!" Obviously, recycling is good for many reasons. We can reduce the amount of trash ⓐ (throw away), use less energy than we would to make new products, and conserve natural resources by recycling. However, recycling is not a perfect way to manage waste. It still requires large amounts of energy to purify used resources and ⓑ (convert) them into new products. So, what about trying to creatively reuse, or "upcycle," them instead? This new approach is becoming more popular since it is even more environmentally friendly than recycling. What's more, it can also be fun! Here ⓒ (be) some inspiring examples of how people have creatively upcycled old, used things.

16

윗글에서 필자가 주장하는 바로 가장 적절한 것은?

① We need to avoid consuming soft drinks for our health.
② Recycling is by far the best way to protect the environment.
③ To become new products, used resources must be cleaned.
④ To manage waste, we should try to reuse products creatively.
⑤ By recycling, we can achieve many benefits to protect the earth.

17

윗글 다음에 이어질 내용으로 가장 적절한 것은?

① 친환경 제품 활용법
② 중고품 기부 예시
③ 창의적 사고를 기르는 방법
④ 재생에너지의 중요성
⑤ 창의적인 업사이클링의 사례

18

윗글의 ⓐ~ⓒ에 주어진 단어를 알맞은 형태로 바꿔 쓰시오.

ⓐ _____

ⓑ _____

ⓒ _____

다음 글을 읽고, 물음에 답하시오.

Along with small everyday items, much bigger things can also ⓐ upcycle—even old buildings that cannot be used for their original purpose anymore. The German government showed us an excellent example of this with a former steel plant that ⓑ close in 1985. Rather than destroy the plant's buildings or abandon the entire facility, they decided ⓒ give it new meaning as a series of useful public structures. ① Many of the buildings kept their original shapes, but received extra equipment and new designs in their surrounding areas. ② For instance, old gas tanks became pools for divers. ③ Concrete walls of iron storage towers ⓓ turn into ideal training fields for rock climbers. ④ When it comes to rebuilding the public buildings, the priorities must be set among conflicts of interest between the different professions. ⑤ Can you believe a building for melting metal is now a viewing platform with a gorgeous 360-degree view? The final result is the Landscape Park Duisburg Nord. It has almost 570 acres of land filled with gardens, cycling paths, and pretty lights at night, in addition to its creatively repurposed buildings. This park proves that it's possible ⓔ preserve the heritage of a place as well as the environment.

19

윗글의 ①~⑤ 중, 전체 흐름과 관계 없는 문장은?

①   ②   ③   ④   ⑤

20

윗글의 밑줄 친 ⓐ~ⓔ를 어법상 적절하게 고치지 못한 것은?

① ⓐ: be upcycled
② ⓑ: closed
③ ⓒ: to give
④ ⓓ: were turning
⑤ ⓔ: to preserve

다음 글을 읽고, 물음에 답하시오.

Through upcycling, a seemingly useless object can (A) transform into / be transformed into something completely different that is ⓐ helpful for everyday life. What do you think can be done with old truck tarps, car seat belts, and bicycle inner tubes? ⓑ Separately, these things look like trash, but with a little imagination the Freitag brothers, Markus and Daniel, repurpose them for something totally new: very strong bags. These bags are ⓒ suitable for bicyclists going to work every day in all kinds of weather. Similarly, a man named Kyle Parsons and his partners have been creatively reusing old motorcycle tires from Bali, Indonesia. A shocking number of tires (B) gets / get thrown away there every year, and they are a serious environmental problem since they cannot ⓓ propose or be recycled. To ⓔ handle this problem, Parsons and his team are turning them into sandal bottoms. They then use canvas and natural materials (C) make / to make the other sandal parts. What a great reuse of resources!

21

윗글의 밑줄 친 ⓐ~ⓔ 중, 문맥상 어색한 것은?

① ⓐ   ② ⓑ   ③ ⓒ   ④ ⓓ   ⑤ ⓔ

22

윗글의 (A), (B), (C)의 각 네모 안에서 어법상 맞는 표현으로 알맞게 짝지어진 것은?

	(A)	(B)	(C)
①	transform into	gets	make
②	be transformed into	gets	make
③	be transformed into	get	make
④	be transformed into	get	to make
⑤	transform into	get	to make

[23~24]

다음 글을 읽고, 물음에 답하시오.

When artists add their own creative touches, things that most people consider junk are ① reborn as beautiful works of art. The giant pictures ② made from trash by environmental artist Tom Deininger are one of a kind. Up close, these brightly colored creations look like a mixed-up mess of broken plastic, unwanted toys, and bent wire—all things ③ what cannot be recycled. From farther away, however, they appear to blend together into marvelous landscapes or other paintings. There is also an artist who shows ④ that even disposable cups can be reused as artistic material. For years, Gwyneth Leech has turned ⑤ used coffee cups into brilliant art exhibits. After a cup is used by someone, she paints a unique design on it and hangs it with many other painted cups in front of a window or pretty background. These works from Leech and Deininger are not only pleasing to the eye, but they also naturally provoke an interest in environmental conservation in people.

23

윗글의 밑줄 친 부분 중, 어법상 틀린 것은?

①   ②   ③   ④   ⑤

24

〈보기〉의 영영풀이에 해당하는 단어를 윗글에서 찾아 쓰시오.

〈보기〉 to cause a particular reaction or result

_____

[25~27]

다음 글을 읽고, 물음에 답하시오.

Every day during lunch, Jamie enjoys a soft drink and ⓐ has a decision to make: What should he do with the empty can? Many people would answer, "Recycle it!" Obviously, recycling is good for many reasons. We can reduce the amount of trash ⓑ throwing away, use less energy than we would to make new products, and conserve natural resources by recycling. _____(A)_____ these benefits, recycling is not a perfect way (가) to manage waste. It still requires large amounts of energy to purify ⓒ using resources and convert them into new products. So, what about ⓓ trying to creatively reuse, or "upcycle," them instead? This new approach is becoming more popular _____(B)_____ it is ⓔ a lot more environmentally friendly than recycling. What's more, it can also be fun! Here are some inspiring examples of how people have creatively upcycled old, used things.

25

윗글의 빈칸 (A), (B)에 들어갈 말로 가장 적절한 것은?

     (A)   (B)
① In addition to – if
② Despite   – although
③ Despite   – since
④ Due to   – if
⑤ Due to   – because

26

윗글의 밑줄 친 (가)와 쓰임이 같은 것은?

① He broke the promise to give the book back within a week.
② She pretends to understand all.
③ To offer words of consolation was difficult for me.
④ I worked overtime to meet the deadline.
⑤ I work out every single day to stay healthy.

27

윗글의 밑줄 친 ⓐ~ⓔ 중, 어법상 어색한 것의 개수는?

① 1개　　② 2개　　③ 3개　　④ 4개　　⑤ 5개

28

주어진 글 다음에 이어질 글의 순서로 가장 적절한 것은?

> Through upcycling, a seemingly useless object can be transformed into something completely different that is useful for everyday life.

(A) What do you think can be done with old truck tarps, car seat belts, and bicycle inner tubes? Individually, these things look like trash, but with a little imagination the Freitag brothers, Markus and Daniel, repurpose them for something totally new: very strong bags. These bags are perfect for bicyclists going to work every day in all kinds of weather.

(B) In order to solve this problem, Parsons and his team are turning them into sandal bottoms. They then use canvas and natural materials to make the other sandal parts. What a great reuse of resources!

(C) Likewise, a man named Kyle Parsons and his partners have been creatively reusing old motorcycle tires from Bali, Indonesia. A shocking number of tires get thrown away there every year, and they are a serious environmental problem since they cannot decompose or be recycled.

① (A) – (B) – (C)　　② (A) – (C) – (B)
③ (B) – (C) – (A)　　④ (C) – (A) – (B)
⑤ (C) – (B) – (A)

29

다음 글의 밑줄 친 ①~⑤를 알맞게 고치지 못한 것은?

When artists add their own creative touches, things that most people consider junk ① is reborn as beautiful works of art. The giant pictures ② are made from trash by environmental artist Tom Deininger are one of a kind. Up close, these brightly colored creations look like a mixed-up mess of broken plastic, unwanted toys, and ③ bending wire—all things that cannot be ④ recycling. From farther away, however, they ⑤ are appeared to blend together into marvelous landscapes or other paintings.

① → to be　　　　　② → made
③ → bent　　　　　④ → recycled
⑤ → appear

30

다음 글의 밑줄 친 ①~⑤를 알맞게 고치지 못한 것은?

Through upcycling, a seemingly useless object can be transformed into something completely different that ① be useful for everyday life. What do you think can be done with old truck tarps, car seat belts, and bicycle inner tubes? Individually, these things look ② alike trash, but with a little imagination the Freitag brothers, Markus and Daniel, repurpose them for something totally new: very strong bags. These bags are perfect for bicyclists ③ go to work every day in all kinds of weather. Similarly, a man named Kyle Parsons and his partners have been creatively ④ reuse old motorcycle tires from Bali, Indonesia. A shocking number of tires get thrown away there every year, and they are a serious environmental problem since they cannot decompose or ⑤ recycle. To solve this problem, Parsons and his team are turning them into sandal bottoms. They then use canvas and natural materials to make the other sandal parts. What a great reuse of resources!

① → is　　　　　② → like
③ → going　　　　④ → reused
⑤ → be recycled

2회

01

다음 문장의 밑줄 친 단어와 바꿔 쓸 수 있는 것은?

> The sunset over the ocean was absolutely gorgeous.

① upset
② brilliant
③ depressing
④ disposable
⑤ frightening

[02~04]

다음 글을 읽고, 물음에 답하시오.

Every day during lunch, Jamie enjoys a soft drink and has a decision to make: What should he do with the empty can? Many people would answer, "Recycle ⓐ it!" Obviously, recycling is good for many reasons. We can reduce the amount of trash thrown away, use less energy than we would to make new products, and ① conserve natural resources by recycling. However, it is not a perfect way to manage waste. ⓑ It still requires large amounts of energy to ② purify used resources and ③ convert ⓒ them into new products. So, what about trying to creatively reuse, or "upcycle," ⓓ them instead? This new approach is becoming more popular since it is even more ④ environmentally friendly than recycling. What's more, ⓔ it can also be fun! Here are some ⑤ inspiring examples of how people have creatively upcycled old, used things.

02

윗글의 주제로 가장 적절한 것은?

① a creative approach to solving the problems of recycling
② specific solutions to avoid the environmental pollution
③ a systematic approach for encouraging recycling
④ creative solutions for ecological restoration
⑤ an innovative approach to systematic waste recycling

03

윗글의 밑줄 친 ⓐ~ⓔ가 각각 가리키는 대상으로 옳지 않은 것은?

① ⓐ: the empty can
② ⓑ: recycling
③ ⓒ: used resources
④ ⓓ: new products
⑤ ⓔ: this new approach

04

윗글의 밑줄 친 ①~⑤의 영영풀이가 어색한 것은?

① conserve: to use more of something than is necessary or useful
② purify: to remove bad substances from something to make it pure
③ convert: to change something from one form to another
④ environmentally friendly: not harmful to the environment, or trying to help the environment
⑤ inspiring: exciting and encouraging you to do or feel something

05

다음 대화문의 내용과 일치하지 않는 것은?

M: Hey, Michelle. What are you looking at?
W: It's an advertisement for a handy new product: a flexible power strip.
M: I've never heard of that kind of thing. How can a power strip be flexible?
W: Well, it is divided into sections so that it can be bent into different shapes.
M: Oh, I see. Maybe that will make it easier to fit it in small places.
W: That's right. Isn't it amazing how one small change can improve a product so much?
M: Definitely. It is a clever invention.

① 여자는 신제품 광고를 보고 있다.
② 남자는 flexible power strip에 대해 처음 듣는다.
③ flexible power strip은 여러 부분들로 나눠진다.
④ 여자와 남자는 신제품에 대해 감탄하고 있다.
⑤ 남자는 내일 신제품을 구매할 것이다.

06

다음 중, 밑줄 친 부분의 쓰임이 나머지 넷과 <u>다른</u> 것은?

① The creature <u>that</u> has a horn is called unicorn.
② AI has powerful effects <u>that</u> can change the world.
③ She said <u>that</u> she would meet us at the restaurant.
④ She suggested an idea <u>that</u> helped us solve the problem.
⑤ He is doing his task <u>that</u> will be put forward tomorrow.

07

다음 글의 밑줄 친 ⓐ~ⓔ 중, 어법상 어색한 문장을 찾아 〈조건〉에 맞게 고쳐 쓰시오.

〈조건〉 – 어색한 부분만이 아닌 문장 전체를 다시 쓸 것
      – 새로운 단어를 추가하지 않을 것

ⓐ <u>As you can see, creative thinking has the power to make many positive changes to the environment.</u> By giving old products more value, we can lessen the amount of waste in a way that is even more eco-friendly than recycling. ⓑ <u>So what would you say to Jamie now as he decides what to do with his cans?</u> ⓒ <u>Perhaps he could upcycle them to make lanterns, toys, or sculptures for his friends and family.</u> ⓓ <u>The options are endless, and all that he need are a little creativity to think of them.</u> ⓔ <u>In the same way, stop and think before you throw something out.</u> Who knows? Maybe you can turn that trash into treasure.

(   ) _____

_____

[08~10]

다음 글을 읽고, 물음에 답하시오.

Through upcycling, a seemingly useless object can be transformed ⓐ_____ something ① <u>complete</u> different that is useful for everyday life. What do you think can be done with old truck tarps, car seat belts, and bicycle inner tubes? Individually, these things look ⓑ_____ trash, but with a little imagination the Freitag brothers, Markus and Daniel, ② <u>repurpose</u> them ⓒ_____ something totally new: very strong bags. These bags are perfect for bicyclists ③ <u>going</u> to work every day in all kinds of weather. Similarly, a man named Kyle Parsons and his partners have been creatively ④ <u>reusing</u> old motorcycle tires from Bali, Indonesia. A shocking number of tires get thrown ⓓ_____ there every year, and they are a serious environmental problem since they cannot ⑤ <u>decompose</u> or be recycled. To solve this problem, Parsons and his team are turning them ⓔ_____ sandal bottoms. They then use canvas and natural materials to make the other sandal parts. (A) 얼마나 훌륭한 자원의 재활용인가!

08

윗글의 밑줄 친 ①~⑤ 중, 어법상 틀린 것은?

①   ②   ③   ④   ⑤

09

윗글의 빈칸 ⓐ~ⓔ에 들어갈 말로 옳지 <u>않은</u> 것은?

① ⓐ: into
② ⓑ: like
③ ⓒ: for
④ ⓓ: away
⑤ ⓔ: out of

10

윗글의 밑줄 친 우리말 (A)를 바르게 영작한 것은?

① What a great reuse of resources!
② What a reuse of resoruces great!
③ How reuse of resources great!
④ What great reuse of resources!
⑤ How a great reuse of resources!

11

다음 글의 (A), (B), (C)의 각 네모 안에서 어법상 알맞은 말로 바르게 연결된 것은?

Through upcycling, a seemingly useless object can be transformed into something completely different that is useful for everyday life. What do you think can be done with old truck tarps, car seat belts, and bicycle inner tubes? Individually, these things look like trash, but with (A) a little / a few imagination the Freitag brothers, Markus and Daniel, repurpose them for (B) totally new something / something totally new : very strong bags. These bags are perfect for bicyclists (C) gone / going to work every day in all kinds of weather.

　　　(A)　　　　　(B)　　　　　(C)
① a little – totally new something – gone
② a few – totally new something – gone
③ a little – something totally new – gone
④ a few – totally new something – going
⑤ a little – something totally new – going

12

다음 글의 (A), (B), (C)의 각 네모 안에서 문맥에 맞는 낱말로 가장 적절한 것은?

As you can see, (A) imaginative / obsolete thinking has the power to make many positive changes to the environment. By giving old products more value, we can (B) reduce / increase the amount of waste in a way that is even more eco-friendly than recycling. So what would you say to Jamie now as he decides what to do with his cans? Perhaps he could upcycle them to make lanterns, toys, or sculptures for his friends and family. The options are (C) limited / infinite , and all he needs is a little creativity to think of them. In the same way, stop and think before you throw something out. Who knows? Maybe you can turn that trash into treasure.

　　　(A)　　　　　(B)　　　　　(C)
① imaginative – reduce – limited
② obsolete – increase – infinite
③ imaginative – reduce – infinite
④ obsolete – increase – limited
⑤ obsolete – reduce – limited

13

주어진 글 다음에 이어질 글의 순서로 가장 적절한 것은?

> When artists add their own creative touches, things that most people consider junk are reborn as beautiful works of art.

(A) From farther away, however, they appear to blend together into marvelous landscapes or other paintings. There is also an artist who shows that even disposable cups can be reused as artistic material. For years, Gwyneth Leech has turned used coffee cups into brilliant art exhibits.

(B) After a cup is used by someone, she paints a unique design on it and hangs it with many other painted cups in front of a window or pretty background. These works from Leech and Deininger are not only pleasing to the eye, but they also naturally provoke an interest in environmental conservation in people.

(C) The giant pictures made from trash by environmental artist Tom Deininger are one of a kind. Up close, these brightly colored creations look like a mixed-up mess of broken plastic, unwanted toys, and bent wire—all things that cannot be recycled.

① (A) – (C) – (B)
② (B) – (A) – (C)
③ (B) – (C) – (A)
④ (C) – (A) – (B)
⑤ (C) – (B) – (A)

14

다음 글의 (A), (B), (C)의 각 네모 안에서 어법상 알맞은 말로 바르게 연결된 것은?

Can you believe a building for melting metal is now a viewing platform with a gorgeous 360-degree view? The final result is the Landscape Park Duisburg Nord. It has almost 570 acres of land filled with gardens, cycling paths, and pretty lights at night, in addition to its creatively (A) repurposing / repurposed buildings. This park proves that it's possible to preserve the heritage of a place as well as the environment.

When artists (B) add / will add their own creative touches, things that most people consider junk are reborn as beautiful works of art. The giant pictures made from trash by environmental artist Tom Deininger are one of a kind. Up close, these brightly colored creations look like a mixed-up mess of broken plastic, unwanted toys, and bent wire—all things that cannot be recycled. From farther away, however, they appear (C) blending / to blend together into marvelous landscapes or other paintings.

	(A)	(B)	(C)
①	repurposed	add	blending
②	repurposed	add	to blend
③	repurposing	add	blending
④	repurposed	will add	to blend
⑤	repurposing	will add	to blend

15

다음 글의 제목으로 가장 적절한 것은?

This beautiful bookshop used to be a theater featuring magnificent paintings on its ceiling. In 2000, it was repurposed. The cinema seating was removed, and rows of bookshelves were installed in place of the original balconies and floors. The red stage curtains, theater boxes, and many other architectural details still remain, making this building a historic and luxurious place.

This museum is housed in a former power station. After it closed down in 1981, the government decided to transform it into a museum instead of destroying it. Now this museum holds the national collection of modern British artwork and is famous for its modern and contemporary art.

The aquarium was founded in 1984 on the site of a former fish canning factory. After the fishing industry collapsed, a team decided to reuse this building but still retain its historic character. Now, it holds thousands of plants and animals, with more than 600 species on display, and is enjoyed by both residents and tourists.

① Transformed Space: Upcycled with Its History
② Treasures Hidden in Old Buildings: Species Diversity
③ The Government's Plan for Urban Development
④ A New Type of Tour: Exploring Old Buildings with Locals
⑤ A Guide: Restoring a Collapsed Old Building

16

주어진 글 다음에 이어질 글의 순서로 가장 적절한 것은?

Along with small everyday items, much bigger things can also be upcycled—even old buildings that cannot be used for their original purpose anymore. The German government showed us an excellent example of this with a former steel plant that closed in 1985.

(A) The final result is the Landscape Park Duisburg Nord. It has almost 570 acres of land filled with gardens, cycling paths, and pretty lights at night, in addition to its creatively repurposed buildings. This park proves that it's possible to preserve the heritage of a place as well as the environment.

(B) Rather than destroy the plant's buildings or abandon the entire facility, they decided to give it new meaning as a series of useful public structures. Many of the buildings kept their original shapes, but received extra equipment and new designs in their surrounding areas.

(C) For instance, old gas tanks became pools for divers. Concrete walls of iron storage towers were turned into ideal training fields for rock climbers. Can you believe a building for melting metal is now a viewing platform with a gorgeous 360-degree view?

① (A) – (C) – (B)
② (B) – (A) – (C)
③ (B) – (C) – (A)
④ (C) – (A) – (B)
⑤ (C) – (B) – (A)

17

다음 글의 밑줄 친 부분 중, 어법상 <u>틀린</u> 것은?

Every day during lunch, Jamie enjoys a soft drink and has a decision to make: What should he do with the empty can? Many people would answer, "Recycle it!" Obviously, recycling is good for many reasons. We can reduce the amount of trash ① throwing away, use less energy than we would to make new products, and conserve natural resources by recycling. However, recycling is not a perfect way ② to manage waste. It still requires large amounts of energy to purify used resources and convert ③ them into new products. So, what about trying to creatively reuse, or "upcycle," them instead? This new approach is becoming more popular since it is ④ even more environmentally friendly than recycling. What's more, it can also be fun! Here are some inspiring examples of ⑤ how people have creatively upcycled old, used things.

18

다음 글의 (A), (B), (C)의 각 네모 안에서 문맥에 맞는 낱말로 가장 적절한 것은?

Through upcycling, a seemingly useless object can be transformed into something completely different that is (A) invaluable / valueless for everyday life. What do you think can be done with old truck tarps, car seat belts, and bicycle inner tubes? Individually, these things look like trash, but with a little imagination the Freitag brothers, Markus and Daniel, (B) repurpose / reduce them for something totally new: very (C) useless / strong bags. These bags are perfect for bicyclists going to work every day in all kinds of weather.

	(A)	(B)	(C)
①	invaluable	repurpose	useless
②	invaluable	reduce	useless
③	invaluable	repurpose	strong
④	valueless	reduce	strong
⑤	valueless	repurpose	strong

[19~21]

다음 글을 읽고, 물음에 답하시오.

When artists add their own creative touches, things that most people consider ① junk ⓐ is reborn as beautiful works of art. The giant pictures ⓑ making from trash by ② environmental artist Tom Deininger are one of a kind. Up close, these brightly colored creations look like a mixed-up mess of broken plastic, unwanted toys, and bent wire— all things that cannot be ③ recycled. From farther away, however, they appear ⓒ blend together into marvelous landscapes or other paintings. There is also an artist who shows ⓓ that even disposable cups can be ④ deserted as artistic material. For years, Gwyneth Leech has turned used coffee cups into ⑤ brilliant art exhibits. After a cup ⓔ uses by someone, she paints a unique design on it and hangs it with many other painted cups in front of a window or pretty background. These works from Leech and Deininger are not only pleasing to the eye, but they also naturally provoke an interest in environmental conservation in people.

19

윗글의 제목으로 가장 적절한 것은?

① Wastes: Obstacles to a Rich Source of Inspiration
② What Are the Conditions of Art Materials?
③ Imaginative Artistry Brings Life to Rubbish!
④ Huge but Attractive: Creations Made from Trash
⑤ What Do Environmental Artists Think about Upcycling?

20

윗글의 밑줄 친 ⓐ~ⓔ를 어법상 바르게 고치지 <u>못한</u> 것은?

① ⓐ → are
② ⓑ → made
③ ⓒ → to blend
④ ⓓ → which
⑤ ⓔ → is used

21

윗글의 밑줄 친 ①~⑤ 중, 문맥상 낱말의 쓰임이 적절하지 <u>않은</u> 것은?

①   ②   ③   ④   ⑤

22

다음 글의 밑줄 친 ⓐ~ⓔ 중, 어법상 쓰임이 적절하지 <u>않은</u> 것의 개수는?

Through upcycling, we ⓐ <u>can be transformed</u> a seemingly useless object into something completely different ⓑ <u>that</u> is useful for everyday life. What do you think can ⓒ <u>be done</u> with old truck tarps, car seat belts, and bicycle inner tubes? Individually, these things look like trash, but with ⓓ <u>few</u> imagination the Freitag brothers, Markus and Daniel, ⓔ <u>to repurpose</u> them for something totally new: very strong bags. These bags are perfect for bicyclists going to work every day in all kinds of weather.

① 1개   ② 2개   ③ 3개   ④ 4개   ⑤ 5개

23

다음 글의 밑줄 친 부분 중, 문맥상 낱말의 쓰임이 적절하지 <u>않은</u> 것은?

Every day during lunch, Jamie enjoys a soft drink and has a decision to make: What should he do with the empty can? Many people would answer, "Recycle it!" Obviously, recycling is good for many reasons. We can ① <u>reduce</u> the amount of trash thrown away, use ② <u>less</u> energy than we would to make new products, and conserve natural resources by recycling. However, recycling is not a ③ <u>perfect</u> way to manage waste. It still requires ④ <u>large</u> amounts of energy to purify used resources and convert them into new products. So, what about trying to creatively reuse, or "upcycle," them instead? This new approach is becoming more popular since it is even ⑤ <u>less</u> environmentally friendly than recycling. What's more, it can also be fun! Here are some inspiring examples of how people have creatively upcycled old, used things.

24

다음 글의 밑줄 친 부분 중, 어법상 틀린 것은?

Along with small everyday items, much bigger things can also be upcycled—even old buildings ① <u>that</u> cannot be used for their original purpose anymore. The German government showed us an excellent example of this with a former steel plant ② <u>where</u> closed in 1985. Rather than destroy the plant's buildings or abandon the entire facility, they decided to give it new meaning as a series of useful public structures. Many of the buildings ③ <u>kept</u> their original shapes, but received extra equipment and new designs in their surrounding areas. For instance, old gas tanks became pools for divers. Concrete walls of iron storage towers were turned into ideal training fields for rock climbers. Can you believe a building for melting metal is now a ④ <u>viewing</u> platform with a gorgeous 360-degree view? The final result is the Landscape Park Duisburg Nord. It has almost 570 acres of land filled with gardens, cycling paths, and pretty lights at night, in addition to its creatively repurposed buildings. This park proves that it's possible ⑤ <u>to preserve</u> the heritage of a place as well as the environment.

25

다음 글의 밑줄 친 부분 중, 어법상 적절하지 않은 것은?

When artists add their own creative touches, things ① that most people consider junk are reborn as beautiful works of art. The giant pictures made from trash by environmental artist Tom Deininger ② are one of a kind. Up close, these brightly colored creations look like a mixed-up mess of broken plastic, unwanted toys, and bent wire— all things that cannot ③ be recycled. From farther away, however, they appear to blend together into marvelous landscapes or other paintings. There is also an artist who shows that even disposable cups can be reused as artistic material. For years, Gwyneth Leech ④ has turned used coffee cups into brilliant art exhibits. After a cup is used by someone, she paints a unique design on it and hangs it with many other painted cups in front of a window or pretty background. These works from Leech and Deininger are not only ⑤ pleased to the eye, but they also naturally provoke an interest in environmental conservation in people.

26

다음 글의 (A), (B), (C)의 각 네모 안에서 문맥에 맞는 낱말로 가장 적절한 것은?

Along with small everyday items, much bigger things can also be upcycled—even old buildings that cannot be used for their original purpose anymore. The German government showed us an excellent example of this with a former steel plant that closed in 1985. Rather than destroy the plant's buildings or abandon the entire (A) facility / morality , they decided to give it new meaning as a series of useful public structures. Many of the buildings kept their original shapes, but received extra equipment and new designs in their surrounding areas. For instance, old gas tanks became pools for divers.

(B) Abstract / Concrete walls of iron storage towers were turned into ideal training fields for rock climbers. Can you believe a building for melting metal is now a viewing platform with a gorgeous 360-degree view? The final result is the Landscape Park Duisburg Nord. It has almost 570 acres of land filled with gardens, cycling paths, and pretty lights at night, in addition to its creatively repurposed buildings. This park proves that it's (C) possible / impossible to preserve the heritage of a place as well as the environment.

	(A)	(B)	(C)
①	facility	– Abstract	– possible
②	facility	– Concrete	– possible
③	facility	– Concrete	– impossible
④	morality	– Abstract	– impossible
⑤	morality	– Concrete	– impossible

27

다음 글의 밑줄 친 ⓐ~ⓔ 중, 어법상 틀린 부분을 포함하고 있는 것은?

Every day during lunch, Jamie enjoys a soft drink and has a decision to make: What should he do with the empty can? Many people would answer, "Recycle it!" Obviously, recycling is good for many reasons. ⓐ We can reduce the amount of trash thrown away, use less energy than we would to make new products, and conserving natural resources by recycling. ⓑ However, recycling is not a perfect way to manage waste. ⓒ It still requires large amounts of energy to purify used resources and convert them into new products. So, what about trying to creatively reuse, or "upcycle," them instead? ⓓ This new approach is becoming more popular since it is even more environmentally friendly than recycling. What's more, it can also be fun! ⓔ Here are some inspiring examples of how people have creatively upcycled old, used things.

① ⓐ ② ⓑ ③ ⓒ ④ ⓓ ⑤ ⓔ

28

다음 빈칸에 들어갈 말로 적절하지 <u>않은</u> 것을 <u>모두</u> 고르시오.

Along with small everyday items, much bigger things can also be upcycled—even old buildings that cannot be used for their original purpose anymore. The German government showed us an excellent example of this with a former steel plant that closed in 1985. Rather than destroy the plant's buildings or abandon the entire facility, they decided to give it new meaning as a series of useful public structures. Many of the buildings kept their original shapes, but received extra equipment and new designs in their surrounding areas. For instance, old gas tanks became pools for divers. Concrete walls of iron storage towers were turned into ideal training fields for rock climbers. Can you believe a building for melting metal is now a viewing platform with a gorgeous 360-degree view? The final result is the Landscape Park Duisburg Nord. It has almost 570 acres of land filled with gardens, cycling paths, and pretty lights at night, in addition to its creatively repurposed buildings. This park proves that it's possible to preserve _____.

① not the environment but the heritage of a place
② either the environment or the heritage of a place
③ both the environment and the heritage of a place
④ the heritage of a place as well as the environment
⑤ not only the environment but the heritage of a place

29

다음 글의 밑줄 친 ⓐ~ⓔ 중, 의미하는 바가 나머지 넷과 다른 것은?

As you can see, ⓐ thinking in a creative way has the power to make many positive changes to the environment. By ⓑ giving old products more value, we can lessen the amount of waste in a way that is even more eco-friendly than ⓒ recycling. So what would you say to Jamie now as he decides what to do with his cans? Perhaps he could upcycle them to make lanterns, toys, or sculptures for his friends and family. The options are endless, and all he needs is ⓓ a little creativity to think of them. In the same way, stop and think before you throw something out. Who knows? Maybe you can ⓔ turn that trash into treasure.

① ⓐ ② ⓑ ③ ⓒ ④ ⓓ ⑤ ⓔ

30

다음 글의 밑줄 친 부분 중, 어법상 <u>틀린</u> 것은?

When artists add their own creative touches, things that most people consider junk are reborn as beautiful works of art. The giant pictures ① <u>made</u> from trash by environmental artist Tom Deininger are one of a kind. Up close, these brightly colored creations look like a mixed-up mess of broken plastic, unwanted toys, and ② <u>bending</u> wire— all things that cannot be recycled. From ③ <u>farther</u> away, however, they appear to blend together into marvelous landscapes or other paintings. There is also an artist who shows that even disposable cups can be ④ <u>reused</u> as artistic material. For years, Gwyneth Leech has turned ⑤ <u>used</u> coffee cups into brilliant art exhibits. After a cup is used by someone, she paints a unique design on it and hangs it with many other painted cups in front of a window or pretty background. These works from Leech and Deininger are not only pleasing to the eye, but they also naturally provoke an interest in environmental conservation in people.

정답표

자세한 해설

리딩 본문[1]

문장편 최중요 연습 문제	문단편 최중요 연습 문제	기타 연습 문제
01 ⑤	01 ⑤	01 ⑤
02 ③	02 ④	02 ③
03 ④	03 ①	03 ④
04 ①	04 ③	04 ②
05 ⑤	05 ③	05 ③
06 ③	06 ⑤	06 ②
07 ⑤	07 ④	07 creative reuse → creatively reuse
08 ①	08 ④	
09 ⓐ has ⓑ conserve ⓒ to manage	09 ①	08 ④
	10 ⑤	09 is still required → still requires
10 ①	11 ②	10 ①, ④, ⑤
11 ④	12 ④	
12 ②	13 ①	
13 ②	14 ④	
14 ③	15 ④	
15 ④	16 ②	
16 ④		
17 ③		
18 ③		
19 ①		
20 ⑤		
21 inspiring		
22 ①		
23 ③		
24 ③		
25 ②		

리딩 본문[2]

문장편 최중요 연습 문제

01 ④

02 ③

03 ①

04 ③

05 ④

06 ②

07 ④, ⑤

08 ②

09 ②

10 ②

11 ①

12 ②

13 ②

14 ②

15 ③

16 ⓑ it → them ⓒ go → going

17 ②

18 ①

19 ③

20 ⑤

21 ④

22 ④

23 ①

24 ④

25 ④

26 are turning them into sandal bottoms

27 ③

28 What a great reuse of resources!

29 ②

30 ④

문단편 최중요 연습 문제

01 ④

02 ②

03 ②

04 ③

05 ①, ②

06 ②

07 ②

08 ②

09 ③, ⑤

10 ①, ④

11 ④

12 ①, ④

13 it is feasible for useless things to be changed into different objects that are valuable for daily life

14 ③, ⑤

기타 연습 문제

01 ③

02 ③

03 ⑤

04 ②, ③

리딩 본문[5]

문장편 최중요 연습 문제

01 ③

02 in a way that is even more eco-friendly than recycling

03 ③

04 ②

05 ②

06 ④

07 ①

08 ⓐ As you can see, thinking creatively has the power to make many positive changes to the environment.

09 ④

10 ⑤

11 ④

12 all he needs is a little creativity to think of them

13 ⑤

14 ③

15 ①

문단편 최중요 연습 문제

01 ④

02 ⑤

03 ④

04 ②

05 ④

06 ②

07 ④

08 ③

09 ②

10 ③

기타 연습 문제

01 ③

02 (A) changes   (B) creativity (C) trash

03 ③

04 ②

기타 본문, Listen & Speak, Grammar & Vocabulary

기타 본문 최중요 연습 문제

01 is

02 ③

03 ④

04 retain

05 ④

06 to reuse

07 ④

08 ②

09 ②

10 ④

Listen & Speak 최중요 연습 문제

01 ③

02 ④

03 ⓔ Aren't they → Isn't it

04 You can say that

05 ③

06 ⑤

07 ④

08 ⑤

Grammar & Vocabulary 최중요 연습 문제

01 ④

02 (1) ⓑ designing → designed
　 (2) ⓓ who she → who

03 (A) written on the book cover
　 (B) painted in red

04 ③

05 I like most of the works made by the writer.

06 ①

07 ③

08 ②

09 The researcher has studied tigers which were cared for by people when they were young.

10 ②

1회

01 ⑤

02 ④

03 ③

04 ④

05 ④

06 ③

07 ⑤

08 ④

09 ②

10 ③

11 ④

12 make → made

13 ④

14 ④

15 ②

16 ④

17 ⑤

18 ⓐ thrown away
   ⓑ (to) convert
   ⓒ are

19 ④

20 ④

21 ④

22 ④

23 ③

24 provoke

25 ③

26 ①

27 ②

28 ②

29 ①

30 ④

2회

01 ②

02 ①

03 ④

04 ①

05 ⑤

06 ③

07 ⓓ The options are endless, and all that he needs is a little creativity to think of them.

08 ①

09 ⑤

10 ①

11 ⑤

12 ③

13 ④

14 ②

15 ①

16 ③

17 ①

18 ③

19 ③

20 ④

21 ④

22 ③

23 ⑤

24 ②

25 ⑤

26 ②

27 ①

28 ①, ②

29 ③

30 ②